FOREWORD

Game Changer

---

noun

A newly introduced event, idea, element or factor that changes an existing situation, or activity, or the manner in which one thinks about something in a significant way.

> *"I show my scars so that others know they can heal."*
>
> **— Rhachelle Nicol', Sunday Mourning**

I have always been in awe and have great respect of the Game-Changing Moments in my life and in the lives of others. You know, those moments when everything you thought you understood all of a sudden doesn't seem so crystal clear? Where something happens, and then nothing can ever be the same again?

Sometimes, you are fully aware that you are in the middle of an incident that will change your life or your perspective in a meaningful way. But most times it is not until you have *come through* an experience that you can see what the Game-Changing Moment was. I mean, after all, **"The only way out is through!"**

Some Game-Changing Moments are devastating, some are joyful, and some almost feel insignificant, but end up having a huge impact. Some Game-Changing Moments hit you like a ton of bricks, and some sneak up on you quietly, as soft as a feather, and unbeknownst to you.

But whatever those moments are for you, I truly believe that it is important to **acknowledge**, **accept**, and **receive** the lesson so that you can integrate it into your life expeditiously and move forward with a new purpose and a better understanding.

Now, I am not saying that will be easy! But I have found that the faster that I seek the lesson, gain a fresh perspective, and interpret the meaning, the readier I am to recover, shake it off, and integrate the lesson into my life.

I have fully embraced the Game-Changing Moments in my life. I like to separate them into two major categories that I refer to as the "Yummy" and the "Yucky."

One of my favorite "Yummy Game-Changing Moments" is the night that I discovered that I should become a comedian. When I was a participant in a pageant for "fluffy girls," I made a comedy routine about regular-sized, skinny girl pageants, and I won first runner-up! It was truly a magical night—I discovered my true gift of performance. It was the Game-Changing Moment that set me up for what I do to this day. As an actress every time I book a job, it becomes a potential Game-Changing Moment, especially if the show is a success!

My "Yucky Game-Changing Moments" range from being in two intimate relationships riddled with physical and emotional abuse to experiencing financial ruin, owing to a debilitating depression and money-draining shopping habits. And to top it off, all of these Game Changers happened while I was already "famous!" **NOT FUN.** I kept silent at first because I did not want *anyone* to know that I was *broke* and *broken*.

> *"You have to be transparent, so you no longer cast a shadow but instead let the light pass through you."*
>
> — *Kamand Kojouri*

I now share in books and speaking engagements what I refer to as my Transparent Truth, because I learned that by sharing it with others, I release myself from the pain and from the shame and open myself and others to the possibility of Change and restored Joy.

Of course, the Yummy Game-Changing Moments are more pleasant, and they leave us with good, warm, fuzzy feelings, and a positive impact. And yes, the Yucky Game-Changing Moments are difficult and at times devastating. But by embracing these defining moments, however, I am wise enough to know now that I would not change anything that I've been through *for anything in the world*! Each moment makes up the Mosaic of the Fabric of Who I Am. And this is the same for you as well.

I am so grateful to be a part of this Project. This Yummy Game-Changing Moment originated from a simple girlfriend conversation with Samira, and now a few months later, here we are with beautiful stories that will inspire and create a movement. I enjoyed watching Samira step into this project with grace, integrity, leadership, and unwavering commitment. She is a true gem. And I'm so proud of all of the authors in this book for sharing their transparent truth with others. They are brave and beautiful.

This is what I predict will happen while you are reading these transparent truths:

You will see *yourself* in the stories. You will see great wisdom, courage, greatness, vulnerability, and authenticity in these authors. More important, you will see these qualities within yourself over and over again. And if you don't see them, go look again, they already are in each one of us. Search within your own Game-Changing Moments and without judgment, ask for the significance and the lesson.

It's all about *your* perspective. **You** get to choose, and that makes all the difference in *your* life and the type of impact you will have on the world.

"One of the most important things you can do on this earth is to let people know they are not alone."

— **Shannon L. Alder**

Enjoy!

Kim Coles

Kim Coles

DEDICATION

I'd like to dedicate this book to each of the contributing Authors. For some of you this is your first publication and my hope is that it will not be your last. For others this is a continuance of you sharing your elevation with the world. Continue inspiring others. Your stories will never get old and are leaving a legacy in your name for others to remember you by.

Also, I would like to dedicate this book to each of our family members and friends who have supported us while on this journey, whether it was holding it down while we took time away to focus, being our cheer squad, or just being there in general. Whatever that support was, we thank you.

A special shout out to my lovely Aunt Elaine who just celebrated her 95th birthday August 7th. No matter the occasion, when I rise, she rises with me, because had it not been for her and the other Angels in my life who stepped in to save me when I couldn't save myself, this book would not be. I am forever grateful, forever humbled, and forever blessed because I'll never forget what God has brought me through and who he brought me to.

There will be many stories in this book. There may even be a story you can identify with yourself. With that being said, I also dedicate this book to you, our readers. It is our goal to encourage you to take your own Game Changing moment and use it to not only better yourself, but to better others in the process.

Welcome to the Game Changer Life, *The Anthology*

Visionary Author,

Samira Jones

Samira L. Jones

A WORD FROM THE VISIONARY AUTHOR

When I talk about the Game Changer Life, I am talking about when life happened, and how we can take that reality to create something great and meaningful from it. As we know, life experiences happen in cycles. There are your peaks and there are your valleys. I'm sure you can think of a moment or two, maybe even three, where something significant took place that created a shift in your perspective on what that thing, situation, or experience was. Often times, it's those Game Changer Moments that ultimately shape us to be WHO and WHERE we are today.

My name is Samira Jones, and this is my story. Today, I operate a successful coaching business for Authors and Entrepreneurs, with a couple of other ventures on the way. I'm also a single mom of two amazing teenagers and the caretaker of my beautiful Great-Aunt, who just recently celebrated her 95th birthday. Sounds great, however, just 5 years ago I would have never imagined that my world would get rocked in the way that it did. You see, at that time I was a happily married wife, with what they call the American dream (minus the dog). Life was great, then everything was snatched out from under me, like a rug from underneath my feet, just like that. I felt displaced physically and emotionally, because everything as I knew it for the last 10 years of my life prior, was no more. I had to adjust to this "new normal." It was the welcoming to my Game Changer Life.

During this shift, I decided to get still and crawl my way through the fire, making the best next decision, then the next, and the next after that. You can either break or have a breakthrough. I decided to breakthrough and bring along other men and women who also held onto powerful stories that needed to be shared. This book was an opportunity for ordinary people just like you and I to take those stories and make a difference in another's life, because too often we devalue ourselves, and our experiences, feeling that our stories do not hold a special place and are no different from someone else who has experienced the same things.

No one's story is the exact same, and certainly not the same in how we approach and share them. There is a lesson in that. The Game Changer Life is about *human connection*. We are all connected regardless of ethnicity and origin…

Before we get into these amazing stories of faith, triumph, courage, and legacy, let me share with you some of the tried and true practices that I've been able to use in shifting my circumstances from these things that are happening to me, to what is there to learn in this. Sometimes it is not the situation itself that is the lesson. The lesson could be how we respond. We may not get to choose what happens to us, but we certainly have a say in how we react.

Let's perform an exercise.

What is your Game Changer Moment? This would be that pivotal moment that stands out in your mind often as the first memory of something significant that has taken place at some point in time. What was that? Be specific and directly to the point. This "something" can be either a great or not so great experience. Kim Coles likes to refer to this as your "Yummy" or your "Yucky"!

_____

_____

_____

_____

_____

How did you feel in that moment?

_____

_____

_____

_____

_____

If you looked at this situation as an opportunity to learn and grow from that experience, what did that look like?

_____

_____

_____

_____

_____

_____

What were some of the things you started doing or what opportunities presented themselves because of that Game Changer Moment?

_____

_____

_____

_____

_____

Yes, Game Changer Moments are opportunities. They are callings upon our lives to make a decision. I was 12 years old when I was abandoned by my mother after several occasions of sexual abuse at the hands of her current husband. When they decided to drive and drop me off in another state to a family member unbeknownst to me, to live, it was GAME CHANGING. That moment changed my perspective of my mother's love and concern for my well-being, it changed how I felt about myself, now feeling rejected I felt unloved and unworthy. To distract my mind from my reality, I became heavily involved in the extracurricular activities in school. I was in the band, played basketball, and enrolled in JROTC.

Those years were very confusing for me, because while I was transitioning into my teenage years, I was also living in survival mode. That state where I was dropped off like Tuesday's garbage, LITERALLY having my clothes in garbage bags, was East Orange, New Jersey, a.k.a. Brick City!

Walking the cold concrete streets of this city in the mornings to go to school, I was always on guard for just about any and everything. Not only was I dealing with my internal hurt and pain, it was difficult to make friends, because the type of people at the schools I attended were not the type of people I felt were good company. These kids were ROUGH!

So even with the odds stacked against me and not in my favor because of the situation in which I came from, I was still mindful enough to want to make the right decisions for myself when it came to the company I kept. To this day, I still have that same discernment, and you should, too. The company you keep is vital to the decisions you make and the path you'll be led on in life. Now, I didn't always get it right, but I did dodge a lot of wrongs.

Time passes, and the waters calmed for a while as I got older, had a family, settled down, and got married. Ask me, I'd say that life was content. There were no major issues, and I was at peace until July 18, 2014, when it felt like I was in a magnitude 9 earthquake. The seemingly loving husband that I'd known for the last 10 years of my life uttered these words, "I love you, I just don't love you the same and have to go."

Wait! What? Where was this coming from? It literally felt like his words fell out of the sky like a ton of bricks. Everyone was in shock, including family and friends.

Game Changer right? What do you do with that? What do you do with a situation that reveals itself to be infidelity and the co-culprit has the audacity to appear in all of your divorce hearings as they continue to shatter your world like a careless wrecking ball? All the while, you are adjusting to the changes, and making certain that the children feel as little as possible from this major life change.

I'll tell you what you do.

You show up POWERFULLY and DENY defeat! Denying defeat doesn't have to look ugly either. It can be quite casual actually. That denial is your PEACE. Yes, your peace! Once you step into your peace zone, it acts as your armor and you see the world and the situations you're faced with, combatting as the other person's problem and not yours. So, I want to encourage you to seek solace when life happens, create a standard for yourself of what you desire, and make it happen. I like to tell others to create your ONE word. Your one word is an anchor to hold onto when those moments arise. It is your core, your center that refocuses your energy on obtaining that one thing.

So, my next question is this. What is your ONE word and why?

_____

_____

_____

_____

_____

Your one word should be so deeply rooted within you that no storm can break you. You're a living being, so it may shake you up a bit, but never break you. Hold onto that one word and speak it consistently until it becomes who you are. When I say who you are, I don't just mean when life happens. Your one word should resonate through your spirit and the person you show up as in the world each and every day. YOU get to make the decision of how life will affect you. No one else is that powerful and should not be given that much energy to do so. #jotthatdown

As you begin to read the chapters ahead, think about your Game Changing Life, that pivotal moment. What was it? How did you define it or allow it to define you? What would you now do differently going forward based on the experiences and stories shared in this book?

Embrace. Educate. Elevate.
The Game Changer Life

TABLE OF CONETNTS

GAME CHANGER LIFE

Violet Davis

The Game Changer Life

I have so many moments in my life that I consider a game changer; however, there is one in particular that I want to focus on---the power of words. It started when I was finally locked up. I say *finally* because when I was hustling in the streets, I told myself, and everybody else, that when I went to jail I was going to be sitting down for a hot minute. I didn't realize at the time that I was prophesying over my life. I didn't attend church, so I didn't truly appreciate the power of my words. So, when I finally got locked up, I took it with ease. I was mentally ready for whatever.

Prison Life

I had just been picked up from MCI-W by the interstate connector. I was currently serving a 2-year sentence in the maximum-security facility in Maryland for a drug charge I had caught, but I had other charges in two other states that I had been running from for several years. I was to be taken back to Pennsylvania to await some charges I had caught for handgun possession---yeah, I actually had the piece on me while traveling back to Ohio from Maryland. When I arrived at the Pennsylvania facility, I had a bad report from the first time I was there, so they treated me like trash. I was the only black female the whole 9 months I was there, and I experienced so much racism that I it led me to get new charges while I was waiting for sentencing for the old charges. I was placed on lockdown 8 of the 9 months I spent in the Pennsylvania facility, and the only time I was able to leave my cell was to take a shower and to attend church service. I could have books, so I did a whole lot reading. Jail was the place I fell passionately in love with reading. The first set of books I started reading in this place was the left behind series. This is where I started to know more about God. These books opened my mind up and then I wanted to know more. I ended up asking for a bible and started reading everything. Not only was I reading, but I started applying what I had read (James 1:22). The first thing I applied my faith to was getting money back that was wrongfully taken. I went to God in my early morning prayer and spoke from a position of already receiving what was taken. I believed that God was getting that money back, and 2 months later every dollar was returned. Another issue I applied my faith to was receiving a reduced sentence---and I did! I read Matthew Chapter 6 and was wowed. Immediately, I started to do all that was said in the word (Deuteronomy 6:6). I asked God to show me how to walk this way once I got back on the streets. I told Him that I wanted to live a life where I was serving Him with my life. I began to minister the words to the other ladies in jail, praying with all prayer and supplication, being watchful to this end with perseverance and supplication for all the saints (Eph 6:18). My light was shining, and people really started to listen as I poured out the word of God.

Nine months later, I was sentenced and returned to Maryland to complete my sentence at that facility, which included a few more months on my sentence since my time didn't stop while I was at the Pennsylvania facility.

Faith Tested

I was naturally high on the word of God when I walked backed into the Maryland Correctional Institution for Women. I had money and I had Jesus! I had a glow that I didn't have when I left. I was housed in a room that was challenging but I didn't let that stop me from washing the feet of my cell buddy and ministering the word to her. She was a lifer and I took to her. We became cool while I was her cellmate. However, she was a homosexual and I didn't know at the time that she was actually a spirit who would attach itself to me. But I learned this as time went on. During my time in that cell I began to see my behavior change. I still went to church and read my bible, but I also started to receive unneeded attention from other women. I also found myself having conversations with my cellmate about the new attention I started receiving from this white girl. Throughout my entire life, I had never desired women. They never caught my eye, but for some reason I started liking the attention and felt the need to try it out. So, I started entertaining this girl with little notes and slick eyes. I would tell my roommate, who was fully involved with another life and lived as if she was a guy. One day, I was asked by another lady who I had become cool with, to move to her dorm. It was cleaner and a better living environment, but when I told my current cellmate she was upset and began to tell me her background about the relationship she had with her. She told me they had been really good friends for years but fell out over something really small. So, I decided to help them mend their broken friendship during the move, which worked for a while. But they ended up falling out again, so I just left it alone after that. I continued to be friends with both of them until my old cellmate betrayed me, and then I cut her off completely. The moment I told my new cellmate Ro about the girl that had shown an interest me, she frowned and said, "Wow! I wouldn't mess with someone like that," which placed doubt in my head about her. Little did I know that Ro and I would soon be in a relationship while living

3

together. I didn't know at the time that girls would get you moved in their room, either because you had money, or they liked and wanted to date you. The reason why I was chosen consisted of a little bit of both.

Remember that I said before I left, I had no money and had to work to take care of myself. From the minute I returned, I saved and was paid---it was like the women smelled the money. Seriously! After some time, it wasn't comfortable for me in that room because of the fights and arguments, and I wanted, no needed, some relief. So, I took a job in the kitchen. I would wake up at 3:30 am, go to work until 11:00 am, and then attend school for my GED just so I wouldn't have to deal with some of the drama. Don't get me wrong, not all of the days were filled with drama, but I did notice that I didn't attend church as frequently because I was tired---then again, my focus wasn't on God anymore but the prison drama. At that time, I didn't know it was a spiritual battle for my mind and for my soul---I just knew that it was life happening. After about 4 months, me and Ro just couldn't live together. It was too much, and I started planning an escape. Eventually, I was able to get moved, which hurt her because she didn't think that I would leave. In prison, people want to be as comfortable as they can be so it's best to be in a cell with somebody who works and carries their own weight because then you can put some things together, which made life a whole lot easier. I worked in the kitchen, so I had a little side hustle going on where I would steal onions, green peppers, cheese, and whatever else I could sell to the women, and I was able to get a name for myself. Selling items from the kitchen was like selling drugs on the streets, so I was in my lane. I supplied most of the campus, which lasted almost until my release.

One day when I was in the gym with some other women who I was cool with, they had a friend hanging around who was going through a breakup. I thought I could befriend her and help her get through this tough time, and because of that we ended up messing around, which only lasted for a short time. And, since Ro started up so much drama behind it, I ended up getting into a fight and pretty much stayed on lockdown. Ro didn't like the new relationship I had formed, and throughout one of my lock ups that new relationship failed. For the very first time in my life, my heart was crushed. But the beauty that was discovered through this pain was my reconnection to God. I didn't know how far gone I had separated from Him until I was in the worst pain of my life, and it was God who saw me through. My time did come to an end a few weeks later, and I didn't look back.

Living a Lie

When I returned to the Pennsylvania Correctional Facility, I knew I had entered another world that would require me to conform to its ways. I had to play a certain role to survive, and I played the role of a man. When I first arrived at Muncy State Correctional Institution, I immediately noticed the difference between the prisons. This one was mostly run by whites, and the prisoners had to wear brown uniforms---the identical colors I wear today working for UPS, all the way down to the black boots. When I first arrived, I wasn't focused on the word of God the way in which I was before returning to the Maryland Correctional Facility. I was back in a worldly mindset, on top of the past following me. You see, when I was in the county jail, I had gotten into a fight with the correction officers and although I had been saved and forgiven by God, the system wasn't as quick to forgive me. What I had done while awaiting sentencing followed me to the state prison. It was as if the correctional officers were waiting on me.

The mindset of the staff and the women in Muncy were different than those of the women and staff in Maryland. The women in Muncy were much more negative and aggressive. I knew I would have to fight to prove a point and to show all of them that I didn't take any mess because this was the type of place where you couldn't show any weakness, and I mean *none*.

The first 5 days were challenging because I had a target on my back from what I had done in the county lock up. It didn't take any time for me to be singled out. One day when lunch was called, and I left the lunchroom to ask a question, trust me when I say that's when all of the drama started. A disagreement broke out and I was instructed to return to my cell without my food. I said, "No, I have a right to eat." One of the officers told me to lock in. However, because I knew he was on, I returned to my cell but not without grabbing a form to write up what had just transpired. Not too long after this, the same officer came to my cell and told me that I would be going to the hole for disrespecting him and still wouldn't be getting anything to eat. (Whenever you go to the hole you have no voice but if you are on the prison campus, then you have an opportunity to fight from a winning standpoint.) So, I asked a Sergeant for assistance, and he denied me that right. Therefore, when he told me to cuff up, I said no. He then entered my cell and grabbed my arm. For a minute I thought about fighting back but quickly remembered that fighting was the reason I was in there. So, I gave in and let him cuff me. The minute he had me cuffed, he twisted my arm and whispered in my ear, "If this was back in my day, I would have hung you from an oak tree." I told him, "If this was back in my day, I would have busted you in the mouth"! Once I got to the hole, I didn't see the prison campus until 6 months later.

When I received my write up, it contained so many lies that I couldn't believe it, but nevertheless, I stayed there for months and couldn't do anything about it. My time in this prison was both transformative and detrimental. I say detrimental because I had to become someone else while doing my time. I dated the wrong women for the wrong reasons and suffered emotionally. But once again I reconnected with God. It was in this place when I first heard God speak in an audible voice. I KNEW he had called me to do something great! I just didn't know what. I stayed in that prison for about three-and-a-half years, experiencing many ups and downs---at times I felt like I was never getting out. I would spend months at a time in the hole for fighting or for disrespecting an officer. But I was able to get my GED in only

2 months once I was released from the hole the first time. I also picked up a trade.

New Faces and New Changes

During one of my visits to the hole, I met a woman who was on death row. She and I became very close, quickly forming a bond. She made sure that I had extra food and would buy me things such as books and other items that you could only get through mail. Because she could have commissary, she made sure that I had some too. (When you are in the hole, you can't have commissary.) (Although I was in a relationship with this crazy woman, and at times felt trapped because of the things she would do, I had no way to break it off with her, which was very traumatic for me because I had no way to escape--- the only time I had any peace was in the hole. It was a crazy season in my life. Looking back, even now, all I can say is, "Thank you, Jesus"!) Because I knew the women on death row would be coming off soon, I knew that I would be able to break away from my current situation, so I started messing with her and was able to get away from the crazy one---at least while I was in the hole.

TIME PASSES... I had 3 months until I would be released from this place. I did not know where to go, had only a few bucks in my account, and had no vision for a better life--- My plans were to go back out into the world and hustle. That's all I knew prior to coming to prison. I was released from the hole, and caught a cab to my girl's father's house where I had a cashier's check waiting on me for $1,000---and a start. I had never been in that city before, but I was determined to get back all that I had lost plus some. I had a plan and that was to make the best of my stay. I knew I would return to selling drugs the minute I walked out of that prison, which is a hard truth, and at the time that is where I was in life. I walked around Williamsport with a hunger and begin to scope the area and plan out my stay. I went to the phone store, bought two cell phones, and then went to a few homeless shelters to see what type of clients I would be serving. I went to a few churches that give clothing and shoes to people who are just released from prison, and then I went to the welfare office to apply for assistance. When I left the welfare office, I went to the Dollar Store to buy some hygiene items. As I was shopping, I ran into the girl who was locked up with me. We only spoke in passing during our stay in Muncy, and when she saw me she knew I had just come home because of the sweat suit I was wearing. I asked her about the town and she told me about the going on, etc. Then, she asked me where I was staying, and I told her I found a shelter, but that I had to be home by a certain time. She then surprised me when she told me I could stay with her and her little girl. They had a one-bedroom apartment located not too far from where we were. I thanked her and told her that as I made money, I would "hit her up" with some. I also told here that I didn't know how long I would be staying, and she had no problem whatsoever---she actually said that however long I needed to stay would be fine. I told her what I was trying to do as far as getting "some work." She made a few calls, but to my dismay we couldn't get any coke. However, I also knew that $1,000 was only going to take me so far, so I bought a bundle and did what I needed to do. I ran through what I had and went back and bought two more bundles with all of the money that I had made---I did that until I was about to buy a brick. But when I returned to purchase the brick, I encountered an obstacle. The dudes had never seen a girl move the way that I moved---and that bothered them. They didn't want to see me advance in any way, so they told my friend they didn't have any more once I reached that level. We tried to cop some drugs from different people but were told the same thing. Nobody did coke, and I couldn't find no dope in a city where that was the only drug people did. So, my home girl introduced me to her New York connection, and I made plans to call him later. After a few days, I knew I had to get out of that town.

At the time I was living as if I was a man, and I didn't like the vibes I received when I was out. I had this feeling that if I didn't leave, something was about to happen. I couldn't put my finger on it, but I made a mental note to hop on a bus smoking back to Maryland within the week. I made a few calls to plan my arrival and left. When I arrived in Maryland, my cousin had a smoker come and pick me up. While I was locked up, she was doing her thing and had made a name for herself in the drug world. She put me on the work I had been looking for when I was in Pennsylvania, and it didn't take any time for me to jump back into rotation. When I reached a few ounces, I reached out to the New York connection and it was on like hot buttered popcorn. Once I came back to Maryland, I reached out to my child's father's family to reconnect with my daughter, and when I saw her, the joy I felt was unimaginable. My baby had grown so much! The moment I laid eyes on her, I knew I had to get some REAL money because I needed her---and more important, she needed me. I spent a little time with her and made plans to come back the next day to spend more time with her. The next day, her dad reached out to me, so we made plans to meet up later that day and talk. I could tell from the look in his eyes that he was hurt because of my appearance. He had never seen me look the way that I was, like a dude, and I could only imagine what he and his lady friend, who he introduced to me, were thinking---she was giving me the eye and her greeting was a little too friendly. But hey, those were his issues now, and this was the life I was living now. He gave me some weed, we promised to meet at a later time, and then he left.

SOMETHING HAPPENED... I remember when I was just starting out and selling drugs. My dream was to retire from the drug game, but my goal was to buy a whole key. Those were the two things I had often thought about. I never imagined I would spend five-and-a-half years in prison. But to get to that point, that's the way it happened. I had been dressing like a dude and living like one, too. I had a girlfriend at the time, but I knew it wasn't going to be like that forever. As I said before, I knew that if I stayed that way, it wouldn't be good. I just had a notion that something was going to happen. So, I begin to slowly transition back into being a woman where I knew I would be in more control in where I was headed and what I was trying to do. I couldn't put on my charm dressed like a man.

TIME PASSES... Everything seemed to go by in lighting speed; however, there were two obstacles in my way: my child's father and my background. Once I returned to Maryland, I knew I couldn't stay in a hotel room. That happened to be the reason why I fell the first time. I had the money to get a place, but I didn't have the paperwork and my child's father was hurt behind the fact that I didn't want to be a family with him. So, staying with him wasn't an option. About 1 month later, my child's father called and asked me to come over his house so that we could discuss our daughter's behavior in school. I promised him I would come over by 8:00 pm but by the time I hadn't yet completed making my runs, so I didn't show up until 11:30 pm. By the time I showed up, both he and is lady friend were good and drunk, but I still stayed for a while to see if he wanted and could still talk. As I continued to sit there, his friend wanted to make small talk and eventually asked me if I wanted some take-out food, and I said sure. While she was making me a plate, my child's father began to wrestle with me. I told him to stop playing but he wouldn't stop. It got to the point where his friend asked him to stop, too, and he finally did. So, I got up and went into the kitchen with her. Our daughter was in the other bedroom sleep when I peeked in. I sat at the table, his girlfriend brought me my plate, and I begin to eat. As I sat there eating, I could hear my child's father and his girlfriend going back about how he was all over me---trying to wrestle with me. The girl explained that she felt disrespected, so the next thing I knew my child's father was standing over top of me telling me to go. I looked up at him, didn't say one word, just grabbed my phones, and started walking toward the door. When I made it halfway across the room, he hit me, and I fell on the couch. When I tried to get up he started raining down blow after blow, and all I could do was to protect my head. I thought for a second, "Kick him and then hit him with the lamp!" But then I thought about our daughter sleeping in the other room, pushed him off of me, and ran for the door. He tried to stop me from leaving, but I was able to get away. When I got to my car, I was in shock even though I knew he had done that from a hurt place. It was a lot for him to deal with. I remember him calling my phone as I drove down the street trying to gather myself. He was crying and saying that he was sorry and that he wanted me to come back. He said that he loved me and wanted us to be a family and that he didn't know why he had done that. I knew from that moment on that he was going to be a problem. I calmly told him that I wasn't coming back but that I would talk to him later. He kept pleading, and I ended up hanging up on him. However, he kept calling and calling. I went about 1 week without seeing our daughter and when I finally saw her it was through a visit with his mom. My eyes were opened after that and I started thinking that I couldn't continue to live as if I was a man. I was no longer comfortable. So, as the days went by, I completed the full transition back into my comfort zone. I felt like I had been freed from something all over again. I had my confidence back and things took a different turn. I still dealt with women, but it wasn't like I used to. Because I only wanted my daughter, her father's mission was set to stop me in any way that he could from seeing her. The way he tried to keep my daughter from me put me in a position to try and work things out with him, even after the attack. In my mind I had to play a game to get what I wanted from him. So, I played the part to have our daughter be a part of my life too. I knew he and I would never work because of the type of person he was and the way in which he was living. We both dealt drugs but not the same kind. He had been shot, so he was addicted to pain pills and he liked that bottle---those were two things that I just didn't get down with. A few months later. I had finally reached the point where I cut him off, obtained a good lawyer, and was granted joint custody.

New Beginnings to Running for My Life

I met this nice guy and things seemed to be going great. He had a few things going for himself such as a driver's license and good credit, both of which I didn't have, so he was prefect for my next move. He didn't work but his sex game was on point, so I was all in! In addition, he thought he was the son of God, literally, so we were good. I didn't overlook the crazy part of him because I was after something. And, like I stated previously, the sex was mind blowing so I literally couldn't see beyond anything else.

We eventually ended up getting a place together, so that I could leave those hotel rooms alone. I bought him a car so that he could drive me around and so that I wouldn't have to pay for car rentals. For the first 2 months things were great, until he became possessive. It first started because he didn't like the guy I bought my weed from, so I started getting it from his guy. He always spoke about having a third eye and being the son of God. Again, I overlooked this as not being as serious as it eventually turned out to be---I was brainwashed by the incredible sex and my life almost ended because of it. My mom called me one day and asked me to meet her so that we could talk. This was after he tried to kill me in the car with my daughter in the back seat. She gave me a stun gun, some brass knuckles, and told me that I needed to get out that relationship because she knew that he was going to kill me. I told her that I felt it too, however, this wasn't the type of person I could just walk away from. I told her I had to have a plan and that I had to do this right if I was going to come out alive. So, first I put him in a position to make some money because I knew if he depended on me to buy his food, it was going to be hard to get him away. Once he started to make his own money, I knew that he would become overconfident, do something that would create a disagreement between us, and I could then walk away for good. Unfortunately, my plan had the opposite effect.

I literally stopped having sex with this guy, and the moment I did I was able to see him for the demon he was, and I was afraid. I didn't know how I would get out of this, and there were times that I thought I wasn't going to make it out alive. I hadn't made it to the point to even think about seeking God, so I tried to come up with what I knew would work when it came to men and their pride, but see I didn't know that this situation was not of this world. It was spiritual and at the time

I didn't know it was the enemy trying to take me out of the game. Every step I made, once my eyes were open, was strategic and well thought out. When was home, I didn't go.

Fireside Reflections

Keywords and Takeaways:

1. Power of words

2. Faith Tested

3. Something Happened, Time passes, Something Happened, Time Passes

4. Attaching Spirits

5. Reconnection to God

As Violet mentioned, she knew her words had *POWER*. She spoke life into a situation that ultimately ended her somewhere she didn't desire to be for the next 5 ½ years of her life, *prison.*

The Bible says, "Death and Life are in the POWER of the tongue. (Proverbs 18:21, KJV).

Do know that your words have power to either work for you or against you. So why not change the tune of your tongue to be something fruitful? Speak life!

Use the power of your own words and write down something amazing that you want to achieve in the next year and claim it with authority!

_____

_____

_____

_____

_____

Faith Tested. Think of a time when you felt the pressures of life and where you may have wondered if God forgot about you. Isn't it the evidence of the past that assures us that He will see us through again? Name a time when your faith was tested.

_____

_____

_____

_____

_____

_____

What was the favorable outcome in that situation?

_____

_____

_____

_____

_____

_____

Now the next time something happens, remember what you wrote and rely on that as your evidence that if He did it once, He can do it again. However, my FAITH must be in alignment with what I SAY I believe. *#jotthatdown*

1. Something happens. Time passes, and something happens, and time passes. That's usually how it works. That is why number 2 is so important. Each time "something happens", be sure to happen to *it!* This is when that mustard seed faith comes in and because of that type of faith you feel reassured that everything is going to be alright.

2. Attaching Spirits. One thing to be careful of is the direct and indirect energies of other people. Whether you realize it or not, energy is transferrable, so it is imperative to be careful of the people allowed in your space for this very reason. I have a bold request. I want you to think about and list either the people or activities you partake in that you know do not make you feel good. Next, I want you to make the decision whether you'll

continue to travel down that road or not. Simple. Your decision. Period.

_____

_____

_____

_____

_____

_____

_____

We often find ourselves looking to reconnect with God or some other source of power when we need to retreat from our pains, anxieties, and hardships. We do this because the attachment to those sources act as our anchor. We have something bigger than us to rely on in those moments. Let's aim to stay connected and not get disconnected when distractions enter our lives and we are left with choosing between what we know is good for us and what we know we want right now. Read that again.

FAMILY ADDICTION AND EMBRACING EMPATHY

My Game Changer

Bernadette "Ms. B" Willis

From birth through five years of age I was placed in foster care. I never quite knew why, nor did I ask...

As a child I was often told that I was too sensitive. My siblings would often tease me and say, "What's wrong with you? Can't you take a joke?" I was often teary eyed and cried a lot. One day when I was in school, the building of which consisted of both our middle school and high school classes, I had pissed off some girl in class earlier in the morning. I can't recall what I did, but I do recall her saying *she was going to kick my ass after school.* I dreaded the school day coming to an end. I was just as terrified as Mike when he touched Alicia's butt in "The Wood" and Alicia told Mike that her brother was gonna get him after school. Mike watched the clock all day, sweating. Well, that was me! In every period, all I could feel was the dread of losing a fight---terribly. We had about 8 class periods each day, and it was in the seventh period that the brother of an older female friend, LaFonda Anderson, spotted me in the hall between classes. I tried not to, but my eyes welled up. She asked, "You still crying?" She had heard I was threatened earlier that day. Gossip about possible fights after school spread like gas on a match at Roosevelt High in New York. LaFonda made it her business to find the young lady who threatened me and told her not to bother me. It worked, because the young lady I angered stayed away from me that day! My peers often viewed me as weak and overly sensitive. The adults around would often whisper something about me being "special." Simultaneously, I would hear echoes of the essence of my being weak and special. But the voices that believed were of "weaknesses" and that noise appeared louder than my "specialness."

In July 2019, I published my first book titled, "Debra's Daughter: A Memoir of Perseverance through Family Addiction." In that book, I chronicled my childhood on fun and games with my siblings and neighborhood children from the ages of 5-12 years old. It was my mother and my five siblings who lived in a three-bedroom house on Long Island with a full basement and a big, beautiful backyard. What contributed to this separation was that our landlord wanted to sell the house my mother rented from him. So, at the age of 12 our family broke up. My three brothers went to live with our father in Freeport, and it was now my mom, my little sister, and I. The crushing reality was that my mom rented a room for us in a crack house. That was our home from the age of 12-17. That time consisted of us routinely being kicked out, being homeless, and me often being separated from my sister and mother. Frequently, I was on my own, although my sister and mother stayed together. I often lived from pillar to post with different family members and elementary school friends, which was a stark contrast from the three bedrooms, full basement, and backyard that I had grown accustomed to. I was also used to my older brothers being around and protecting me. The residents of the house we moved into were alcoholics, crack addicts, wife and spouse abusers, and drug dealers. Domestic violence was prevalent. But despite these vices and dynamics, we were a family and we acted like one. The specifics of good and bad memories are chronicled in my memoir. We broke bread together, joked around, and had fun. At the same time, witnessing what took place in the crack house was torturous to me---and I was miserable. To top it off, my mother was neglectful and spiteful toward me. My physical punishments were often unjustified---I really felt that my mother hated me and favored my little sister. This was a cold, dark, evil environment but it was "home." My sister and I received refuge at church and at the houses of friends. We did all that we could to avoid our "home." At that time, I was depressed. I didn't know it then, but I was also very angry. At 16 years old, I became pregnant and was still very active in the church, singing as a soprano in the choir.

One Sunday, we had a guest preacher who I noticed had been staring at me periodically from the pulpit as I sat in the congregation. Sometime during his sermon, publicly he talked about different parts of my life and prophesied how I was special. He had confirmed to me a visitation that I had from a heavenly being. I am going to call it an angel. Very few people know this about me. The only other person who I had told about this visit was my pastor almost 30 years ago. One time while reading the bible, I found myself frozen and unable to move. On my left I could feel a wind and breeze. So much so that the pages of my bible began to lift and to turn very slowly without assistance. I felt a peacefulness and calmness for a minute or so. It was coming from my left, but I was stuck and physically unable to look and see what was present but I could feel the breeze, and I could see the bible pages move because the book was in front of me.

During that time, "Baba" was the father figure who I had in my life. He was the owner of the house and he also lived there. My biological father was alive and lived in the next town; however, he was a passive parent and only stepped in to assist my mother when she needed

19

money to send us to Alabama to live with our grandmother. My biological father did not visit or check on me during that time. Maybe he justified his absence in that *Debra has the girls and my responsibility are the three boys*. Baba and I had a loving yet strained relationship. I was placed in a home for unwed mothers at 17, and it had been some time since I had seen him. I missed him. Although Baba was still in Roosevelt, I lived in Malverne at the time. I intuitively felt when he died. We were on good terms before he passed away, and we had talked on the phone periodically. He kept asking me to come see him because he was becoming ill. I always said I would, but I didn't. One early afternoon while doing my chores at MOMMA'S HOUSE I will never forget I was cleaning the bathroom and wiping the shower walls when a strange, unsettling feeling came over me. It was a cold feeling of peace. I stopped scrubbing the wall and without thinking said, "I feel death." Later, I learned that "Baba" had passed away the same day I experienced that "feeling."

Some would say I had a traumatic childhood. As a little girl, whenever adults would ask me what I wanted to be when I grew up, I would either say a *singer* or a *nun*. It was always my desire to help people. Despite being an adolescent who was often homeless due to the dynamics of crack addiction and also being a teenage mother, I attended college. I chose physical therapy as a major because as a kid I thought the television show "The Million Dollar Man" was awesome! Also, I had watched another television program on physical therapy and I loved the idea of helping patients walk again after bad car accidents and hearing doctors telling them that *partial or full recovery were was impossible*. I guess I LOVE the prospect of Miracles.

My grades in high school were ok. So, I had to gain access into the physical therapy program by mastering the liberal arts major, then transitioning into a physical therapy major. I struggled with biology while my psychology, sociology, and African history courses were easy A's. I then decided to change my major to sociology with a concentration in human services. After interning as an HIV/AIDS educator, I got my first job in social work as an intensive case manager for an alcohol and drug treatment nonprofit organization. In this role, I helped women who had lost custody of their children due to their addiction. I worked with these women to help them get their children returned from foster care and into a safe, recovering home with their mothers. I loved this job but it was very taxing on my spirit. Although most women took advantage of the services, getting to NA/AA meetings, and attending parenting classes, there were those who just weren't ready to submit to their sobriety and to admit they were powerless against their addictions. Their children paid horribly for a product they did not ask for. As a result, their children were often shuffled from family member to family member, and foster home to foster home. As I type this, I am realizing that's exactly what happened to me. It's a harsh reality, but true. I remember one woman in particular who had agreed to go to inpatient rehab. This was a last-ditch effort from the county before they would petition the court to terminate her parental rights. She swore she would do what was necessary, and she had made monumental progress toward her goals. She had agreed to go to treatment. We talked the day before and the morning I was coming to drive her to rehab. We loaded all of her things, mostly clothes, toiletries, and personal knick knacks in my car. We had loaded everything into my car, even filling the back seats. It was an inpatient treatment facility and the minimum stay would be 6 months. We packed her whole life in that car! She told me there was one thing left to get and she went back into her apartment. Five minutes, 10 minutes, then a half hour had gone by before I realized she had not yet returned. Did she hurt herself? I rang the bell, then I called her on the phone. She ignored all of my attempts for contact. I was diligent and a little naive, but I refused to give up on her. I remembered the words she uttered about truly wanting to get her son back. So, I rang her bell and knocked on her door for about 4 hours. Then, I got hungry! I unloaded her belongings on to her porch, drove back to the office, and notified my supervisor.

After that position, I worked for a few alcohol and drug treatment facilities, and some pretty tough places, including a state prison and a state run juvenile detention center. During my employment at the prison, they initially trained me away from the inmates. But, eventually, I was trained and assigned closer to where the inmates resided. I will never forget the first day I saw the inmates from the program. My responsibilities included supervising three drug treatment inmate dorms and six program assistants. The inmates were in the yard, and I was headed there to introduce myself to them before count time. My heart bled and nearly broke at the sight of all of those black and brown men in one place; all wearing green jumpsuits. In awe and disbelief, I said to myself *So, this is where they all are*! It felt to me as if they were missing from the community, that no one knew where they were, and that I just happened to work in the place where they were found. I was shocked and profoundly saddened, simultaneously.

To this day, when I see an African American man in that dingy, forest green, from top to bottom, I feel angry and disgusted. It is important for me to note that my anger is not toward the men---but it is targeted toward the system. I have actually spoken with strangers who I didn't know and discouraged them from wearing that color because of what it can ultimately represent. What was also disturbing when I worked at the prison though, was the high rate of deaths of the COs. When a CO died, the facility would run the American flag at half-staff. It seemed like every week a CO died. One time during my tenure, a CO committed suicide by blowing his head off while working in the tower. Needless to say, I had a tough time working in that position and always receiving bad news. I had practiced Christianity and had a positive outlook on life. Those sentiments, however, were not welcomed by my colleagues. I loved working with the inmates. It was the staff that made working at the prison difficult. I had about a 30-minute drive to work. Every morning and afternoon, I would have to pray during my commute. This was done to prepare my mind and spirit before I arrived at the prison and to ensure that I didn't bring any negativity energy into my home, where I lived with my daughter. The negative energy and the constant pressure to not be myself was a little too much for me to deal with.

I also worked in juvenile detention centers where I physically had to restrain children who were 5-18 years of age. This had to be done to keep them from hurting themselves intentionally through self-mutilation or from assaulting staff or other residents. Physical restraints had to be placed on them to keep both the children and the people who worked around them safe. I HATED restraining children, regardless of whether they were built like adults. I was physically fit for the job but many of the employees were both bigger and stronger than myself. It just always felt like a violation to me to put hands on people. I once witnessed a teen girl go into a traumatic flashback during the restraint. She was a bigger girl and during the restraint her pants exposed her buttock slightly. She immediately stopped resisting, put herself in a fetal position, and started to wail a curling cry. I was convinced that at one time she was raped or experienced some type of trauma, and that being in the restraint triggered her memory of the incident. Her physical and emotional response were witnessed and acknowledged not only by me, but by social workers and the psychologist. Unfortunately, her response was not included in her record, even at my urging.

When we were trained at the juvenile detention center, we were able to experience how it felt to have the restraints put on. So I was handcuffed, foot shackled, and chain restraints that were connected and wrapped around my waist were connected with chains around my feet. Under these circumstances, a person's movement is restricted to shuffles only. I wondered if that was how blacks on a chain gang or even how slaves felt. While placed in those restraints and even some of the "holds," I hated it. I had to internally talk to myself and do deep breathing. At that time, I had never experienced an anxiety attack, but I'm sure if I wasn't breathing deeply I would have probably had one. Because I detested restraining children and breaking up teen fights, I became a master at de-escalating and negotiating crises. It was about preventing them before the situation escalated. A child could literally be throwing items, feces, or whatever, and regardless of where I was stationed, I was always called on the walkie-talkie to come and assist the team. I could convince the toughest gang-affiliated teen to walk back to their room *without* being escorted. Most of the time, the child simply wanted to be heard and validated. It boggles my mind how some of my coworkers didn't even attempt to use the psychological training we were taught for that type of situation. For some of my colleagues, it was straight to hands-on FIRST, which led me to believe some workers wanted to restrain the children almost like bullies. A short time later, they shut this facility down. I then went to work with a younger population of children. This facility was NOT run by New York State. My coworkers there were very experienced and professional and utilized the psychological training; however, I was still often called to the scene. It was then when I realized maybe this is a strength & gift that I have.

Fast forward about five years. I am becoming burned out and disillusioned with the state and non-profit system. As an experienced social worker, I had always told myself that the minute I started to become calloused and cold that I would get out of the field. People who experience vulnerable life circumstances need caring, nonjudgmental staff. We can push someone over the edge easily into suicide or violence when we act unprofessional toward those in need. I never wanted to be one of those angry, judgmental social workers.

For most of my career, I have frequently worked at more than one job at the same time. During my last position with the Department of Health and Human Services, I had changed to per diem, while working another daytime position. I was fired from my per-diem job for advocating for the kids in the residential program who didn't have any soap to bathe themselves. In addition, the children were unruly, physically abusive to the other children, as well as the staff. No one seemed to take a leadership role during this shift, and the staff weren't on the same page.

On top of that we were short staffed. I had stayed 3 hours after my clock out time to help the house run more smoothly. That day, I participated in 3 restraints. Remember, I used that as a last resort. So, you can imagine the chaos and disruption that took place in the house. I called everybody on that supervisor list and informed them of the disarray when I arrived at work. The cops had already showed up three times to help us find children who had left the premises. They said they weren't coming back that day. Somebody had an issue with my calling. I simply wanted the supervisors to ask people to come to work or to come and help us. And as anticipated, I received a voicemail message the next day stating that my services were no longer needed. When I called them back to challenge their decision, I was informed that I was being let go because I needed an internet training and missed the deadline to complete it. As you read this story, it is safe to assume that no such training existed and if it did, that no one ever reached out to communicate that I needed to take this training. I was genuinely heartbroken. For the last 5 years, I enjoyed spending the holidays with the children in the residences. It was one of the few times when they were treated like children. Many churches and other civic groups would volunteer during those times and buy the kids gifts and other tickets for special events. These were special treats because the nonprofits could not afford to do such things. Most of the children didn't have memorable, fun-filled holidays when they celebrated at home. I enjoyed watching them open their presents at Christmas time. Although I didn't like the bullshit excuse to dismiss me, I was convinced my time at this agency had come to an end.

My other job was at a call center where I helped customers and insurance navigators with their health insurance accounts. Because of the bureaucracy and the many intricacies that could cause a problem with a client's account, it was my philosophy to do my best to solve the problem while I had the customer or client on the phone.

I never transferred a call to anyone since I wanted to be the one to help and resolve their various complaints or issues. I received many awards and kudus from customers and insurance navigators on how I helped them by going above and beyond the call of duty. I instinctively put myself in the person's shoes of the individual who was on the other end of the phone line.

I now live in Albany, New York, which is the capital of New York and where for the last 10 years a buzz around careers in Science, Technology, Engineering & Math (STEM) has grown louder and louder. There were and are many initiatives in upstate New York to mimic Silicon Valley. There are also business partnerships with many colleges, universities, and STEM businesses resembling Silicon Valley with what they call Tech Valley. Millions of dollars had been and continues to be invested in the initiative and in our area. I knew that my career as a counselor was ending so I signed up to participate in the Entrepreneur Boot Camp with Albany Colonies Chamber of Commerce. This was a 12-week intense business course and business plan competition. While attending the boot camp, I was working on edits for my memoir that I had mentioned earlier.

In the book, I alluded to me understanding why my mother was the way she was toward me. But I never said why or elaborated more on that topic.

My mother Debra was born in 1952 and raised in Birmingham, Alabama.
She was friends and went to school with two of the four little girls who were murdered by the Ku Klux Klan in the 16th Street Baptist Church bombings…

Trauma

My mother was the oldest of my grandmother's 10 children. Stories from my aunt and uncles indicate she was more of a mother than a sister to her siblings while both of my grandparents worked. I would imagine she never had the chance to play with a doll since she was responsible for doing her sister's hair. Make believe cooking was replaced with real cooking for her siblings. Pretend diapers were replaced with real, demanding babies and children who were hungry and required care … No childhood (I'm sure that was traumatic).

She later met and married my father as a young woman. I don't know what happened, but by the time I was born, he was no longer living in the home. My mother was a single mother of 5 children who often worked 2 jobs.

I was born in the 70s, raised during Reaganomics, and the strategic placing of crack cocaine into the black communities across the United States. Church and Hip-Hop music made things much more bearable! When I began to look at my mother through this lens of circumstance and see her as a woman who is so much more than just my mother, I began to release a lot of resentment and fear, which ultimately led to forgiveness. *This, my beautiful people, is called empathy.*

So, I am attempting to participate in this brutal entrepreneurial boot camp, finishing up my memoir, and wanting to ride this Tech Valley wave. My business plan was going to consist of being a coach to minority (underserved) clients who work in STEM fields. But creating and understanding this business plan in structure was more than difficult for me. Also, for the first time ever that winter, my asthma was acting up really bad. All my life I never had asthma flare ups or needed any breathing treatments. That winter I had to go to the emergency room at least six times and sometimes they kept me overnight. This was detrimental to my attendance points at my job with the call center. They were becoming frustrated with me, and I was growing frustrated with working for other people. I was at negative attendance points with no chance of redemption. If I ever wanted a raise, a promotion, or to simply make a lateral move within that organization, my negative attendance points made this impossible. I went to work the next day and submitted paperwork for an absence. They simply claimed that they did not receive it. It was at that time that I decided that *I am quitting and today is my last day*. So, I did. I completed my day and five minutes to the close of my shift, I sent an email to my supervisor and to human resources. (Please note that I do not recommend quitting your job for entrepreneurship unless you have an exit plan.)

With my new-found freedom and time, I devoted myself to marketing my book, perfecting my business plan, and watching YouTube videos, Podcasts, and webinars, and attending trainings dedicated to entrepreneurship. I did nothing else. No television. No partying. No dating. No hanging out. No wasting time. No job. No income. No hair. And no nails. No BS. As entrepreneur Gary Vee would say, *I ate shit*. I was learning about myself in a new-found way. And I worked on my business plan, which consisted of me serving as a life coach with minorities who work in STEM. So, that's what I worked on. I worked on me, listening to my intuition and learning about myself for about 4 months.

During the judging of the entrepreneur boot camp competition, I presented the story of my book, which would soon be published as well as my business plan. The judges told me that my pitch presentation for the business plan did not match my overall vision. They were not aligning. I knew what they were saying. They were able to see what I was failing to acknowledge. I wanted to help people, but I also wanted the financial gain of working with that specific target audience. I was so sick and tired of working in human services. As I attended more trainings, I began to acknowledge that I needed to make a choice. One of my favorite influencers is Evan Carmichael, who is an entrepreneur/business owner who believes that one of the world's biggest problems is *untapped potential* and wants to help entrepreneurs reach their full potential... By the time this is published, he will have close to 2 million YouTube subscribers. I was watching one of his live trainings, and there had to be at least 3,000 people watching at the time. Toward the end of his event, he opened it up for a Q&A session. *I was feeling torn between a business that worked with the alcohol/drug population versus minorities in STEM.* I wasn't very specific but I put out my question in the Q&A, and low and behold he answered it! He told me that I wanted to follow my heart, but that I wasn't following my intuition and wouldn't be happy until I did. I was stoked. Evan Carmichael said my name and answered my question! That same week, something very similar happened to me while watching an online training. However, this was a spiritual influencer. What are the odds of that! I took it as a sign. Again, any work or research that I was doing related to learning and promoting anything STEM related *wasn't working*. I kept coming across the word Empathy and emotional intelligence. I read and studied more about it. Then, I started to take online quizzes about Empathy. I started to read books that confirmed without a doubt that I am an Empath. What we put energy toward grows. So the more I learned about myself and empathy, the stronger my gift became. I looked over my life and realized why I was so able to de-escalate crises among the inmates and the children that I worked with. The adults who saw my light when I was a child and my peers simply didn't know how to take me because they didn't understand me. I could be so calm when they were livid or highly disappointed. I refused to let the negative energy of others affect me. I then began to take an empathetic view of my life. Specifically, with the people who had hurt me. No one relationship has impacted my life more than that with my mother. My book Debra's daughter (http://bit.ly/debrasdaughter) is a tribute to her and the legacy of the strength of my ancestors. I am forever grateful. Those things that others saw as weak and what I sometimes saw as a curse (caring too much) was and continues to be *my ultimate blessing*.

The same is true for you. If you persevere through the hard times and listen to your intuition. Your gut feeling. Your instinct. You will pull through. We all have intuition. And it manifests itself through dreams, visions, and prophecy. It is a GOD-given gift. You do have it... It's just that the more we are disconnected from our true selves (for example working at a job that we hate, eating unhealthy foods, watching negative TV and internet shows, being around low-frequency people), the more difficult it is to hear that inner voice and to feel your true soul and spirit. Choosing Empathy is the Game Changer that's going to change the world. I am excited and blessed to be a part of it. Martin Luther King, Jr. had a dream. A big dream. Although, his dream has not come true YET, he continues to make a significant shift in the world.

I changed my business plan and name from Willis Wellness to Empathy Empowers. We are a life coaching company that teaches people how to cope with an alcoholic, addicted, or a recovering family member. We teach coping skills and healthy boundaries. Empathy is our major tool. The only person we can change is ourselves. That is the mission. The vision is to enhance the world by making it more empathetic. This will be accomplished through time, relationship building, and strategically managing resources. When a person is born they receive a new name. I renamed myself with a title that has purpose and defines me.

Allow me to introduce myself. My name is Ms.B. I am the Goddess Of Empathy. The name is for you, the title is for me. You can just call me Ms.B. I am the proud CEO of Empathy Empowers. At empathy empowers we understand how family addiction and alcoholism can devastate the family, and we have more than 20 years of experience in the field. If you or someone you know need help in managing alcoholism, addiction, or recovery with a family member, feel free to reach me at msbempathy@gmail.com.

Peace and Blessings...

Fireside Reflections

Keywords and Takeaways:

1. Forgiveness

2. Empathy

3. Gift

4. Persevere

5. Healthy Boundaries

Ms. B speaks about forgiveness as she began to understand more about having empathy for others, namely her Mom. Forgiveness is an important tool to be able to have because it is freeing and allows you to move forward with life in a way that you would not have if you had not forgiven someone. At the same time forgiveness can mean I forgive you, but that also doesn't mean that a person must remain in your space. At the end of the day, it is for you as much as it is for them.

Who in your life needs to be forgiven so that YOU can move on and thrive? Below write their name and let them know that you forgive them and why.

_____

_____

_____

_____

_____

_____

_____

Empathy is anchoring word here in this chapter. Ms. B explains that she discovered her gift through empathy. Allowing yourself to empathetic opens your eyes with a wider lens in how you view and handle the world. You never know why someone is the way that they are, so try to be less judgmental and more empathetic as a whole.

In what ways will you practice being more empathetic?

_____

_____

_____

_____

_____

_____

Often times, our gifts are tied to the things that we do not realize our gifts are. As mentioned before, Ms. B discovered that her gift was empathy. If you are unsure of what your gifts are, look closely within versus outward into the world trying to discover something that you have had inside of you all along. It's a matter of paying attention to yourself and patterns. There you will find out and become more in tuned with who you really are.

Do you know your gift? What is something that you do effortlessly or something that you enjoy doing and would do without even getting paid to do it?

_____

_____

_____

_____

_____

_____

Persevere is one of those words that will show up without a doubt in each of our lives. It is one of those words that is important for us to heal, manage ourselves, and to get to our next levels. It is a word that encourages us to forge through!

Continue to push through life's obstacles. Each time that you do, you are strengthening your muscle to be able to push through even harder the next time and the time after that. Remember, these are only moments. They come and they go. *#jotthatdown*

Healthy Boundaries! This could be its own chapter. Creating healthy boundaries is vital to your success whether in life or in business. Creating those boundaries allows you focus on what's important. Depending upon the situation, those boundaries look different for each of us. However, it is simply a way to create a space to ensure that we are our best selves.

What healthy boundaries have you created, or will you start implementing right away?

_____

_____

_____

_____

_____

_____

BUILDING BLOCKS

Jay Barr

It's 3:53 am on the first Monday morning after we *lost* an hour due to spring forward. I am awake, laying in my bed as usual and waiting for my 4:00 am alarm to go off so that I can start my day. This day is no different than any other. I did not feel the effects of the lost hour and because I heard so many people complaining about it, I wanted to prove that I was not going to let it affect me and that I would continue my routine as normal. I did just that! I did not skip a beat. I got up, got dressed, and was in the gym by 4:30 am to begin my workout. I got a great workout in and headed back home to shower to take my girls to school, then head back to the house to begin my workday, which would last until I got done, somewhere between 6:30 pm and 9:00 pm. I work so many hours because most of my day is not my own. Most of my day belongs to the people who need me, my decisions, my input, my guidance, my time, my approval, as well as my mentorship. At some point I accomplish the things I need to do for us to further expand our company. You see, I am the Executive

Vice President and part owner of the company that I've been with for the past 10 years, and my workdays are intense, stressful, demanding, rewarding, and, believe it or not, fun! It's fun because I love what I do, who I help, who I do it for, and the difference I make day in and day out for our staff, customers, partners, and our organization as a whole. I do not even view it as work. It's just a part of life, just as much as me doing anything for my family and loved ones, I do it for our company, and I wouldn't have it any other way. This 4:00 am routine has been my routine for the past 5 years, not coincidentally, the past 5 years have been the most productive ones of my life.

By all accounts, and life's measuring sticks, I am "winning" in life. I'm extremely successful in business, make a great living, have a loving and beautiful family, the stereotypical big house, and oddly enough only basic cars because I travel so much that I do not really see the value in owning an expensive model, since I am in a rental pretty much every other week or more. Most people that I come across tend to like and respect me owing to my unwavering, positive outlook on life regardless of trials or circumstances. Life is pretty good! I know it sounds like I am just another person bragging on how awesome he is, but I promise *that is not the case*. Things are going fantastic now, but things were not always that way. To appreciate where I am now, we need to discuss what led me to this point because for as much as I used the word "I" in this lead in, this journey is not about me. My goal here is to tell my story in an effort to reach that person who has walked that walk and inspire him or her to take a few more steps.

I will begin at a pivotal point in my life, which left me scarred mentally, shook generally, and probably forged in my heart a desire to push for success. It was a 90-plus degree day, in the summertime, on the west side of Baltimore City, Maryland, where I was living at the time. I was 12 years old and had just walked to the corner store to buy something cold to drink. If you grew up in any inner city, you likely know the type of store I am talking about. It has the long bulletproof glass or whatever material that was, and all of the things you want to buy are behind it. So, you *have* to ask for it, the clerk gets it, then you put your money in the plastic cylinder that they spin toward you so you can place your money in. Then, they spin it back around to themselves, take your money, place your item in it, spin it back, and you grab your stuff and go... Sound familiar? That is where I was, somewhere around midday, on this steamy, hot day. The store set up was like a long hallway, which couldn't have been more than 6 feet wide if that, but it was long enough to fit about 15 people in a straight line, but behind the glass there was much more space where all the things you could buy were located. I was in the store with two other guys. One of them I knew, and he was a neighborhood drug dealer named "Fat Derrick," and the other guy I'd seen around the way but didn't know his name. Both of them were older, maybe 19 or 21 years old. I was in line behind Fat Derrick. (Derrick was really fat, I mean the kind of fat that you can't see around him kind of fat!) I was looking down in my hand checking to make sure I didn't drop any of my quarters on the way up to the store, and the other guy was standing in line behind me but further back. He sounded like he was rapping some NWA lyrics or something and sorta bopping to the beat he had going on in his Walkman. I could tell he also sold drugs because he was way too *fresh* to be around the way like that, for any other reason.

So, while I was checking my change, the door opened. I heard a loud boom, a click, then another boom... I could barely see around Fat Derrick, but I saw a big gun smoking and two guys, one on the trigger and another one who was with him. I heard a thud, looked back to see the fresh guy hit the door at the end of the hall area of the store, then slump to the ground. As soon as he hit the ground, he bounced back up, and then boom! Again, I hear Fat Derrick say in a low tone, "Stay down," but I guess the guy was panicked and doing what his instinct told him to do, which was to try to get up. He got back up twice but did not get up a third time after that last shot. There was not much left of the back of his head after that last shot. I was 12 years and scared shitless! I just wanted my mommy, but I also was not trying to get shot, so I was literally pressed against the glass as hard as I could, hoping the shooters couldn't see me past Fat Derrick. I could see them and I could see them look at Fat Derrick, with a sort of short stare as if they were saying, *I know Fat Derrick, and I can't kill him because he's connected.* So, they turned around and left, but they didn't run like they had just shot someone to death; they just turned around like they were doing their business and began to go on their way. I heard the door close back, and the people behind the counter were bugging out and I guess calling the police. I couldn't understand or make out what they were saying since I was still in shock myself. I waited maybe for 5 or for 10 seconds, which felt like 5 hours, and then I started running. I was super-fast and hadn't yet lost one single race in my entire life. So, I full-out sprint to the door, and just as I am about to open it, I get yanked up and pulled back hard, damn near off my feet by Fat Derrick.

Now, I mentioned he was fat, right? And I am super-fast, right? I have no idea how Fat Derrick managed to move fast enough to catch me at the door, but he did and quite frankly had he not, I wouldn't be here to write this story. I am flailing around, telling Fat Derrick *let me go,* because all I wanted to do is run all the way home and just get to my mother. I was frantic and he slammed me against the wall and says, "If you run out there right now, they will think you are running to tell on them and they **WILL KILL YOU**." Have you ever talked to someone, they say something to you, and you have no doubt that what they are saying is the truth? You know that tone, that inflection that leaves little to no doubt? Well, that's how he said that to me, and even at 12 years old, I knew he *meant* what he said. So, I snapped out of it real quick, and I waited in there with Fat Derrick. We may have waited for several minutes, but not for too long. And then he walked out, then motioned for me to come out. He said, "Shorty if you smart, you **ain't seen nothing today**… **YOU were never here**." I took that for what it was and slow walked a few steps... then broke out into a full sprint all the way home. I never told my mother, never said one single word about what happened that day… but I had some rough nights, replaying the way that fresh dude lost his life. That was my first time seeing someone get killed but it wouldn't be my last. It was that experience that solidified in my brain that I wanted more for my life, and I would live it to the fullest because no matter what you do, you never know when it's your time to go. I knew I would give myself and my kids a better life and do my best to make sure they didn't have to live through the experiences that I did.

However, just because I wanted a better life, and I knew I would get there, the *how* was a bit of a mystery because the only people I knew who were doing "well" were the people in the drug game. All of the adults in the neighborhoods who went to work had jobs that paid them enough to be broke. That didn't make sense to me, and it was the complete opposite when talking to my friends in school. You see, in second grade it was clear they had to skip me or figure something else out because I was blessed with mega smarts! My mother worked it out for me to get bussed over to the other side of town to a school that had the G.A.T.E. program… That stood for Gifted and Talented Education. I met all kinds of kids from all kinds of backgrounds, some like me from the hood, and others from different countries and yes a bunch of white kids who seemed to have *perfect lives*. I can admit I was jealous of the things they would tell me about their lives, and I would often lie to keep up with them. That school was one of the best things to happen to me because it gave me a perspective that extended beyond my block. Growing up in the inner city, far too often all we have exposure to is our own neighborhood. So, there is a continuous cycle of "no hope."

The G.A.T.E. program gave me hope, which would play a big part in my life as the calendar turned. Having in the back of my mind that other things were truly possible definitely helped me through the tough times growing up. We didn't have Facebook, Instagram, or other social media to help us escape our realities, but luckily I had school. However, when I returned home, it was back to reality. The reality of a father who lived with us but who was not really present. He was an on-the-road tractor trailer driver so he was always on the go, which probably wouldn't have bothered me but when he was home, he was not terribly interested in me. He was not bad or mean to me, and I have some really good memories about him, albeit but they are relatively few, considering the 16 years he had me living in his household. My dad had two vices, alcohol and women. So, when he was in town, he was often drunk, and if he came home at all, it was after being with who knows how many women. As a kid, the women never bothered me because I didn't know any better. I just knew my mother cried a lot, and I didn't like that at all. But when I was older, I would see him, because he had other women in our neighborhood that he used to "be with," so it was kind of embarrassing. I always wondered why I wasn't important enough to get his time like these women, and why he couldn't put down the bottle long enough to build with me. But as I grew up, I understood that my father was a young man and did not have life figured out either. So I do not hold any grudges against him. Just the void of him being there, but not being there, I think that hurt more than if I didn't ever have him in my life at all. At least not having him would have eliminated the hope of him caring for and about me, and him being there for me. It was really tough to see him, but not see him, and even tougher to have him not see me, if you know what I mean.

I also did not have my dad around to talk to when I had a babysitter touch me repeatedly and even force me to have sex with her at a really young age. I have no idea what this older girl saw in a little skinny-ass boy, but it was her sickness, not mine. I struggled with owning that pain as my fault for years, but later exercised those demons. She used to touch me and get me excited; I was young and couldn't control that thing if I wanted to. She always commented on how much I was a little boy, but with man features. I knew what she meant. I was a little boy, but I had a man-sized package. No worries, this is not me advertising the size of my junk. I was a small boy and ultimately, I grew into it and I will leave it at that. However, I had to deal with that alone because I would never talk to my mother about it. I wanted to talk to the man, my father about it, but he was just not available for that type of a conversation. Also, I wasn't sure if I was going to get into trouble for it. Couple that experience and the way that he treated my mother, it really screwed up my view of women. In fact, this is likely a message for all women: *Be careful with what you put up with in a relationship with a man in front of your kids*, because watching my father constantly disrespect my mother, and her constantly take it, caused me to devalue women and in my head somewhere I thought that was how you treated all woman. I am sure that plus my experience as a smaller child didn't lend a hand to me thinking of women very highly, but I definitely liked girls, probably a bit too much, as life would show me over time. Anyway, the final straw with my dad was when he had another kid outside of the relationship with mom. At that point I wanted to be done with him, but it wasn't because of that that. It was because he let our phone get cut off so I couldn't talk to my girlfriend. Everyone thinks I wanted out because I was so angry at my father about him making my sister outside of the marriage with my mom. I didn't like that because he already wasn't there for me the way in which I wanted, and now he had another one. Add that with the fact our phone was off because he chose to spend the money on the women, and not our house, and that really pissed me off! We left him shortly thereafter to go live with my grandparents. Unfortunately, the fact we had no money and no phone, and life as I knew it was turned upside down, led me to the streets. The family business was cocaine, and it was very easy to get involved. I am not proud of those days, but believe it or not that life taught me more about life and business than anything else. I had a good mentor who told me to always keep a job, no matter how much money I was making, and this taught me that if it doesn't feel right, look right, sound right, then it "ain't right," and to walk away from anything that fit that criteria no matter the amount of money involved. Advice like that actually saved my life on more than one occasion.

Within a year of us leaving my father, I had a kid of my own on the way. I was 16 years old. As I was dealing with that reality, a huge tragedy rocked my core. It was March 17, 1993. This day nearly broke me. This was the day I lost one of my best friends, Big L. Murdered. I was completely numb. I began living with more purpose after this, but not initially. Initially, I just wanted revenge. I was reckless for a good bit, sincerely looking for trouble and for someone to take the pain out on. Luckily for me, I showed up too late, when his killer was spotted. I received the call that this piece of shit was at McDonald's, and I got there, he had already left. My mentor in the game who convinced me I needed to get my mind right told me *You can't be a dad behind bars*. I took that advice, got a job, and started doing more of the right things. But, I still was reeling from the loss of Big L. As was the case pretty much throughout my life, I always struggled with "both sides of the fence." My mother and grandparents always instilled very positive things and thoughts into me, and I would often hear my mother's voice right as I was at the edge of doing something I shouldn't do. But that didn't stop me from taking all the preceding steps and running full speed toward that edge. So, just as I was getting a job and working as I should, given the fact I was going to be a father, I still was out doing destructive things. After the close call with Big L.'s killer, I did some really basic crap... I played corner boy for a night, which really was not my thing. Even when I got in the game young as a "Time Out" boy, just yelling to my crew when the police were around so people would get low or not do anything that would get them shaken down or arrested, even then I really was not much of a corner boy. I always felt that was too risky and back then if someone my mother knew saw me, they would tell on me, and I would get "hemmed up." You could say I was more worried about dealing with my mother or Granny, than I was about dealing with the police. Nevertheless, I was more about moving the packages, not the hand-to-hand so it was a different game. More time was involved, but much less time exposed to get caught. Literally, it involved making a quick trip, move from here to there, and then being done for days, sometimes weeks, if a re-up wasn't needed. That made far more sense to me than hanging out on the corner all day and all night just to give much of what you pulled to the dude you worked for. Nah… I would stick to my in-and-out roles. Anyway, one night, I was with my right-hand man, Meat, who was close with Big L., too. A month or so prior to this night, we schemed and got ourselves some guns. So, pretty much every time you saw me, I was strapped. Well, the thing about being a corner boy is that if you are holding the work, you don't want to be holding a gun, too. That's two charges if you get rolled up on. Either way, I didn't feel comfortable going on the street without it, but I did because my man said it wasn't worth the risk this night and we would be alright. Of course, Murphy's Law hits and a guy gets out of a cab and says *we must be crazy to be on his block working*. A few words were exchanged and BANG… he pulled out and blasted, one of the guys named Ant we were with fell down, I looked at Meat, who was standing either in anger or shock, but then he turned to run, then I ran. Ant got up and ran as well. Turns out that even at that close range, the shooter made a poor shot and he missed everybody. None of us were hit, but it did help me snap out of the "bad boy/good boy world." I took my ass back to work.

On August 1, 1993, a star was born. My first "why" bullied her way into this world by disrupting her baby shower to try and join the party! Having a child completely changed my outlook on life because it was no longer about me. My drive was renewed, that feeling I had when I saw the fresh dude's brains laying out of his head, and I said that I would work my ass off to make sure my children would not have to see the things I saw or live the way I lived. The birth of Camaree sparked my string of jobs as I was trying to find my way, and, yes, I had one hand in the streets and one hand in the right lane as I was sorting things out.

It was June 24, 1997, and I had just turned 21 years old on June 1st. I had a great surprise birthday party, and I was on top of the world! I got into a beef with a drug dealer at a basketball game the Sunday before, and there was no doubt that we were going to have to finish this beef at some point. When I came home from this altercation, I told my mother about it and went about my business. Little did I know that at that time my mother had a vision about me being in the hospital, which you will find very eerie as I lay out this next series of events. I went to work as normal, and then it happened. I was doing line clearance for the gas and electric company, clearing trees and branches from the power lines. I was on the ground and my foreman cut a tree, which landed right on me, hitting me in the head, knocking me unconscious, and causing amnesia. This experience is the one that ended up setting up the life I live today. I thought life as I knew was over, and in many ways that was true. I went through a year-long rehab to get myself back together. I battled depression, I lost weight, remember I said I was already a skinny kid, and I couldn't leave the house, I was in a third-floor apartment and walking down the stairs made me dizzy. Up until that time, I always prided myself in being a rather sharp guy, my brain was my asset but after the accident, I was anything but sharp. I lost 3 years of memory, and I was no longer the super-sharp, quick-witted guy. I literally had to search for words, and struggled with remembering and retaining information. I felt hopeless.

The fact that my brain is not what it once was still gets to me. But back when it was really fresh, it was crippling. Just imagine anything you were really good at, I mean something that you know if you were involved, it was going to go amazingly well for you… Now imagine whatever that thing is, you are now, no longer as good at, overnight... You are now 70% as good as you were before, and it's not like you got older and can't do things like you used to. It's that you are young, in your prime, about to hit your stride, and **boom**! Now, you operate at about 70% of what you excelled at…. So if you are a speed reader, overnight you have slowed down some, maybe you are a great singer, and overnight you can't sing as well, or maybe you are extremely gifted in arithmetic, and overnight it takes you longer to figure things out. I can keep going with examples to try to make you feel what I am relaying, but in my case, it was my mind. Now notice, I didn't say you could no longer do these things, you can still read fast, but just not as fast, you can still sing, but just not as well as you know you can, and you're still good at math, but maybe instead of solving problems in 5 seconds it takes you 15 to solve the formula. Seems inconsequential, right?? Not if that is what you are *really good at*, not if that is what makes you go, not if that is what makes you tick... *Your own super power has diminished.* The fact is the changes may not even be noticeable to the outside world, but internally, you know you are slipping even if the world doesn't acknowledge it. My mind was different, and has never returned to its original state. Prior to the accident, I remember while I was in the hospital, them repeatedly asking me questions to check how lucid I was and how much damage had been done. "Who is the president?" "What's your phone number?" "What's your address?" "Where are you?" I knew something was crazy wrong when whatever answer I gave, in return I received a vacant response. With my brain beat up, I was able to still read people, and I could tell their reactions, although attempting to be stoic and non-reactive, it indicated I was not only wrong but that I was way off. This went on for a while, as they kept running mental and physical tests to assess my damage. Fortunately, there was no bleeding or anything like that. There was also talk of *if I could just get more "with it, he may be able to go home.*

So, I proceeded to compensate for what I couldn't trust my brain to get right with some good-old-fashioned manipulation. The good thing about baseline tests is they can tell you how a person is progressing; the bad thing about baseline tests is they are predictable. So I pretty much got every answer wrong. When *What's your phone number?* was asked, I gave them my grandmother's number. Why? I have no idea, but it was the number I knew, and I thought it was mine. I gave them my address from maybe 2 or 3 addresses ago, and the president? Now I may have said *Reagan.* I was all over the place, BUT what I realized is I could solve this riddle, and I could crack this code. So I did! I asked for a pencil, and someone brought me some paper. What I began to do was write down the questions and I would ask them to my unsuspecting visitors. So, each question someone answered correctly, I would write down on the paper, then read it over and over to myself until I memorized the answer. I realized quickly I had what they call "CRS"= Can't Remember Shit! So, I needed to come up with a system and come up with it fast, so I could get out of the hospital. I began writing things on the paper in a certain way, such as this in the middle that on the left or right etc. Before long, even though I may not have actually remembered the information, I remembered middle, and I would take my brain to the middle of the paper and there was my answer! Before long, I was able to do that in my head and I was able to *give the illusion* I was remembering things and possibly coming out of it. Boy did I have those nurses and doctors fooled! They thought I jumped into some accelerated recovery and that everything was clicking again. Not a chance. I was literally clueless to the answers I was giving, I just knew they were right and more right answer equaled Jay going home.

So, I continued on this path for a bit and then it happened. To this day, I do not know if the doctor planned this or strategically put himself where I could hear him, because he became hip to my game or he was legitimately serious about what he was saying. All I know is when I heard him say, "Well, we were going to keep him for further observation, especially to ensure no aneurysm would occur, but he seems to really be coming around. So, we should be able to release him." Hold Up! Wait! Time Out… *I was just bullshitting* is what I was thinking, but I told on myself, or Sherri did once I told her. I am not sure which was which. All I know is that I *was not released.* The huge take away from this incident for me in that moment was that even in the most deficient status, you can create systems to overcome your adversity or challenge, and that was the genesis of not letting anyone know my mind was slightly off from where it was. I did not want anyone to think they had the upper hand or get the upper hand due to my deficit. I would level the playing field with my systems. I have systems for EVERYTHING You think I am operating on a high mental level, and it's just my systems carrying me. For instance, I travel a bunch, so I have a system for my travel items. As a result, I never leave or lose anything on the road. I place everything in the same exact place every time I go anywhere so I do not have to think,

I do not have to check, I simply work my system and I appear to the outside world as a highly functioning and really detail-oriented person. This skill or ability I was able to build to mask my deficiency was born out of a necessity to never let anyone see who I was, that I was not as sharp as I used to be, and to take away any advantage you may have or think you have... Bottom line it was not going to beat me and will not be my excuse.

There was a moment where I began to feel a little better about my situation, I was on a good run. I remember being home and my good friend Tony stopped over. He had recently purchased a Diamante, which was a pretty dope car back in the day. So, I managed to get myself down the stairs, or he helped me down, I do not really remember that detail, but we got outside. I was very happy for him and complimented him on the car with genuine excitement. He looked at me with a strange look, and I asked *what the look was for.* He told me that he had already showed me the car before maybe a few weeks or a month ago. I was crushed. I had no recollection of seeing his car, ever. That was it for me! I spiraled hard out of control into a depression. If it wasn't for Sherri being there for me every step of the way, I do not know if I would have made it. I had to see a therapist and do tons of exercises to get myself back into the world. I needed to get back to work somewhere because I needed to earn some money. Once I was able to drive again in 1998, I was only driving short distances, there was a car dealership about 5 minutes from my house, so I applied there and got a job selling cars. Ironically, my time at the dealership is why I am a successful executive today. During that time, I was in the "Why Me?" mindset. Turns out I needed that tragic moment to create the space I am currently in today.

I sold cars, and I loved it. I was really good at it, and was making some real money legitimately for the first time in my life. I really enjoyed working with customers and helping the managers. The car life was great for me. However, Sherri and I began to get super serious, and even though I was making good money, I was not always disciplined as a 22-year-old, so I didn't keep what I made. In the car game, if you don't sell you don't eat. I needed to get a consistent income and consistent schedule if I was going to keep Sherri around. She was already working and going to school to be a nurse, so me spending 12 hours a day minimum at a car dealership was not conducive for maintaining a healthy relationship. I stuck it out for a while but eventually I left the car business although I ended up back in it, on the credit side. A couple of years later I got out of the day-to-day car dealer life. The great thing is that while I was there, I learned a ton about the industry and loved it. There were guys making insane money, and these guys were not as smart as I was. They were not as gifted either, but boy they could sell! It showed me that you do not have to have all of the assets, you just have to grind and never give up on yourself. Guys with marginal education levels, absolutely killing it, making six figures, it was inspiring. If I can say anything about myself as I became more self-aware in life, and I begin to look back at the different life experiences that have shaped me into who I am today, I do believe I had a strong ability to see things and to read them well. But the best part was I always had takeaways that were meaningful if I saw any value in what was happening, whether I did anything positive with that information or not, I always recognized it. It would have been easy for a young egotistical kid to say, "I am smarter than them, and I have more talent than they do," and then create all kinds of excuses for why they were winning more than I was at the time. Who knows, maybe I did to some extent back then, but deep down I knew and recognized then that hard work, works, and you can literally grind your way to success. I needed that life lesson.

To balance things out timewise and still make money, I returned to the side hustle of the streets. Nothing too crazy but at this point things were huge and I didn't have to do much to pocket some serious coins. I got a decent job, had solid money coming in, and was living sort of reckless. I was not fully addressing my depression, forging my mindset, which is the cornerstone of my resolve but really not a healthy way to live when you have issues that need to be dealt with, otherwise you will be a ticking time bomb. I went through several phases of self-destruction, I was volatile, I definitely was not taking care of myself, and I was not the man I should have been on any meaningful level. Luckily, I had Camaree and she afforded the opportunity for me to always have an underlying purpose. Even if I couldn't shake what was in my head for me, I could compartmentalize and be *how I needed to be to be a good father to my kid*. That skill still exists in me today, and I don't know if it's from the "Gemini" spirit that lives within me or as a defense mechanism or maybe even developed out of necessity since I absolutely had to go through things but also had to go forward. Who knows? Maybe everyone has this ability. But all I know is for me it is a way of life, which is both productive and rewarding, but also highly destructive and dangerous.

Here is what I mean... I can give people the best of me, help them, inspire them, be what I need to be for them while at the same time be amazingly self-destructive for myself, and literally separate the two worlds as if there was a visible wall with a door, and I just walk back and forth, depending on where I am. Now, this doesn't mean that I am not genuine and definitely doesn't mean I do not practice what I preach or somehow that I do not apply what I learn and teach to myself. If any of that were true, I would not have any success. Plus, people can see through that facade. I am exactly who and what I say I am. I do everything I tell others to do. But what no one sees is the pain and likely depression-type things that exist behind the scenes that I just suppress and likely don't deal with. I just may drink too much one night, or not sleep for a few days or entertain women, or get around the wrong crowd, all of the things that I know better than to do but allow myself to drift to in moments when this other piece creeps into my head.

I worked and was in and out of the game as needed, but largely I just lived day by day without much of a care about finances, and always stayed pretty comfortable but never flashy or extra. Things continued that way through my series of jobs. One job for a popular rental furniture and merchandise company led nowhere, but it was in one of the toughest neighborhoods in Baltimore City, and that was just what the doctor ordered for my frustrations and built-up pain. Nothing spectacular happened here, I mean I have some crazy stories about that time, but that's for another day. The most important takeaway from this one was that this is where I met my best friend, who became my brother, who just so happened to share a name with my fallen friend Big L. My brotherhood with EL is one of the most pivotal relationships in my life because it appeared that both of us were lost and looking for what the other provided, that balance of realizing we were not crazy for being the way we were, and that is true to this very day.

Let's talk about how things began to change for your boy. So, life was going well, and I needed to get a good job and completely leave the game. Given the fact that most of my family was already in prison, and many of my friends were in and out, and everyone in the world would be snitching soon as the football numbers were thrown at them. So it really was just time to get out, get legit, and live life as it was intended to be lived. So, I realized Real Estate Appraisal was where it was at. Loans were plentiful, so I knew if I just got in the game I would be able to clear $350-$450 dollars per appraisal. If I did a couple per day, I would be writing my own ticket. I took the appraisal course based on the advice of a cousin, who knew I was interested and also told me he would work with me to get my hours. You must work with someone for a certain amount of hours as a trainee before you are able to get out on your own (at least that's how it was back then). I graduated and was ready to roll, but the original deal agreed to did not happen, so I was a man without a home in the appraisal game. I also was not the by-any-means-necessary, whatever-it- takes person I am today. So instead of figuring out how to get it elsewhere, I just focused on being angry and bitter about not getting what I was told from my cousin. He did say that full disclosure would help me get hours, but it had to be the right way to stay with compliance. However, the only thing was *2 black guys coming up to a house for appraisal*. He couldn't stop his momentum for me, but he could find a way to hook me up with trainee hours. Unfortunately, I was looking for tutelage and experience, and not just hours because I really did need to know what I was going to do. This was going to be my way to run my own business and create a legit legacy. Well, my immaturity and whatever really kept him from truly helping me left me discouraged, and I was ready to get back out there and just make it happen again until I figured it out. I was beginning to think the only thing I would be good at was the dope game, and looking back on it, I certainly am not mad at my cousin for not doing what I wanted him to do, *he had all the risk,* and I had a history of being mercurial. So, I may not have done business with me either, haha!

Again, I received a favor because another friend opened a Mortgage Brokerage Firm and offered to hire me. I made quite a few loans quickly and earned a higher commission split than most rookies would be offered, and man, I was making legit money but on a hustler-type of level so I was loving life! The people in the bank knew who I was, and I did so well that I was able to move my family out of the city and into the suburbs so that my girls could receive a solid education without the distractions. In addition, I needed to get myself away from distractions. So, I proceeded to sell loans. But the problem was that I was not building relationships. I was literally sending loans to whatever bank would say *Yes,* the fastest, and not building any alliances. So, when that industry took a hit and fell hard, I had no connections to keep me afloat and I was extremely low. I had no idea what I was going to do, and I was lost. I was in the bathroom because I could be alone and just be in that place that many men have been where you have all this success, but then it's gone--- you still have all these things, this life you built, this family looking at the Lion to figure it out---and I was just low. Sherri was always there to pick me up though, encourage me to go on, and just told me to go be happy. She told me to find something in addition to money that would make me happy. She was a nurse and told me that she would figure it out while I figured out how I would be great. So, I tried the car biz, and the mortgage biz, and both of them were taking hits as the economy was in bad shape. I knew that I needed to get into something that was "recession proof" and "future proof." I did not want to get into the medical field like Sherri because while I love people and all, I also don't like people at times, and the stories she shared with me confirmed that just wasn't my calling. So getting into the computer field was the only logical conclusion.

There was a popular computer training school in our area that I mulled over attending. Then, I finally applied. The problem was that I needed to get a loan to get in, and I really did not have the income or credit to be able to get this sizeable loan even though it was a student loan. So, I tried using cosigners and my grandfather, who I respect more than any human being alive, I mean to the point where I would not ask him for assistance even though I knew he had perfect credit and never missed a bill in his life. However, I was totally out of options and I asked him for help. He thought about it and came back with a *Yes*. The reason I am telling you this is because this was another Game-Changing Moment, as I will explain when I tie it all together here shortly. Grandpop said he would do it and that we should go up to the school. There was literally one slot left in the class, and me and one other person were trying to get in. Grandpop and I got in first, and I got the last seat in that class.

Fast forward, I absolutely killed the class, I was stupid focused, and success was the only option. The school had a job placement department, which scheduled an interview for me with a travel training company that installed and trained software. I rocked the interview so well the job told the school they would hire me. But they had a person from within the company who also applied for the position, and they had to go with that candidate, which I respected. This job paid $60K a year. I was looking forward to that money because I knew I could do some things with it. This turned out to be one of the best jobs I didn't get, because it left me open for what happened next. The job placement lady told me the report she received from this other company and said, "Hey, can you do me a favor and go interview at this other technology company?" I said, "Sure, but why is it a favor?" She told me they would not pay me nearly what I could make elsewhere but they wanted to send me because the place was pretty good about interviewing and even hiring people from the school. However, many people had poor interviews, so she wanted to show them she was not just sending the "bad options." So, I took the interview, didn't do my normal pre-interview prep to even learn what the company did, knew they wouldn't pay, and I needed money. But, I would do the school that favor. I interviewed and was waiting so long for the next person to interview me that the VP came in and interviewed me himself because he felt sorry for me for sitting there so long. I had a really strong interview with the VP, and I must say we caught a rhythm.

I was in a groove! I was really enjoying the line of questioning and also learning more about the company and sharing more about my background. He found out I had a car background, which I discounted because it had been years since I worked at the dealership, even though *once a car guy, always a car guy*. When you've had to close a deal so your kid can have Christmas gifts, you are never the same. In addition, I had several years on the finance end so I was much more experienced in the industry than most people who come to a tech company. This is important because the company provided software for car dealerships. After the interview, they made an offer, and, yes, it was pretty much laughable. For me to take the job, I would have to take a $27K pay cut, which I was not comfortable with, given my financial goals and the fact I needed to get back on top. However, the brilliant Sherri tells me *you liked the interview, you have car experience, don't worry about the money, just see if you will like it, it sounds like you will like it*. Well, she was right. I LOVED it!

I started at the bottom, and I didn't care, I loved the job and I had a history of being an impact player over time no matter where I was.

So, I figured I would get to that level at some point here, too. The other side was weighing me down because I was 100% legit at this point, struggling financially, but otherwise I loved the gig. So, what do I do? No idea. During my first few months at the job, the school that got me this job closed down, which means I got the last seat in the last class at that school, and if I didn't get that last seat, none of this next part would have ever happened. Since I had responsibility of the girls, I kept showing up late for work, and Sherri was working trying to pay bills so that we wouldn't be broke and me, miserable. The company adjusted my start time to try and help me out, but my performance was still inconsistent; however, once I was there I was certainly a stand out performer, to the point where the VP came back to me and said there may be a chance for me to earn some extra money. This was contingent, though, on whether I could come to work consistently on time and be reliable. So, I focused and figured out the things that were in my way and kept performing. All of this was fine but, I still wasn't making real money, and eventually, I received word of some really big money opportunities back on the street level of course. This is where the big Game-Changing event happened.

Now to fully appreciate this, it's important that you remember I got into the school as the last seat in the last class that graduated before they shut their doors mid-session on the next group of students. I don't get a job, I totally crushed the interview for, and that led me to do this "favor interview" at this company where I meet the VP and find out that it's tied to the car business. So, the universe is conspiring to help your boy out, as long as I stay out of my own way, but that would be too easy and too much of a happy ending if I simply stayed out of my own way. As had been my pattern, something good was going on, and I had to reach back into the bad bin and look for something else. This is super significant because the company I was working for literally feels like I was a part of something, like the ground floor of something major that will take off and be something incredible. So, I was feeling that energy and loving it, but I was still looking back because I needed some more money. I knew that if I just made a couple of moves that I would be able to get our lives back on track and get back into things clear headed at work. So, I meet with my people a few times, and on one occasion I was in the house while it was being watched. I didn't realize it at the time but there are more drugs and money in some nearby suitcases than I've ever seen in my life. I still don't have any of the details about my role, but it was going to be important enough to earn a significant amount of cash but not so vital that it falls apart without me. Turns out someone else had this role, and I was a timely replacement who could be trusted since moves this big could not get off schedule. I sleep on it and am not needed for a couple of days. Of course I started thinking of how much I could use the money to get back on track, to get some breathing room, and to focus on making myself valuable at work. Our company had several six-figure positions despite being a small organization, and one of them belonged to the on-the-road trainers. I wanted in, but they never promoted anyone to this role. They typically hired dealership guys or industry names to get out there and do it. All I knew is *I wanted it* and it was dangled slightly by the VP. But it was not going to be his call. Only our CEO could make that kind of a call, as it was risky to put a relative unknown out on the road to be a face of your organization. As I sat in bed weighing my options, I was still 100% committed to making this run, because once you are in, you don't get to pull out, at least not without consequences. It was no turning back, and I actually felt good about it. As with most things, you are not supposed to do, you only seem to see the best-case scenarios and ignore the peril.

The very next day, I was having lunch in our conference room as we did on Fridays because our CEO bought the staff lunch and we ate together. This particular day, I do not leave when everyone does, I just hung back and continued to chat with the VP. Then, the CEO began a conversation with the VP, which was way over my head. I really wondered if I should even be in the room based on the information being discussed, but I didn't get up. I sat there mostly because I was not finished talking to the VP yet, but also because it was kind of cool to be in the room with these power players talking about *big boy things*. Out of nowhere the CEO asks the, VP "When are you getting the big guy out on the road?" The VP and I lock eyes, big-eye style like neither of us saw this coming, and he says, "Funny you should say that! I was going to tell you how well he is doing and that I was considering giving him a shot." He approved, and just like that, I was given the break of my life. Oddly enough, when I checked my phone after lunch, somewhere midway through this talk, Sherri texted me and said, "I feel like your life is about to change." I have no idea where she gets these feelings from, but she was 100% right and that still freaks me out to this day. I did not get the 6-figure salary right away because I was an unproven talent, but I kept grinding and got something way more important than money. I got exposure and experience. The VP told me if I performed well, I would be able to write my own paycheck in 2 years. *That's all I needed to hear and I was charged up*. Obviously, after this encounter, I pulled out of the run and was allowed to because I was a working man, and not an active D boy in the game, so I was just a convenient option, more of a luxury than necessity. So things could go on without a terribly different trajectory for everyone. This decision turns out to be the most important Game-Changing point in my life. I skip it because I really want to see if I can run with this opportunity at work and become something special. I did not want anything possibly knocking me off track so I committed everything to it.

Less than 10 days later, I receive the dreaded phone call. Everyone involved in the run was arrested. Apparently, the entire operation was being watched, and they were just waiting for them to make the next move and arrest everyone involved. I said everyone, and I meant everyone. Every single person involved, people I knew and people I didn't, were all taken away. Turns out the person I was replacing actually set everyone up, because he was caught on a previous run. Just like that, it all was over. There is zero doubt that had I followed through with it, I would not be writing this story right now and I still would not be home from federal prison. This is not one of those "close calls" that you hear about---this was a 100% definite if I do this, I am done thing. I ended up with my hands on legal documents that showed surveillance notes from the night I was in the house, and had they come in, I would have been swept up in that mess, but they were looking to take down the whole operation, so they needed more action. I was actually listed as an uninvolved party, a basic visitor, likely because I hadn't been there before. I was not into anything but a full-time job with a struggling financial situation if they looked into me. I had the biggest pit in my stomach after hearing about this complete takedown. I have been forever grateful that I was not involved and routinely look at this opportunity at this job as a *life saver*. I work hard at it as if it represents the second chance I did not have to have.

That was the last warning shot I needed about that life and I have not revisited it since that time. I have also parlayed my full focus and attention into becoming not only one of the best trainers and consultants to ever perform in the position, but based on my overall desire to impact lives, I have grown into leadership role after leadership role over my decade with the company. Not that there hasn't been adversity along the way, of course there has been, but I remained diligent and changed my thinking, which changed my life. I stopped letting myself off the hook, and refused to accept the excuses I used to believe in, that totally limited my ability to "be great." I have been on a consistent climb ever since, and now I am at the top of leadership at our company. I am not just a leader, I am currently the Executive Vice President, who runs the daily operations of this company, and in 2016, I was made an equity holder in our company. Like the Jay-Z lyric, this means that *I play for the team I own*. Not so bad for this Baltimore kid who has seen some of the worst that life has to offer. I now get to see some of the best and take as many people as I can with me.

Now if you are keeping score... to bring this whole thing together:

- I witnessed a brutal murder at 12 years old, and Fat Derrick saved my life by not letting me run out.

- I see several more murders in my time in my neighborhood.

- My father is present, but absent.

- One of my best friends is murdered, and I am shot at point-blank range within months of this incident.

- I had my first born at the age of 17.

- A tree is cut down on me, and I lose my memory and functional skills for nearly one year.

- I cannot drive longer than 15 minutes, so I get a job located 5 minutes from my apartment at the car dealership.

- I am in and out of the drug game to supplement income.

- I get into a legit business making serious money and move myself and family away from the distractions and reach my breaking point when it all falls apart.

- I am the last person admitted to the last graduating class of a school that closed down unceremoniously midway through their last session, and I only get this opportunity because Grandpop cosigned for me.

- I take the interview for a good job that I don't get, which leads to an interview at a job I was not supposed to take due to low pay.

- I struggle with finances and decide to hop back in the game real quick to set myself up so I can work at the company I am at now.

- Less than 2 weeks until I am about to do this run, I am given the opportunity that set up my life, so I pull out of the run and when they do the run I was supposed to be on, everyone is arrested.

- I maximize my second chance at life, and I now am a successful executive, working on major deals, running day-to-day operations, and impacting lives every single day.

My journey has had some trauma, but largely I have a bunch of self-inflicted wounds, perhaps spurred on by my trauma. But, I do not charge it to that, I just charge it to *bad choices*. I am extremely blessed to be here, able to do what I do, and I do not take a second of it for granted. Had that tree not hit me, I wouldn't be where I am now. Sometimes, *what happens to you, happens for you*. I live my life now to practice what Granny told me, "Your gifts are not for you. Your gifts are for you to give away."

So, if anyone can draw inspiration from understanding that if you are going in the right direction, the universe does conspire to give you what you want/need. It doesn't mean that you won't face adversity along the way. It just means that it's all a building block to YOUR success.

Fireside Reflections

Keywords and Takeaways:

1. Tell my story

2. Create systems

3. Self-aware

4. Building relationships

5. Building blocks

Yes, tell your story. Your story is more so for others than it is for yourself. Your story is evidence of what God can do. We all have a story. Embrace it as a part of the building blocks that created you to be the person you are today.

Create systems. I personally love this one, because I am a total systems person! Systems can do so much for your organizational skills, time management, and well-being because they create structure. Once that structure is locked in, it makes everything else easier. Decide what areas of your life where you need to create a system. Start now by writing 3 below, then on a separate sheet of paper build out what each of those areas will look like going forward.

_____

_____

_____

_____

Self-aware. When you are self-aware, you are in position to make better decisions and choices that affect you and everything attached to you. You are able to articulate what your needs are and understand you own compass. What does self-awareness look like?

1. Know what creates joy in your life.

2. Know what your strengths and weaknesses are and seek to improve in those areas while seeking opportunities to thrive at the things you are great at doing.

3. Self-awareness is knowing all these things and living life according to those things.

Building relationships is one of the most important connecting tools you can do in your life. In large, your success is connected to who you know. Of course, it is also a divine blueprint as well. However, solid relationships lay the foundation for the chances of having a solid future. #jotthatdown Don't be lazy and take them for granted. Take a genuine interest in the people you connect with and see how you can better their lives as one day it can come back to bless you and they can also better yours.

Jay's story was full of Jenga moments. Remember Jenga, how you stack the blocks to build a tower and as you pull from the tower, the blocks will eventually come crashing down until you start all over again? Yeah that game. Many of our lives replicate Jenga, and that is okay. View each of those falls as an opportunity to grow and thrive instead of an opposition of failure and welcome the circle of LIFE!

YOU MAY HAVE WON SOME BATTLES
BUT NOT THE WAR!

Tracion Flood

I, a beautiful, strong, intelligent, black queen, was living the life of a crack fiend and standing in the rain without an umbrella or hat. My clothes dripping wet, I had been running around in the streets with the same clothes on for days. Oh, shit! There go my people, "Go home, Tracey!" But in the streets I stayed. This black queen stood on the street corners looking for crack, walked away from my babies, walked away from my job---and worst of all---walked away from my God. Yes, I still didn't look back. I was mesmerized. I had crack eyes. I didn't want to feel the pain, so I took a hit of cocaine. I didn't want to face the past, so I took another blast. Of course, I asked God a hundred million times maybe 3, "Why couldn't I be more like Carolyn, Pam, or Angie"? The cocaine didn't take away the pain but what it did do was eat at my brain and just about caused me to go insane. But, all praise to God, He didn't let go when I did. He ever so softly whispered for me to remember what His word said. See, all I needed was a mustard seed of faith and an ounce of love and out of my hole I could rise above. Now I've regained my strength and God saved my soul and this time by the blood of my sweet Jesus, I won't let go. So, to you "Crack Demon," I know you're out there waiting to jump back in, take control of my life, and try to kill me again. You may have won some battles, but the war, the blessed Trinity, and I will win.

This testament-poetry was written on my heart as I lay on a mat in a jail cell wondering how I got here. I remember boarding a Greyhound bus that was headed for Wilmington, North Carolina, leaving the only daddy I ever knew. His name was Miguel DaCruz. I remember the tears rolling down his face, and I didn't understand that this Greyhound trip was like none other because we would never return. My mother did not explain to me that we were moving to North Carolina to help my grandmother take care of my first cousins, who to this day are the same as my brothers and sisters because their mother, 7 years prior, was shot and killed by her husband with a sawed-off shot gun. After the long bus ride, I recall arriving at the worn-down bus station in Wilmington, which no longer exists. Mr. Buddy, who was a friend of my grandmother and I later learned was a pervert, was there to pick us up. When we arrived at my grand-mother's house, my cousins were on the porch playing marbles and jack rocks. They hated me on sight. I felt the same way because I wanted to be back in Brooklyn with my daddy, Mickey, my Aunt Sue, my grandmother's sister and Uncle Edward, her husband. I didn't want to live here! We moved from the comfort of our Queens apartment in Woodside, New York, to my grandmother's 2-bedroom house, with 1 bathroom and 1 TV occupied by 10 people. My grandmother, mother, uncle Lee, uncle Wop, Lemuel, Angie, Pam, Carolyn, David, and myself. Once the reality struck that this was life, I had to adjust and try to make my new family like me. My uncle Lee slept on the couch in the dining area; Carolyn, grandma, my mother, and I slept in the front room. Uncle Wop, Lemuel, David, Pam, and Angie slept in the back room. Again, we had one bathroom and one TV. David and I were the youngest, so we were favored by grandma during those days. David's father was the one that killed my Aunt. All the rest of my cousins had the same father. Therefore, David acted out more than the others because his father killed their mother. I recently learned a family secret that David and I were sisters and brothers and first cousins, meaning the reason my mother moved to New York was because she had a child with her sister's husband. This secret will remain in the grave with David Porter's remains along with the other two men who proclaimed to be my father.

My mother was and, to this very day, is a go getter, who is a strong and determined woman, refusing to settle for anything less than bogie. I recall several of my uncles' friends wanting to date my mother but thank God she was not interested. Then came the day that I will never forget, the day she decided to introduce me to the man she would marry and stay with until this very day. He walked on the porch and shook my hand. I will never forget the disgust I felt from that handshake. I had no clue why but one day I would find out. My grandmother's house was the place where everyone would stop by to sleep, eat, play cards, drink, or simply feel at home. No one was unwelcomed at 208 N 11th Street. He was an old friend of my uncles' and the family. I remember when he and my mother started dating. He was very possessive and abusive. I remember the black eyes he gave her, and the big sunglasses she wore to cover them up over the weekend. However, I believe my mother saw a "partner" and wanted out of sleeping with her mother or on the floor, especially after a roach crawled in her ear and she had to call big cousin Joyce to take her to the emergency room. Imagine, a filthy roach in your ear! That must have been awful. But, no matter how awful that may have been, the fights and the black eyes must have been better than living at grandma's house. The next thing I knew, we were moving up the street into an apartment with Harvey Jacobs who beat my mother like nobody's business. I remember one fight when he put her head through a wall, stabbed her arm with a pitch fork, and as I stood in the middle yelling leave my momma alone, he delivered a 6 piece to my young ribs, knocking the breath out of me. I ran down the hill to my grandmother's house, and when my uncles came to protect us, she jumped on their backs. To this day, she will still say, "We didn't fight that much."

My mother always spoiled me and made sure I had the best. She worked the hardest hours, from 11 am to 7 pm, 3 am to 3 pm, or 4 am to 4 pm. She wasn't only taking care of me, she was conforming this country boy who dropped out of high school. She took care of me and him. I will never forget the first time he took advantage of me. I was in my beautiful room with a pink canopy, and my record player in the cubby consisting of Michael Jackson, Diana Ross, Donna Summer, Smokey Robinson, and Millie Jackson 45 s. My mother was at work on those shifts. He asked me if I wanted to sleep with him. I was only a little girl, so I said, "Yes." The most disgusting thing happened---he began to grind on me, and once I realized what was happening, I jumped up and ran to my room. I was in fourth grade, attending Bradley Creek elementary school. The next day, I decided I was going to run away and never come back. Why should I? After all, she never left him even after all of the beatings he gave her, so how was she going to leave him for me? The next day I wrote a letter telling my mom that I was running away. This was one of the first and last beatings I received from my mother besides actual fist blowing fights. First, I had nowhere to go. While she beat me, she told me she had an abortion because of me and that I wasn't going anywhere. Later, they found a house down the street at 613 N 11th Street. It was an old home, which required a lot of work. I couldn't believe we were going to live in that house with him. However, we did, and the renovating began. He was good with his nasty hands, although my mother paid for the renovating materials. Once we were settled he appeared in my room almost every night. This was when I learned it was much better to hang at my grandmother's house or in the streets around 10th Street Park or at Ms. Ruth's store corner than be home with this disgusting individual my mother called "her husband." And, so the abuse continued. I specifically remember one day when I was at my grandmother's house and she said, "Oh Lord, your momma down there saying she gone kill herself." I ran all the way home terrified. I arrived home to find my mother sitting in a chair with a black dress on holding a rifle wrapped in plastic. I wanted to leave and never live under their roof again. I believe those days were when the suicidal thoughts started.

Then, the summer I turned 12 years old were when my prayers were answered. My big cousin Joanne and her husband Rufus came down from New York to visit. I was determined that when they left I was getting in that car with them and never coming back. Joanne thought I was going to stay with her in East New York, but I had other intentions. I was going to Aunt Sue and Uncle Edward because they loved me, and I just knew they would allow me to stay for as long as I needed. Once we arrived in Brooklyn, I jumped out, grabbed my suitcases, and headed for 470 F. They lived in Lafayette Gardens, also known as LG, Bedford Stuyvesant, "Bed Stuy: Do or Die." There, I had my big cousin, more like brother Edward, Jr. who we affectionately called "Jr." or "Wolfie," Rebecca, who I had idolized since I was a young girl, and Jr.'s girlfriend Nadine, who I thought was the coolest chic in Brooklyn. *This is the summer I started snorting cocaine.* I looked older than my pre-teen 12 years of age, and my cousin allowed me to snort cocaine and to smoke weed with them. In the middle of the summer, my dreams of staying were shattered. I got into three fights with Shawn Bailey and cut her with a box cutter. I was charged as an adult with assault with 1 charge being intent to kill. I cut her 3 inches from her jugular vein. I had no intentions of harming her, however. I was protecting myself, and I was scared to death. I closed my eyes and started swinging that blade. The ramifications were that I was banned from New York for 1 year. Imagine being banned from the state of New York at the age of 12? I was given the name "The Butcher." But those people had no clue that I was frightened beyond my wits. I ended up going to Joanne's in East New York because I was in hiding. Shawn's mother had a boyfriend who was in a gang. One man slapped my cousin Rebecca and some other men caught my cousin Jr. in the elevator with intentions of taking him to the roof and throwing him off. Thank God, he knew his building and elevator, jumped out, and escaped. I returned home after the summer with the kids saying she think she's bad. I didn't but I had it in me, and if anyone messed with me, my family, or my friends it was going down---and going down big. Funny thing is the next summer my mother let me go right back to New York. As I look back over those times after having children of my own, there is no way in hell I would have allowed my child to return. However, I now believe she was keeping me out of harm's way because I know she knew about her husband's perversion. I learned to carry blades in my mouth; I could talk and all.

The next person that I marked for life was Monica Thomas. She ran track for DC Virgo, and I truly believe she was Olympic material. I was on the porch practicing spread eagles as a cheerleader for MCS Noble Jr. High School and she was across the street visiting my cousin Mike. I guess I spoke to him or walked across that street and I don't remember exactly what happened, but we started fighting. I took my headband and gold T-earrings off and laid my razor down and we fought. It was a good fight, too. She was as strong in her legs as I was so no one won that fight. I was mad because she gave me a good fight, so I picked up the razor and cut her on her arm, straight petty—the blood that poured from her arm---and she ran home to Taylor Holmes projects. When my mother came home, she took me over to where Monica lived to apologize and I cried, not because I was sorry, but because I had to apologize. I didn't mean it at that time---it wasn't until more than 20 years later when I saw her and that awful scar on her arm that I wholeheartedly meant every word. I cried because I caused that scar, a scar that she, her children, and her lovers would have to see for the rest of her life. Harvey continued to show up in my room. I continued to drink. I continued to smoke a lot of weed. I think back over those days and remember we had a huge hurricane, hurricane Gloria I think, and my mother asked if I wanted to sleep with them. I was scared but since she was in the bed, I thought I would be. In those days, my mother was a big woman and wore sizes anywhere from 18-22. She was in the middle---I woke up to his hands sliding down my stomach to between my legs. When I looked up, he was under the cover over her. How in the hell? If I had a lamp in my hand, I would have busted this negro in the head! I jumped out of the bed, and as soon as my feet hit the floor, the dead arose. She asked, "Where are you going?" I said, "To my room!" To this day, especially as a mother, no one can convince me my mom didn't know what was going on.

I became promiscuous. I felt if someone was going to touch me it would be because I let them. I was 14 years old the first time I became pregnant. One day my mother was in the kitchen cooking, and I got up and fainted. Once she realized that I had not had my period, she took me to get a pregnancy test. It was positive. To this day, she doesn't know who the father was, but she drove me to Jacksonville, North Carolina and words cannot describe the unimaginable pain I experienced. I did not receive any anesthesia or pain medication and I remember the procedure feeling as though my insides had been ripped out. My cousin Carolyn went with us, and I cried the whole way back, lying in her lap. At the time, Carolyn was 15 years old and pregnant with her daughter Shakieal. Shakieal was born on my birthday at 1 lb. 5 oz. and is my first name sake; Shakieal Tracion Davis. She is a constant reminder that I would have a child her age---a heartache I still carry. I can remember about 1 month or so afterward riding in the car with my mother when she said with a laugh, "Trying to make me a grandma at a young age"? I felt nothing but pure hatred for my mother at that moment. I don't know what the abortion she experienced 4 years prior was like, but those people killed me and brought me back to life---*dead.* I have been pregnant 13 times with 3 live births, 1 born dead, and another child died inside of me as New Hanover Hospital would not do a D&C for 2 weeks.

The mental anguish of knowingly carrying a dead baby inside of you for 2 weeks is unexplainable. However, that's a whole other story...

In my last two-and-a-half years of high school, my room had no door, and I had to put a blanket up for privacy. My mother continued as the main source of income, working 12- to 16-hour days. One night when I was home alone on the phone talking to Antonio George, Harvey walked into the house with his brother and demanded I get off the phone because Lumpy (his brother) needed to use it. He snatched it out of my hand. I lost it, and we fought from the kitchen to their bedroom. Why we ended up in there, I don't know. We ended up on their bed with him on top of me---a position I had been fighting to prevent since I was 10 years old, but now I was about 15 or 16 years old. I made up my mind this was going to happen! I was telling, and his ass was finally out of my life. We waited for my mother to come home and when she did, I told her everything as he sat on the couch with his face in his hands. My mother looked at me then, she looked at him, and said the words I can still hear to this very day, "NOT MY HUSBAND!"

My heart, my hopes, and my spirit dropped. It was then that I knew I was truly in this world by myself. I had to fight at home, internally, and in the streets. My mother chose him over me, her only child and a girl child at that. During those days my best friend was Shannon Blair, and her mother Donna, who was like my mom, and her brother Craig, were my family. Their house was normal to me and also my second home. I stayed every chance that I could. Momma Donna was the first person who my mother told that she could "have me." The second was my friend Sequoia's mother Ms. Carol. Momma Donna is also the first person who taught me to eat pizza with a knife and fork! Like who does that?!? Shannon worked at Little Caesar's pizza. I was 15 years old, but I wanted to work, too. I didn't work because I had to, I worked because I wanted to. Besides, I liked to smoke weed and to drink. While working at Little Caesar's, I had a boyfriend named Kevin Corbett. I was attending New Hanover High School at this time. I was in the marching band, ran track, and a JV cheerleader until I beat this girl nicknamed Birdie with a night stick that my cousin Squeaky gave me as she and Carolyn sat in the car and told me to "Handle my business." We didn't play any games back then. Her mother went to the principle to try and get me expelled but we weren't on school property. However, it was through Kevin and his friend Javon Elder that I met one of my best friends in life who was more like a sister, Karen Robinson. They came by the job one night with Karen in the car and we hit it off instantly. Kevin talked my mother into transferring me to Laney. She loved herself some "fine Kevin." He was mixed---Italian and black---gorgeous, and he was her baby.

As soon as I got to Laney, I laid eyes on Steve Holmes and it was over for me and Kevin, who transferred to Brunswick High School. Steve and I stayed together until he graduated and attended East Carolina University. He had his mother, his father, and his sisters. They were a true "Cosby Family" in my eyes. His parents loved me, and I love them to this day. I stayed at their house as much as I could. They took me on family vacations. I was safe with them, but I still had to go home. I was too ashamed and embarrassed to tell them what was going on at my house. Karen lost her mother and lived with her uncle and aunt. She would frequently miss the bus, and I would pick her up. I had my driver's permit at age 15 and drove like I had a regular driver's license. One day, I asked my mother if Karen could live with us so she could go to school every day. I wanted Karen to stay because of her situation but also for myself because if she was there then HE wouldn't come in my room at night. I hated the weekends because Karen would go to her Aunt Jenny's and spend time with her sister Kim. The hatred grew to the point that I worked on a plan to kill Harvey. He had a blue Renault and I would imagine laying in the back seat then once he got in, I would shoot him in the back of the head. I meant that thing, too! But, I never did. Once Steve went to college, I started drinking, drugging, partying, and fighting every day---he truly was my stabilizer.

Eventually, I joined the delayed entrance program with the Army Reserves where once a month I went to drill until I completed high school. I then choose a Military Occupational Specialty (MOS) and went to basic training. I had to attend Saturday school for the entire year to graduate because I skipped school so much. One day Karen and her brother Ricky (God bless his soul) were at my cousin Pam's house drinking Thunderbird and smoking weed laced with crack (we called them "woolies") when her older sister Kim called to say our rivals were messing with them. I said, "I'm sick of them, Ricky, give me your gun"! He did, Karen drove, and I was in the passenger seat in mode 3000. I walked through the center of the Jervay projects strapped and ready to shoot. I told this female I would pop her, and she thought I meant "slap." I pulled that gun out and fired in the air just like in the movies. We walked back to the car and pulled up at the Bob Johnson store. I pointed the gun at Rona and she said, "Shoot me"! Lord, why did she say that? Well, I shot her, and everyone scattered. I told Karen to drive around that block three times and she did. Each time, I shot into the crowd and each time I missed. That incident got me to basic training faster than intended because we were in the newspaper and I had no intentions of going to jail. The police did pay my mother a visit, but she told them they were too late because Uncle Sam had me. God saved me because I was a sharpshooter and I literally shot into a crowd of running people, aiming and firing, and I didn't hit one person (nobody but God).

I wrote home often. In one letter, I told my mother to tell Harvey that I was a lean, mean fighting machine and if he ever hit my mother again, I would kill him. I don't recall him putting his hands on her again. I decided to go to active duty because I didn't want to end up under their roof again. So, I got married at the age of 20 and gave birth to the first love of my life, Tra'Quan. We were stationed in Fort Polk, Louisiana and Tra' got sick with pneumonia. Tony demanded I leave the Army and go to school to pursue my dream of becoming a nurse. I talked to my commander who advised me not to leave. He told me I would become a statistic, that I should send my son home, and remain on active duty. I cried for 3 days straight because I loved the Army, I loved being in one of the biggest gangs in America, and I especially loved being independent and away from Wilmington, North Carolina. However, I wanted my son to have what I did not, which were his parents. Therefore, I was discharged with honors from active duty and enrolled at Central Texas Community College. My husband and I did not factor bills and the fact that we would now only have one income. We always drank heavily but in good spirits not because of stress, which was what he began to do. One day, I walked in the door from school and met his fist in my face. He started punching me and wouldn't stop as I crawled out the door. He continuously stomped me all the way to the neighbor's door, and they called the police. I never imagined our neighborhood would ever be flooded with so many military police. I ended up in the emergency room with personnel taking pictures of his size- 13 footprint on my thighs. All of this because he found a phone number in my notebook. If he had only asked me why that number was there, we would probably be together this very day and maybe life would not have taken the course that it did for me or for him. I ended up back at my mother's house with my son and then returned after 3 months. However, I had no respect for my husband and our marriage was over. I remember the day I made the decision to walk away--- Tra' would hate both of us if we stayed together and if I leave he is going to hate me. I just had to figure out how in the world I was going to raise my son alone. Another game-changing event in my life was about to occur and had I known what I was going to encounter or that my captain was correct in stating I would become a statistic, I would have stayed just like the old generation use to, through hell and high water.

I ended up back in Wilmington under the roof of my mother and stepfather with a son full of resentment and wanting answers to how in the hell she stayed with a man who put his hands on her and lusted after her only girl child. During this time, Oprah had come out with her story of being molested and the conversation was an open topic.

One day, I asked my mother why she stayed. She came up with the excuse that he smoked marijuana and that he drank a lot. Well, I never knew weed turned anyone into a child molester. The next comment was that when my grandmother ran a liquor house, a man fondled her and some things you just have to get over. I could not believe the words coming out of my mother's mouth. She finally said that his aunt molested him when he was a little boy. At that time, I didn't give a damn what happened to him. I wanted to know why she stayed and why she didn't love me enough to keep the many promises she made to me that she would leave him. The thing she said the most that killed my soul was that he used to make sure I "had covers on" or "to check the windows." I was smart and talented in school---I was in ROCAME, ran track, a cheerleader, played basketball, volleyball, played the concert, symphonic, and marching band, yet the man never attended one event nor did he ever give me one birthday, Christmas, or any other type of present. But it was okay for him to check on me at night? This was unbelievable. I came back to the same friends and family doing the same things, selling drugs, drinking, and smoking woolies. I started nursing school at the University of North Carolina Wilmington, but dropped out because crack was taking control over my life. The very words my captain told me were coming to pass. I was in Fort Polk, Louisiana at that time and often wondered if he put a root on me. The thing is this was the crack error and people were more interested in hitting a pipe than crushing the rock up and putting it in a blunt. During those days, I was selling heroin and would be out all times of night because of my crack addiction. I will never forget the first time someone told me I was wasting the crack by putting it in a blunt and introduced me to a mountain dew bottle with aluminum foil over the opening with two holes on the side. I was stuck in her house for 2 days and *I was hooked*. My life took a turn for the worse. I remember Tra' was about 5 years old and was on the bed crying his heart out at my grandmother's house. He said he wanted me to be the way I use to be. At that time, I had no idea how to begin to be the mother he knew. That same day, my mother was there, and I was walking out of the house heartbroken because of the pain I was putting my baby through. She said, "You'll never come back!" meaning I was a lost cause. I stopped and pointed my finger at her, just like Celie did Mister in "The Color Purple, and said, "I know a man named Jesus!" and walked around the corner to smoke crack. The faith of a mustard seed is all we need, no matter what we go through God is, God can, and God will just wait on him. This was during the time I started dating my youngest son's (TyShaun's) father, Keith. Keith was 6 feet 5 inches tall, weighed 280 plus pounds, and his nickname was "Gladiator." I remember the first time that I saw him I told Carolyn, "I'm going to climb that mountain." Keith was a known drug dealer and extremely violent. Yes, I was in the type of relationship I vowed never to tolerate. He knocked me out more times than I can remember, waking up with him kneeling over me, crying. I believe he was crying because he thought he had killed me. Keith was so big that when I called the police no fewer than five cars would come, and he would sling them like rag dolls; I give you my word! One night after going to a revival with Therman Burgess and his wife, who tried to help me with my addiction, I walked into the house and it was as though I was led straight to the back room. I stopped, looked down, lifted a board, and bingo: I found his stash. I attempted to break off a small amount, but it didn't happen that way. I don't know how much I took, but I left the house and stayed gone for about 2 days.

Needless to say, when I returned and stepped onto the porch, he knocked me out as soon as he opened the door. He told me I was the only person he knew who could turn a kilo into a half ounce. Shortly after that he held me in the house with a gun to my head and threatened to kill me. First, he put a milk jug over the barrel, paced back and forth, then as he walked to the back of the house looking for another means to silence the gun. I took my chance and hit the door running. I ran until I got to the bottom. I was 4 blocks from my grandmother's house. I thought I could make it but he pulled up in a car with a crack head and threw me in the car. The person driving was a stud. I begged her to help me, telling her he was going to kill me, but she didn't care. She just wanted the crack he promised her. When we got back to the house I believe he put a potato over the barrel then put the gun in my hands and told me to kill him. I still didn't leave him. The last time he hit me, I was about 4 months' pregnant with TyShaun, and when I woke up that time I decided that was enough. Keith and I got pregnant 3 times and none of the babies made it because of my crack habit. I can remember smoking crack and feeling myself miscarry but would not walk away from that pipe. He would come to the emergency room in utter disgust because he knew. I live with the fact that I smoked crack pregnant with my baby boy. I remember sitting on some steps smoking crack, and he started fighting like he was trying to kick his way out of my stomach for dear life. The next morning, my water broke, and I ended up in the hospital. After 1 week, I started to get an infection, so labor was induced. My baby was born at 2 lbs. and 8oz. He is truly a living miracle, and I am so grateful for his life---I'm so thankful that God allowed him to live. If it had not been for my son walking in and finding me passed out on the floor after my last suicide attempt, I would not be here today. Again, I ended back in my mother's house. Living in that house was always a nightmare for me because I was filled with anger, confusion, pain, and hatred. However, I have a big heart, which I have been told is my biggest downfall.

I am a natural-born empath, who is a person with the paranormal ability to apprehend the mental or emotional state of another individual. Empaths are highly sensitive individuals, who have a keen ability to sense what people around them are thinking and feeling. Psychologists may use the term empathy to describe a person who experiences a great deal of empathy, often to the point of taking on the pain of others at their own expense. Therefore, even though I hated my stepfather with a passion, I felt his guilt and I had compassion for him, as much as I hated him, I cared about his feelings, and strangely, I had love for him. After enduring the constant violations at night and having to stay under the same roof, some kind of way I had the ability to disassociate those feelings of hatred and act normal like they did when family was around or just period. My mother use to say, "You get hurt by people, then you go out and hurt yourself." I often thought to ask her if she knew she was the "people." I couldn't stand being in that house, and I would go out and get high even if it meant leaving my children in the house. I ended my military career to keep them out. The irony of it all was that she ended up raising my children anyway. Harvey would always belittle me in front of my children or say things to her in my presence to let me know he didn't want me or my children in their house. She would say, "Even a cat takes care of her kittens," and I always wanted to say, "Yeah and even a cat protects her kittens from predators, too." During those days, she worked at General Electric during the swing shifts, from 7 am to 3 pm, 3 pm to 11 pm , and 11 pm to 7 am. I would leave and stay out for days, and she would get off work and ride around looking for me in all of the drug areas. There were several times that she did find me, and once she walked into a crack house while they were cooking crack on the stove. I went down, and I went down fast. I didn't know how to stop using drugs. I had experienced suicidal thoughts since I was a young girl and to add to that I began wanting to act more on those urges because I could not believe I had gone down this path. I was committed to the Oaks Mental Health facility a couple of times.

During one breakdown, I remember I had been out in the streets for about 8-9 days, and I was out of my mind. I remember that was one of the many times Harvey apologized to me; however, it was too late for an apology. My life had been ruined. But, just as fast as my life went to the left, things changed for the better. One night at a club, I ran into my old friend Sequoia, who went into the Marines straight out of high school. Sequoia had a son, a failed marriage, and returned to Wilmington as well. She told me that she was in the mortgage business and that I would be great in this field. I asked her to get me in the door and that I would do the rest. I got an interview and was hired. My life took off! I asked my mother to pay for my first advertisement in the AdPak. My smile was all it took and business was great! It was 100% commission, and we were top producers. I was able to get out of my mother's house with my children and live comfortably. However, I still had a serious crack addiction and would leave my sons for the entire weekend. But, I would show up for work. I think about those days, in a suit all week, conducting business with my face in the AdPak, Star News, Yellow Pages, Black Pages, commercials on FOX, and in crack areas and houses on the weekend---I was sick. The company I worked for expanded as a Lender but was eventually shut down by the banking commission. The sad part of it was that we looked at the drawing of the 2 million dollar building we built and would one day occupy and only stayed in it for a couple of weeks. Sequoia and I eventually moved on to the Money Tree Mortgage Group, where she was the mouthpiece and I pushed the paperwork. But, I failed her and the business with my addiction. She got to the point where she couldn't depend on me. We were a dream team, but I could not seem to get my life together. As beautiful, intelligent, and popular as I was, I just couldn't deal with the past hurt. It was a festering tumor on my insides like cancer. Once Sequoia walked away from the Money Tree, I hit bottom.

I could definitely relate to Whitney Houston. I was a local celebrity who was a crack head, and it seemed as though the whole town knew it. At that time, I was in a lesbian relationship with who I thought was the love of my life, Ramona. Today, we are the best of friends or even more like sisters, and I thank God for our relationship. Again, that is another story. But, we broke up and I lost my mind, I left my children, and cut all of my hair off (because she was a beautician, I figured I was cutting her hands out of my head), and went to New Orleans. Of all people, my ex-boyfriend Kevin sent for me and I stayed with him, his wife, and his son, little Kevin. I went during the Essence Festival, and that next afternoon I conceived my daughter, my angel Destani Traci-Anna Davis. Her father, Armond, was Creole, and one of the most gorgeous men I had ever laid eyes on. As I was walking out of the Super Dome in awe because I had never been around that many beautiful black people at one time, he saw I was lost and confronted me. We had a wonderful time, but he wanted too much too fast. I went to New Orleans to get my mind and my life together, so that I could go back and be a mother to my sons, but ended up pregnant. He wanted to get married, and I had to go so I left without telling him I was pregnant.

Once again, I ended up in my mother's house, with two sons, and pregnant yet again. I was in bad shape mentally; I wanted to kill myself. My oldest son was 7 years old at the time, and I remember lying on the bed crying on his shoulder. I told Tra' I was pregnant, and I didn't know what I was going to do. That sweet baby said, "I know what we are going to do" I said, "What?" He said, "You're going to take care of the baby, and I'm going to take care of Ty." I looked at him and said, "Okay." Then, I had Destani, the prettiest baby girl I had seen in my life. She was so pretty that I questioned God, which is something I will never do again in life. At 4 ½ months my baby got sick and was diagnosed with hypogammaglobulinemia, which is an immune disorder characterized by a reduction in all types of gamma globulins, including antibodies that help fight infection. It may be congenital (present at birth) or related to medication; it may be due to a kidney or gastrointestinal condition, cancer, or severe burns. We ended up staying in the hospital for 16 months straight. Starting at New Hanover Regional Memorial Hospital, then Duke, John's Hopkins, Chapel Hill, and Pitt. My daughter went more than 20 times with numerous scares that she wouldn't make it through the night. She was on the ventilator/oscillator 3 times. The day finally came that she was released, which was the scariest day of my life. Three months later, my sons caught the Rota virus from the Annie H Snipes School they were attending at the time, and I knew Destani would get sick. Destani ended up back in the hospital in the intensive care unit on the oscillator, and I made a decision that I question and often regret to this day. My mother, big cousin Joyce, whom I refer to as Auntie, my then girlfriend Tonya, and I sat in that room for 7 hours and 16 minutes waiting for all the life-supporting medicines to exit her system, then the doctor put her in my arms. She took two sweet breaths and my mother said, "She's gone." The part of me that was holding on for dear life died that day. I swallowed the fact that Destani died in my arms, but I did not digest it until 1 year later and had a complete breakdown. I wandered in the streets for 3 months, sleeping in my candy apple red BMW, crack houses, anywhere. During this time, I met Reggie and his goal was to help me get my mind together, get back to work, get together with my children, and to just live again. Six months later, I found him in the trunk of his car---murdered. I was the number one suspect. I asked the detectives if they only had bread and butter would they take away their butter. Reggie was the first and last man to date that took total care of me. My nerves were a wreck, and I smoked all day every day. I could not believe this was life, and I decided I was done. I couldn't do this life thing anymore. I drove to the third street bridge twice with the intent to drive over the bridge, but never had the courage to do it. I was tired of being under the scope of the detectives, my nerves were shot. The night I made up my mind to finally drive over the bridge, I went to see my grandmother because she had just had surgery. When I was leaving she asked, "You coming back tomorrow"? My heart dropped because I had no plans to ever walk in her door again. I replied, "I don't know gramma, I don't know," and walked out the door. As I was driving toward the bridge I did what any other addict would do, I thought maybe one last hit before I do this because I was going out with a bang.

I was stopped by two officers, something I had grown accustomed to at that time and, I was a black woman in a red BMW driving through a known drug area. The officers stated they stopped me because my license plate light was out, but I knew that was a lie. They asked my name, and I gave fake information. I believe I told them my name was Carolyn. However, they knew who I was. I didn't have time for them, though. I was on a mission---to drive over that bridge and leave this world and all the pain it held behind. I cranked my car and put it in gear. The officer on the passenger side dove in my car to try to snatch my keys, but I was already driving off. We rode for a block with him hanging out of my car fighting me over my steering wheel until I looked in my rear view mirror and saw his partner aiming the gun at the car. I took a quick left and lost control, which threw super cop off my car. I jumped out and ran nothing but ass and elbows. I was later found hiding in a house that I ran into. I was placed under a $50,000 bond for attempted murder on a government official with a deadly weapon. Now mind you, I just drove off. I did not drive into nor did I attempt to back into super cop. But again, I was charged with attempted murder on this officer and a few weeks later I was charged with first degree murder and placed under "no bond." The district attorney went before a grand jury, presented the trumped-up charge of attempted murder, and had me charged with Reggie's murder. Yes, they do that, which is a reason so many innocent people are behind bars to this day! I remained in the county jail for 15 months and 5 days, and 3 weeks before the murder trial, the charges were dropped. When I say everyone thought I was going to be found guilty, understand no one believed I would make it out of that charge. I use to tell those gossiping, hating females that the only way I would be found guilty is if "God, Jesus, and the Holy Ghost, were being held captive on the day of conviction" and that is highly unlikely. I was given the maximum time for dragging the officer therefore I completed the remainder of the 2 years in Raleigh women's prison and then to Troy, which was opened because during that time the women's prison was overpopulated. So, they moved people like me under maximum security there. However, that was the best thing that could have happened to me because I started taking classes, which triggered something in me. Everything was taken from me except my mind, even though that was close to being lost I still had it. I got out of prison and went to my mother's house. Three weeks later, she told me to get out and we could go to court over my sons. They were a tax write off, which was the number one factor she was in a tax bracket where she benefited greatly by having two dependents. I am not saying my mother didn't love my sons because she does but the way she cheated me out of raising my children no real mother would ever do that to her daughter. I didn't have a pot to piss in or a window to throw it out. I had no job, no car, no children, and she told me to get out. I refused to allow myself to go back to where I was. I used all the hate and pain I had and mixed it with Jesus and I drank it, which fueled me. Failure was no longer an option!

I learned to let the past go and no longer allow what happened to me as a child control the rest of my life. I learned to walk in faith and keep God first by keeping myself out of the way. I now know that no matter what comes my way I can truly do all things through Christ who strengthens me. I cannot get one day back or change anything by holding on to the past---holding on almost killed me. I learned to forgive by first forgiving myself for allowing a situation to control me for so many years. If I can save anyone from going through 30 years of bullshit, just one person, I will have served a purpose in this life. I know God allowed me to go through everything I went through to help others. The molestation, the alcoholism, the addiction, the abortions, the multiple rapes, the loss of children by the system, and death, divorce, and confusion of my sexuality. I know now that storms don't last forever, and trouble doesn't last always. I know who I am and whose I am. I am a strong, walking, talking miracle, a child of the most high God. Hold on to God's unchanging hand and He will lead you from darkness to the light.

Today, I have a strong relationship with my sons although I do not have a relationship with my mother, even though I sit in the same church with her and Harvey every Sunday. She and I don't even look at each other in the eye. I don't hate Harvey anymore either. I realized something happened to him to make him do those things to me. So, I flipped that thing around. It wasn't what happened to me anymore; it was what happened to you. As far as my mother, I don't know how she sleeps at night and I don't try to figure it out anymore because I gave it all to God and left it with him. The battle was never mine---it belonged to the Lord the whole time. To date, I have earned an Associate's degree in General Education, a Medical Transcription diploma, a Bachelor of Science degree in Business Administration (Management) (summa cum laude), a Master of Business Administration (Management), and I am currently working on my Doctorate in Business Administration (Project Management). I am a survivor. I may have lost some battles in this life, but I will keep striving to accomplish my goals, and help as many individuals as possible so that God will get all the glory and honor. I am who I am, and I am proud of who I have become.

Fireside Reflections

Keywords and Takeaways:

Faith of a mustard seed. Just WOW! Look at all Dr. Tracion Flood had to go through before she saw THIS day, that she would be called Dr. Even in her times of struggle, she knew to call the name "Jesus"!

How about you? Do you have a mustard seed faith story, or are you currently in a situation where this story has inspired you? Remember…all it takes is just a little faith in knowing that this may be my today, but I know that there is a promise as long as I believe, for a better tomorrow.

_____

_____

_____

_____

_____

_____

_____

_____

_____

_____

_____

_____

_____

_____

_____

_____

PEELING AWAY THE LAYERS...
WHY AM I SO ANGRY?

Pella Bradham-Parker

As I laid down on the couch drifting in and out of sleep, I could hear the conversation on the television between the two sisters who began to share their stories of being molested by their father. I could also hear and feel the pain and bitterness in each of them when speaking about the person who molested them. For the rest of the evening, all I could think about was that story. I began to have vivid pictures in my mind of a living room and bedroom setting that I had spent quite a bit of my life in. The memories became clearer as the night went on. I tossed and turned during the night, with my mind clearly seeing myself in vivid pictures of my young life. It was clear I was having flashbacks of some things I had buried deep in my memory bank.

When I woke up the next morning, I began to ask myself questions about myself, such as: Who am I? What happened to me? Why do I feel the way I do? And, why am I angry? With that, I started my morning devotion, and then it was prayer time. I began asking the Lord, "Why am I so angry and sometimes defensive"? As I continued praying and studying over time, more things started to become clear to me, which answered each of the above questions racing through my mind.

The first question, "Who am I" was an easy answer, or so I thought. I was a daughter, wife, mother, sister, friend, and most important, a child of God. That's easy right? Not so. I was also a little girl who had a lot of pain and anger that I was holding on, too. This is where the journey began that I am now on. A journey that drew me closer to God, and allowed me to really see who and whose I am.

As you read this chapter, I pray that you will allow the love of God to reach you right where you are and allow healing to take place in your hearts. I pray that each area covered will be a blessing to you all.

Who Am I?

The little girl who was so loved by her family and grandparents to no end. I knew that I was loved by my grandmother and grandfather who doted over me. Then, one day my grandmother was gone. The fire not only destroyed the home, it also took my grandmother's life. That was a life-changing moment for me. At 4-and-a-half years old, I remember seeing my grandmother laying in a casket and then no more. As I grew, I would watch other people with their grandmothers and wondered why both of my grandmothers had to die. My maternal grandmother passed before I was born, and now my paternal grandmother who I adored was no longer here. I was not at all happy. I was ANGRY!!! This was the beginning of the many layers of pain, hurt, and anger for me.

This same little, angry girl and her mother moved into the projects and all seemed to be better. I still had my grandfather who loved me, my Mommy who loved me, along with the rest of my family. Yep. I did. As a young girl and in my teenage years, I remember spending many wonderful days and nights at my favorite Grand Aunt's home, with her two youngest children. We became like a sister and brother, and I love them to life. My one cousin and I had what I refer to as a love-hate relationship. She loved to hate me! But, she loved and still loves me today, and I love her with all of my heart. I have nothing but mostly good things to remember about my childhood. As they say, the good outweighs the bad.

The move to the projects brought about more good memories as well as bad memories. Let me start with the bad. While spending some time at another family member's home in the projects, another layer of anger was added to my life. The anger from being molested had now crept into my life, and no one knew it. I was afraid to tell anyone what had happened because I was made to believe it was all my fault. I was young, felt unprotected, and all alone, with nowhere to turn. By this time, my mother had become a Christian and I, too, had given my life to Christ at this young age, which I am so glad that I did! With my life now focused on being a Christian, this is what kept me from totally losing myself, as most victims of child molesters do. Instead of becoming promiscuous, I became even more angry and defensive, which was my way of protecting myself from any further harm.

Everyone just kept saying that I had an attitude, when all I wanted was for someone to see I was just hurting and angry and that no one was helping or protecting me from this horrific and devastating act. I hated the days that I had to stay at this family member's home, because I knew what was going to happen. I began staying at other family members' homes when necessary to avoid being in his presence. During this time, people did not seem to listen to children as well as they do now.

Living in the projects made you grow up faster than the average neighborhood kids. Also, I was an only child, so grow up I did. Seeing people doing drugs, getting shot, fighting, and all that came with living in the projects began to happen on a daily basis. The place that once had flowers beds in the little front garden, now had become a totally different place. I began dating at an early age, and had a boyfriend who was very protective and caring for me---he made me feel safe. It was the last day that I had to go to this particular family member's house, while my mom and aunts were out of town, *I had had enough*. I was no longer going to be touched or put in any awkward situations by him, *I was done*. When I saw the person come into the room, I remember freezing right where I was sitting. He came over to the chair and started touching me. I started to cry. I grabbed my things and ran out of the house over to my boyfriend's house. I began to tell him what happened, and he wanted to go over and handle the situation. I begged him not to do anything to harm the person because I felt this would tear all of our families apart. That was the last time I ever went back or stayed in that home over night. I never spoke of the molestation again, as it would have destroyed my family. I just held it in and became angrier. Another layer to my life. I would cry any time I heard of a young child being molested or harmed in any sexual way.

As a little girl where do you go to get help, when you believe everyone will blame you for what happened? Especially when the abuser is telling you the family will be mad at you if you say anything. This is how they get you to keep their horrible behavior a secret. In church, I learned from my Sunday school teacher that you could go to Jesus and tell Him your problems. Even at my young age, He would listen and help me. So, that's what I did. I would pray every day for the Lord to protect me from this person, and He did. That part of my family moved out of the projects, and I never saw the person again until I was an adult. I was able to avoid him at all cost. Although I prayed and did not have to deal with him, the anger had built up and was brewing. First my grandmother was gone, now I was molested. What was next?

Now, let's talk about the good! The next several years of my life I spent going to church and getting closer to the Lord, while still living in the projects and growing up quickly. I was very serious about being a Christian and going to heaven when I die. I joined the choir and participated in many other areas of our youth department. I even began to invite my other friends from the projects to go to church with me. My best friend would stay over and say, "I know we have to go to church." Boy did we laugh at that. Today, she is saved and serving the Lord with gladness. While I was continuing to grow spiritually, naturally I still had that defensive, protective way about myself. I was swift with my tongue and did not care if it hurt feelings. That was only if I was pushed to that limit. One day, I could be sweet as pie, the next I could be a beast! The days I was a beast, I was not happy. I did not like being that person at all. It always made me feel horrible after losing my temper, and it still does today. I always wanted to have a sweet, quiet mannerism. Clearly, I did not get blessed with that. What I did receive was the love of my church family and friends who continued to love me through my growing pains.

Looking back on those early years of my life, I do not regret living through any of it. The projects were a lot of fun when we were not dodging bullets, fighting to protect myself because my hair was different, my eyes were big, and I thought I was cute, or other females wanted to date my boyfriend. Even being with him was a challenge. He wanted me all to himself, but sometimes I thought he chose to be with others when we weren't together. It appeared as if I was always there, but someone or something was in between us. It wasn't a person---*It was the streets*. The very thing he protected me from, was the very thing I was fighting against. It sure taught me a lot, living in the projects. Survival was at the top of that list. Another layer to my life.

As an adult, I needed to find myself and deal with all the hurt, pain, and anger that I had going on inside. As I stated earlier, I began to pray and ask the Lord to help me see me. Show me what was wrong. The old saying is so true. Be careful what you pray for, you just might get it! The Lord allowed me to start seeing all of the layers in my life that made me feel all of the emotions that were in my life. I did not want to be an angry person at all. I needed to have a life-changing moment to help me move forward. The question was, "What would be that life-changing event"? The answer is: The moment I asked the Lord to show me myself, and to change me and take away this angry, defensive way about me, and make me more like Him, and to allow me to become a better woman, daughter, wife, friend, cousin, and niece.

Listening to the ladies on the television had sparked the flame in my life for change. One thing that occurred in my past that caused me major pain was that my boyfriend had gone to prison while I was away one summer. He was snatched away and sentenced to death. I was 16 years old and devastated. My life and senior year of high school were now ruined, or so I thought. I had no desire to go to prom without the one man I had planned to spend that evening with. How could the prom be good without him? However, I did attend the prom because someone else purchased tickets in my name to attend the prom with him. I tried to enjoy myself as much as possible but was ready to go after the first hour. All I could think about was the fact that I should have been there with my boyfriend. I made it through that year with some pain still lingering, and I was missing him like crazy. During my time of prayer, fasting, crying, and studying, the word of God for strength and answers, I discovered another layer in my life of pain: the layer of Abandonment. I realized that when Damon was sentenced to death in prison, I felt abandoned. The one boyfriend who I loved with all my heart had gone to prison. What do you do at age 16? He left me to grow alone. It was not his plan to abandon me, but his choices created pain for me. Although I was a young girl, the love that existed between my boyfriend and I was real, and still is today.

A few years later, at age 19, I met John P. I thought finally, I have met someone again who truly loved me. John and I were married and had two beautiful daughters. I thought I would be with him until one of us closed our eyes on this side of heaven. Well, the love of one of us did die. His love. I guess it was temporary. After 23 years of marriage, he walked into the home and told me, "I am leaving you." There I was standing in the kitchen fixing dinner stunned. The hurt and pain I was in was unexplainable. That pain I felt was abandonment. Here was this horrible pain once again. I began to look at my life and think to myself, at the age of 40, how do you start over? I had no clue. I had the pain of divorce and an emptiness all going on at once. With all of this pain, I once again turned to the one person other than my momma who could help me. That was the Lord.

That was what I thought to be the ultimate layer of pain, anger, and any other emotion that you can possibly imagine. What do you do with all these emotions and feelings bottled up inside you with no outlet as a young girl, or a 40 year old blindsided by more pain? You explode at the most inappropriate times. Whenever I felt threatened or attacked, I would explode. My mother always taught me not to hold things in, but I had to learn how to let them out without losing my temper. I still had not mastered that yet. I was still learning to deal with all the pinned-up pain and learning how to let it out in a positive way.

How do I begin to heal from all the layers of pain, hurt, and anger? What do I do? Where do I go for help? Who do I trust to listen and believe me? Finally, I realized that I needed to ask the Lord for help because no one else could heal any of the pain I was feeling. And, because He is such a good Father, He began to not only answer but to also show me. First, I had to heal from being angry about my grandparents no longer being with me. Second, I had to forgive the person who molested me. Third, I had to forgive Damon for making choices that caused him to abandon me. Fourth, I had to forgive my ex-husband John for abandoning me. And, last but not least, I had to get past being angry with God for taking my Mommy from me. I know I will see her again, but this is a pain that makes all the above pain feel less powerful. In July 2016, I lost my best friend in the whole wide world, my Mommy. Now I am learning that this is another layer of pain that I have had to learn to live with and heal from. This time, just as all the others, I have had to run to the Lord to see me through.

Upon visiting my old boyfriend, I realized that all of my old feelings still remain, and due to his situation, I am still not able to depend on any one to change his situation except the Lord. Again, I can clearly see He is the source, and that His will shall be done.

Through every area of pain, anger, and hurt, I have realized that I have always run to the Lord, who is my strength for my healing. This is how I have overcome all the pain, anger, and hurt that I have gone through. No matter who we are, there are areas in our lives that we must turn to someone for help, and the question is who and or where do we go? I am aware that everyone has their own way of handling the things that happen in their lives, For me, it was my relationship with Jesus that not only showed me myself, but He also helped and helps me to forgive myself and to allow myself to heal for any and all parts I played in the things that may have caused me some of the pain and hurt in my life. That came by peeling away each layer of the pain, hurt, and anger that I have shared. I now look back at each layer and see the positive in each one. I look to see how I can use it to help others to get past hurts and anger that lives inside of us.

I am still in the process of peeling away layers of pain, hurt, and anger because it is a daily process. No one gets over anything in one day. Life is a daily growing process, and I too am growing daily. And, the Lord is with me every day. I have some good days and some not-so-good days, but the layers are peeling away. I am in such an amazing place spiritually and naturally, that I am less defensive---I laugh more, I love more, and most of all, I know God loves me! He is still working on me, peeling away the layers!

Fireside Reflections

Keywords and Takeaways:

1. Journey

2. Healing

3. Peeling the layers

4. Spiritual Relationship

Life is a journey. That journey will take you through some joyful highs and some unavoidable painstaking lows. However, however it is not the journey itself that determines what we are made of. It is how we respond to the journey that does. When life shows up at your door it helps to be mindful as we discussed in an earlier chapter. Your mindfulness will lead to how you make your decisions. Don't forget that!

During Pella's journey she discovered sometimes where devastation has left her in a place of trying to heal. It is so important to allow yourself to heal because what you do not address, will address you and show up in parts of yourself that may be unrecognizable and not who or how you want to be. So, take the time to discover the best way to get the support you need to move forward in life in a healthy way.

When we think about peeling the layers, we think of an onion right? Sometimes you have to peel until you reach the core. Same thing with us. Like Jay shared his building blocks to success, sometimes there are the things that you have to *peel back* and resolve to be able to reach that same level of fulfillment in life. I like the term peeling the layers because it provides us with a vivid picture of what that looks like. Let's practice peeling the layers.

What areas in your own life surface when you think about pain? Once you write those areas down. One by one, begin to work on fixing that problem. Figure out what resources will help you do that then commit to doing it.

_____

_____

_____

_____

_____

Often Pella mentioned her spiritual relationship with God. God was always available when she had to deal with another layer. What are you anchored to when life shows up and YOU have to deal with those layers? Do you have a favorite scripture? What do you do?

_____

_____

_____

_____

_____

EVERY STORY HAS A BEGINNING LOOKING BEYOND THE BREAK

Vivian Jones

Every story has a beginning. So, let me tell you about a little girl who grew up in a home that was broken, dysfunctional, and filled with violence. I remember an incident back then that landed me in the hospital. All I heard was screaming and glass breaking. I ran into the room to help my mom, and a piece of glass went straight through my foot. When I was being taken to the hospital, I was told, "You better scream like you crazy and as loud as you can once we get there"! I'm guessing that's how you get in the back faster to be examined by a doctor? I also heard him lying about what had taken place, remember me being so angry about what happened. But, I was coached not to say anything. This is the same man who would tell us not to lie and what would happen if we did. What a joke! Growing up, I noticed everything, and I do mean *everything*! I was also the one who got into the most trouble. I can say I was fearless and never scared to stir up the pot, as I smiled and would lead my sibling into all kinds of bad stuff. With a smile on my face though, my leadership skills were used in all the wrong ways.

I really don't remember everything with my mother and my father, but the parts I do remember weren't pleasant. As time went on, my mom got sick of the other woman and the ongoing, horrific beatings. Finally, she decided to get a divorce. Like always, my dad was with other women while still married to my mom. It's painful enough to find out about your husband cheating but then to find out about a child who is the exact same age as your child? I can only imagine how that could have broken her spirit, but as mothers we must go on in spite of the heart wrenching pain. I'm sure taking the first step to leave wasn't easy. I'm sure it took time. She didn't leave him right away---we all know how that goes. She was in love I'm sure. With five children by this one man, I'm sure she was scared out of her mind to leave because he was the bread winner. I wish I could say that things got better for her in her new relationship after leaving him, but they did not. I remember it as one big party, with a lot going on--but this time mom was the abuser. What a vicious cycle! We lived in a house on Tuskegee Street, where we experienced serious fighting and a ton of partying---drugs, pills, alcohol, and prostitution. I remember the bad, the ugly, and the good, what little there was of the latter. We had no structure nor did we have a curfew. I was having a good time not knowing all along that a seed was being planted.

As far back as I can remember, my mother was just being the best parent she knew how to be back then. She would always have food on the table, and a lot of the family visited, with some living with us from time to time. I'm sure if my mom had known any better, our childhood would have been very different. She had no idea how to raise children, so we were exposed to *a lot*. There were five children, all close in age, no biological father in the home, and one of our siblings living with an aunt (we will never know the story behind that, but I'm sure my mom was just young). She was on state assistance, with no help from my father. But he would pop up every so often and bring us some money, enough to buy one or two boxes of Cherry Chans or Lemon Heads. I remember seeing him and being so happy---running to the car, then daddy heading off to the candy lady's house down the street. I always felt the visit was for mom and not for us anyway---being his children was just a good reason for him to stop by. He was "In and out." That should have been his name. Oh, and let's not forget the times that he would take us to get hushpuppies! We really thought he was the number one dad then! I digressed---back to the new guy who was living with my mom. For the most part, I was in my own little world sneaking cigarettes and marijuana and breaking into the neighbors' house. Fighting with the new guy and calling my real father on them both---I was just one angry kid. And, if that wasn't enough, two girls, who I hung out with on my block, engaged in a number of inappropriate things, including bringing each other to sexual climaxes, having orgasms at our extremely young age. The sad part about it is that they would be up front drunk and partying---and I was having a party, too. As my sister would say, "Where were their antennae"? Don't get me wrong, we had very nice Christmases, and we went to the park like normal kids, but we had no supervision the majority of the time---everything was just one big party in my head. Almost after every party my mom had to fight him---and her children would help. *This had become our norm.* I didn't like this new guy at all since he wasn't my father, so I rebelled against him. He really wasn't a bad guy---it was my mom's alcoholism. She would constantly beat him, always starting a fight with him.

Every story has a beginning. My childhood played a significant part in my life. I don't ever remember being asked what I wanted to be when I grew up, so I would set fires because my mom would always call on me to do *everything!* So, one day I placed a diaper on the stove and threw it in the garage, setting it on fire. I did the same thing at one of my aunt's houses, but the fire occurred in her bathroom. They found me just sitting in there watching the flames. I had a serious issue that needed immediate attention. Even back then my young life was like a tornado---it would storm across everyone's life, including my own, leaving a trail of damage and breaking up everything in its path. As a child, the best memory that I have is about a lady who lived across the street---she would always have gifts for the kids---that is if you worked for it. She assigned us with the task of opening up the gate when she was leaving or returning home. When the kids saw her coming or going, we would race each other, trying to be the first one to open up the gate. Even now, I'm smiling because I genuinely loved her---although she was a bit eccentric, she sincerely cared about us kids. On some days, though, she wouldn't give us anything and would say, "I don't have anything to give you today, baby." I know now that she was teaching us a valuable lesson---sometimes we just need to do things out of the act of kindness and not always expect something in return. I get that now. We also had an older man who lived in our neighborhood who would call all of us over---but he had a hidden agenda, and we would run from him. He would say, "Come here little girl. Come and sit in my lap. I got some candy for you." As I see his face now, it causes me to cringe and my hair stand up on my arms. I would actually play with him, and one time he *almost* caught me. I was so scared. It's a good thing that he was overweight, or my innocence would have been taken right then and there! Then, there was the third neighbor who could be sweet one day, then very sneaky, waiting on the right moment so he could go in for the kill, the next! He would give me free chili cheese corn chips every day since he had a food truck. One day, he said that I couldn't have any, and I remember being so angry that I set his valued truck on fire! There is no other word to describe that act except for insanity. I don't even recall ever getting in trouble. It was swept under the rug like a lot of things.

Every story has a beginning. Several years passed and these two little girls came to live with us. We never knew the reason why. All we knew was that the two girls were the daughters of a friend of my mom. We would call them our cousins. Then, one day, my mom took me with her to her friend's house, and I wasn't sure why. I wasn't in school, so maybe I was kicked out. I was always into something. Anyway, I overheard my mom telling her that she was going to help. When we arrived, her friend was beaten up so bad, I remember both her and my momma sobbing. Then, I knew why mom had her children---she was with a pimp who had beaten her with a wire hanger. She was stuck to the sheets owing to all of the dried blood and puss. As we slowly pulled the sheets off of her skin, she would scream. Mom tried to convince her to leave, but she would just cry, shaking her head no. That was such a sad day for me. She was so violated, tormented, and frightened, unaware of how to get out, as living in fear and manipulation were her norm. She never returned to get her children who went to foster care and then to an aunt I believe. I always wondered, why was I there? Why did I have to see that? These are the questions that I constantly tossed around. I hated him for that---I was so angry. I had to block that out somehow, as it was just part of the ongoing party that played on and on in my head.

Every story has a beginning. Eventually, my mom started taking pills that her boyfriend was selling and mixing them with alcohol. It's sad but I remember the calls, the sells, and the names of the pills. She had started acting very strange, would come into our room, and just stare at us. She would keep this up for so long that she denied us the opportunity to go to school or to play outside. She wouldn't cook or clean either now, which was not all like the mom I knew. She was paranoid and would say in a timid, yet frightened voice, "Don't go outside! Something gone get y'all." We would look at each other bewildered, wondering what was wrong with our mom. Things had deteriorated so much that her sister and brother would stop by to try and get her to shower. She would scream to the top of her lungs as if they were killing her. This was so heart breaking for me to watch--- as tears flow down my face, I can feel the pain as if it was yesterday. She would repeat the color red over and over, and this would go on for days. Having a mom who was not in her right mind, I started missing days from school. But, when we knew she was back, the party would start back up again---the food and the house started smelling good again---and my smile returned. This type of behavior reoccurred in our lives until the day she died at the age of 32. She was so beautiful and young. She was in a car with a drunk driver who was speeding and lost control of the vehicle. Every bone in her body was broken, and her head split wide open. If she had lived, she would have been a vegetable. She went through the windshield and was hit by the other oncoming cars. The driver had one scratch on his head and received a 5-year sentence in prison. I hated him for years, but I had to let that go. It was part of the ongoing party in my head.

So far, all five of my mom's children have lived beyond the age that she was at her death, 32. When we would come home for school, mom wasn't there and we thought nothing of it. It was growing late and we were told that our mom was in the hospital and that everything was going to be okay. Then, the time grew later and later, and I remember my father saying, "Pack y'alls stuff, your mother just died." I was 13 years old. Angry, confused, and hurt, I had numerous questions that went unanswered. I had just started menstruating, and mom was showing me the correct hygiene to use and how to take care of myself. I rebelled so bad that I would ditch school and steal from my dad's wife. I didn't want to be there! She wasn't my mom, and I wanted to go live with someone on my mom's side. I hated the fact that I didn't have a mother anymore. So, my father allowed me to pack up my bags and go live with my aunt. That was the worst thing I could have ever done! When my journey began, I acted out everything that I had ever seen growing up. I never looked any differently at life. I thought life was just one big party---take the hurt and keep moving forward. My behavior became worse. I was now living with my aunt, giving her hell, sneaking out of the window to have fun with my friends. My aunt's house was boring, and I also had a curfew. She would frequently tell me, "Be home before the streetlights come on." They did not party; they went to church, and I was confused all over again. I was used to having fun, so I created my own. I started hanging out with my best friend, and we did everything together. Now, I was drinking and smoking all of the time and thought I was grown, staying out all night. If I didn't make curfew, I would just stay put.

Every story has a beginning. I met a guy several months after moving in with my aunt. We were both young; however, he was 4 years older than I was. My father wanted to lock him up underneath the jail because I became pregnant at the age of 14, which was very hard on me. You see, no one knew about my pregnancy until I was 6 months along. I was so young I didn't even know what was going on. But I felt something different in my body, and I remember craving oranges. I just couldn't keep them down. My friend would ask, "Girl are you pregnant? I'm telling." And, she did just that. So, with no OBGYN care for 6 out of 9 months, I was still partying. Then, I was taken advantage of and some man gave me a disease that could have resulted in my son becoming blind. I dropped out of high school, and I was always in fights with my sons' father. I remember being so scared of him. I almost lost my son because of the abuse. One minute my son was his, the next minute, he wasn't. The pain I experienced during that time with him was horrible. But I couldn't let go of the fact that he was my child's father and if I left, that somehow I would be denying him something good. I ran away to be with him and my friend, and my dad posted a missing report. Being in and ou

t of the juvenile system was an ongoing cycle at the time. Even after giving birth to my son, nothing changed. I basically raised him without a father. I didn't know how to raise a child at 15 years old. He has witnessed and heard so much growing up. Still, the party never stopped for me.

Every story has a beginning. I remember the first time that I tried cocaine. I walked into a room at my friend's house. I asked, "What smells?" The party was so loud, but what did I do? I joined it, of course. I had been on and off this drug for many years. I remember going to live with a family member who was my only available option at the time. They were doing this drug, as well, but not in a way I had witnessed other use before. My uncle said, "You wasting it may as well smoke the pipe. You just smoking a paper pipe any way." So, the first time I hit the crack pipe was with a family member. I was young, lost, and turned out. His wife would take me with her to the store to steal. I had no alternative but to join her in the criminal act if I wanted to stay in their home. Then she instructed me to tell the men that I was "well qualified" when we were hanging out late nights doing drugs. I am so thankful that I never touched heroin. At one house we used to visit, everybody was doing their drug of choice. I watched a guy light up something on a spoon, tie his arm up, suck what was on the spoon up into a needle, shoot himself up, nod off, and then return to his former self. I was curious about the drug he was taking that would cause him to pass out, young and not knowing anything about the drug or the fact that heroin causes this type of a reaction. He had the audacity to come over and ask me, "Do you want to try it?" My God, after all that I witnessed, he approached me with the needle, and became hysterical--- I went off on him! My aunt came out of the room, observed what was going on, and she went off, too!

I never returned to that house again. My world was so dark. I would stop using drugs, stay clean, and then start back up again. I had guns pulled to my head, was up for days, losing track of time, and spent countless amounts of money. But somehow, I managed to push pass that season in my life and make it to the next journey. The crazy part about all of this is that my only dream growing up was to have fun and to be a "Madam". I thought that lifestyle was amazing. I'm shaking my head because of the insanity of it all. But that's what was instilled in me. Time after time, I've witnessed this vicious cycle in families, even today. I see the repetitive cycle of bad behavior in our children and in our children's children. It has to stop right here! I'm not just speaking to my family, but to everyone. If we see the cycle now, we *must act on it and cut it from the core*. Then, we can begin to look beyond the break. Recognizing that generational curses are very real.

Every story has a beginning. As soon I turned 18 years old, I had my own place and everything became a lot worse. At the age of 21, I received a 10-year prison sentence for leaving my 6-year-old son for 6 years---what a journey that was! But, it became a part of the party in my head, and prison didn't help me at all. I was doing the same thing in prison that I was doing on the street. Some of the prison guards are just as bad, if not much worse, than the inmates. Sleeping with the ladies, bringing us drugs, money, alcohol, and food---the only thing I didn't have on my person were the hard drugs, but the ladies did. I had alcohol and marijuana and was doing my thing; most of the guards didn't say one word. The lifestyle in there was crazy! It's so clicked up: the stud girls had multiple ladies walking the yard like pimps and hoes. But, some had real relationships. I've heard some called "daddy crazy," and others referred to as the "stud's brother," "uncle," "dad," and the "girlfriend's mom." Looking back at the various conditions causing such low self-esteem and manipulation that took place in that environment, it was just crazy. I just could never call any of them a girl, and that's pretty much it. I held on for about 2 years until I finally succumbed and experienced being with a female. Yeah, I played around with girls when I was a child but never experienced "sex" with females as an adult. I went to prison in 1993, she got me in 1995. We were inmates at the same camp, then became separated. Of course, I tried other girls while living the prison life. Then, I went through a "church phase." I was happy praying and reading my word. The test came, though, when they moved me to another prison. Several years later, my former friend arrived, too. Even though she was in a relationship with another female, I didn't care. That's how the game goes in there. Eventually, we got back together up until she was released. I was released sometime after her, and we continued our "romantic relationship" on the streets, not really even knowing each other, and we started our journey. Our relationship was off and on. It was a rough one. We had a lot of good times and bad times---My son was not happy with the relationship that I had with her at all, and I'm sure it shocked the family. But I didn't care what anyone thought or said. This was my lifestyle and I was going to live my life to the fullest. My father would always say that it was an abomination, two girls being together. But I did not understand or listen to what he was talking about. I would just throw up what he was doing in his face and tell him SIN is SIN!

I was not out of prison for a good 6 months before I returned for domestic violence, which was a violation of my parole. Leaving my son again planted seeds of hurt and abandonment. Once again, my addiction had gotten the best of me. I had an apartment and left my son with my girlfriend. My family wanted to get temporary custody of him, but I decided it was best for him to stay home. He got into a lot while I was away. Although I only had 4 months to clean up, it felt like a life time. So, when I returned home, everything was good---we were living the life! My sister had joined the church and she would come witness to me. I would listen but was caught up in my new lifestyle. I decided to go to church with her one day, and I continued to attend because it was something new. In addition, what was being said made way more sense than the way I was currently living. One night, I decided to tell my significant other that we could not live as a couple any longer, and told her that I would help her out with everything so that she would be okay. She asked if I remembered what would happen to me if I ever left her. I always thought that was a joke, but in real life that is how some think. So everyone, take heed to these types of statements---they can change your life forever! She retrieved a knife from the drawer, but nothing happened---that night anyway. I think it was a Tuesday that my son and I were getting ready for bible study. All of her things were packed in the pantry area but she had not left yet. She asked, "Are you going to church"? I said, "Yes." She said, "I want to go." As you can imagine, I was very excited. She sent my son to the store to get some white shoe polish---that was to get my son out of the house so that she could kill me. When my son left, she asked me to go into the pantry to get her white shirt. I said to her, "I'm looking, but I don't see a white shirt." I turned around, and she stabbed me in the neck. I fell against the back door and she continued to stab me. I managed to grab the knife away from her hand, looked her in the eye, and told her that she was hurting me. I was holding on to the knife so tightly that I almost lost my thumb. Thank God she stopped and said, "Let me get rid of the knife." I said, "Okay." It was obvious that she was not in her right state of mind. When she hit the corner, I hit the back door. The strength I had to get up was amazing. She heard the back door open, and I was running losing serious blood by the minute. No one would help me! Everyone just watched as she came behind me with the knife. Finally, a guy asked, "Do you want me to call the police"? I shouted, "Yes, please, please call"! Continuing to run, I finally made it to the street side walk. The police officers saw me and told me to get to the ground. I took off his shirt and wrapped it around my neck---I was losing way too much blood to care what he thought. I happened to think about my son, though. I saw him coming back from the store. He stopped, looking at all of the fall out in a daze. My girlfriend began to apologize to him, but my son said nothing. She was handcuffed and went to jail. My son and I went to the hospital by ambulance. Almost losing my life was crazy! When I was released from the hospital my father insisted that I live with him for a while, so I did. As soon as I healed up, I drove to jail to visit with her a few times. I know you're thinking, "Is she crazy"? No, not crazy--- dysfunctional.

I continued to attend church and stopped going for a while. But, I got back on track, and I was able to forgive her for what she had done to me. I had to look beyond the break and change my way of thinking about what happened. Pushing it behind me allowed me to move toward another chapter in my life. It wasn't easy, but I had to keep going. In my life, there had been a lot of broken pieces and tragedy. Sometimes, I revisit all of the pain so that I can continue to focus on what's best for me and continue to allow God to renew my way of thinking. A changed mind is *powerful*! I see now that everything that took place in my life happened so that I could tell my story and help someone. It took years for me to finally get off this world wind called life. Each time I fell, I only became stronger. Then, my son began to act out the seeds I planted in him. This is why the curse has to be broken. He was in and out of juvenile detention centers, running away from home. He went to Elko for a while. When he was released, for approximately 6 months, he was in trouble again and this time his momma couldn't save him. I told him before any of this happened that one day he would become involved in something that I couldn't get him out. One Tuesday night, I was on my way to church. The news was on. It caught my attention because it was about three boys who had committed a murder, and they began to show photos and say the names---I went numb. My son was facing the death penalty at 16 years old. At this point, he was nowhere to be found---he had ran away. So, I filed a missing report on him, and have heard nothing from him to this day. There are absolutely no words to explain how I was feeling. All I know is that I wanted to be numb to it all. I forgot about everything that I learned in church. I drove to the store, bought me something to drink, and went on another drug mission returning to my norm.

This season of my life I was angry at God---in and out of institutions and mental wards---I even tried to kill myself several times. I felt that life was only meant to deal me pain and sorrow. My only child was gone, so I had absolutely nothing to live for. While I was in the hospital, one of the nurses said to me, "There is a God. In the state you came in here, we didn't know if you would pull through." I woke up to the nurses taking the tubes out my throat. I tried to get up to walk, but fell down. I couldn't even walk on my own. I couldn't die and I didn't feel that I was fit to live. I was hurting so bad. I just knew I was done after this. I didn't even want to fight. Each time I tried, I would lose the battle. I wandered out there in those streets for years, and never became faithful to the church. I was angry yet I still knew there was a God who was higher than me, or I would be dead by now.

I was lost and didn't want to return to church. Then, the shame and guilt started eating at me. So much has happened in my life, and unfortunately, I cannot reveal it all. I was out there not caring, giving up, and pretending to be okay. Then, when I thought I was okay, it still wasn't good enough! My ex-girlfriend was released from prison, and I was involved with her yet again. (Yes, she is the one who almost took my life!) So used to dysfunction that I never knew how to correctly function on a consistent basis. What a vicious, damaging cycle. At this point, I'm sure everybody thought that I had lost it or that I just didn't care. My ex and I continued our relationship for about 2 more years. Then, she disappeared again. I ran buck wild! I came across hundreds of thousands of dollars and blew every dime. Several years later, I decided to attend rehab. I was doing well for a while until I became involved with a guy in the same program. We didn't need each other; we needed healing.

We both left the program and were doing okay---just dealing with a lot of other issues. Guess what? We got married, and I was happy because I thought I was doing the right thing for once in my life. How did I think that, though, and we both had nothing---I'm not referring to only material things, but stability in the mind. We started off strong, then eventually we became active in our addictions. We lied, cheated, and lived with my father. I almost killed him! It truly was hurt after hurt. I got kicked out my father's house, so he had to leave, too. We separated because of all the cheating, lying, and the other women. It's funny to me now how the other women would call me, asking if he and I were still married because he was giving them promises that he couldn't keep---the manipulation was so real. I became sick of all of it, went to a safe house, and divorced him. I stayed there for a while, left, then rented a place and started dating again. The guy was someone who I had dated for years. He was such a sweet person. He never called me out my name in my presence like everybody else, but he had a lot of issues. I sure do know how to pick them, don't I? We lived together, though, up until the day he died--- his death was so unexpected---I never saw it coming. I could not believe what had just happened right in front of me. It was 2013, when he passed away. I was 42 years old... and met him when I was 18 years old. I had started working, then I moved. I was on track somewhat and not doing any drugs. I stayed home, went to work, planned to move, and to buy a new car---I was just doing me! Then, my father starting calling me all the time saying the same thing over and over. I knew that something wasn't right, but I thought his symptoms were owing to old age, so I would take him money, ice, and food. I did notice some weird stuff, but wouldn't say too much. One of my brothers would also tell us about the things my father would do such as eating half-done chicken after cooking it in the microwave, not bathing for days at a time, having accidents in his clothing, dumpster diving for cans, etc. We also noticed that Sunday dinners weren't the same. He would wander off to the back of the room, and we would begin to say, "That's just dad being dad." For months, we had a family meeting about his situation.

I drove to my dad's house one day, and after I walked inside of the house, I saw him sitting at the table sweating like crazy! It was so hot in the house that I could barely breathe. I looked around the house, which was disgusting---if my father was in his right mind, he wouldn't be living this way---there was mold in bathroom, and the toilets and showers weren't working. His bathroom was unbearable! I couldn't stop gagging. I said, "Dad you have to get out of this place! It's not good for your health." He didn't say one word. I knew then that he wasn't well. We would receive reports from people that he would forget his way home, and security informed us that he would go to the casino to gamble with fake money thinking it was real. He was being mistreated and used. When I left his home, I didn't know what to do. Sometimes in life you have to step out of your comfort zone, take the plunge into the unfamiliar, and make a difference in someone else life. God will truly bless you in doing so. I put in for family and medical leave on my job and went to live with my dad at his house. The decision was very hard but eventually, I had him placed in the hospital. I was scared because I didn't know what I was going to do with him when he was released. When he got out of the hospital, it was so hard. I almost gave up a million times and made plenty of mistakes along the way. But this was a game changer for me and such a humbling experience. I had to *look beyond the break* and step into the divine power and strength that God placed inside of me.

I've conducted research on everything written on the internet about dementia. I've spent many late nights learning everything that I could so that I could give him the best of care. I went through a lot when I first got him back home. He would fight and leave out the doors, which eventually we had to place locks on. I would almost get hit by cars so he would be safe because he would run into the streets. Once I got him to the doctors and on his meds I was given some relief, but as the disease progressed, he has declined and his behaviors have changed. My father was a very strong, smart man. But this disease does not have a name. Even during the writing of this chapter of my life, my dad's health continues to decline. He no longer walks and the way in which he communicates has changed. He has been turned over to hospice care. I reached out to one of my cousins for encouragement and who gave me some awesome words of wisdom. I thank her for that because I found myself not writing. I've come too far in my way of thinking to turn around now.

In telling my story, my goal is to help every man, women, boy, or girl who is suffering from generational curses of an addiction. You can change everything about yourself but if you don't change your way of thinking the curse cannot be reversed. I'm a woman who has been through many tough times in life, but I now can speak from a place of peace, forgiveness, and power, recognizing that "I'm unbreakable." I would also like to acknowledge the fact that after 32 years, my son's father has become a part of my son's life. They now have a relationship. It's amazing how life works, and it really doesn't matter when. When things take place, continue to grow and to learn that everything is done in God's perfect timing. It was very challenging for me to accept this at first, but who am I to hold on to what someone did in the past? Anyone can grow, and once I gave it to God and asked him to help me understand, my son's father called and asked me to forgive him for not being there for his son.

Once you look beyond what's causing the hurt and the pain, release it. That's when you can receive the healing and blessings that God has in store for you. I accepted his apology. I can move pass that "break" because I'm unbreakable. It no longer has any power over me. I told him, "Thank you," and was able to encourage him as well. I also let him know I never spoke an ill word to his son about him, and that I would always keep it real simple. I said, "If your father knew how to be a father, he would just be." I didn't feel the need to damage my son any further by talking negatively about his father to make me feel good. That would have caused my son more harm than good.

Always look beyond the break---you are "unbreakable." I promise that if you change your way of thinking, your life will make a significant turn for the better.

Fireside Reflections

Keywords and Takeaways:

1. A changed mind is *powerful*

2. Comfort Zone

3. Forgiveness

Our minds are the most powerful organ in our bodies, because it controls what we think and how we respond to life's situations. The more positive energy that you feed your mind, the more powerful impact it can have on your decision making. What are some of the ways you feed your mind positivity?

_____

_____

_____

_____

_____

This is huge, your comfort zone. At some juncture in life you will be challenged to do something outside of your comfort zone. That thing, whatever it may be will appear to disrupt your "normal" and is often the gateway to your breakthrough or next level, although it may not seem like it at the time. Can you recall a moment when experiencing life shift and being pulled from your comfort zone happened to you? How has it changed or shaped you?

_____

_____

_____

_____

_____

This story is so powerful because we continue to see examples of forgiveness. As stated before, remember that forgiveness is just as much for your healing and being able to move on as it is for the person being forgiven! Who do *you* need to forgive?

_____

_____

_____

_____

_____

AN APOLOGY TO MY BLEEDING HEART

Omozua Isiramen

My story starts with a broken heart.

A bleeding heart to be precise, as that is what I felt when I asked a church elder to pray for me.

Fear not. This is not about anything that was done to me. It is a story of awakening and stepping up into courage from unconscious incompetence to intentional self-discovery and a life in which I thrive as a human being.

You must know I am not what one would consider a fervent church-goer, however, I do believe in God and a higher source we humans get our strength from as life happens.

A Peculiar Sunday

On this Sunday, I was propelled to go to church by something within my soul that felt so unbearably painful, and like my last piece of energy to seek for help, a deliverance of some sort. During prayer time, the church elder I walked toward, took me in her arms like the other elders did to those who came to the front of the altar for prayer. She prayed and I cried as she did so. I heard her words, which were profound and touching. And as strange as this may sound, although I did not understand everything she was saying, I somehow hoped that with the courage that seeped through my legs and walked me to the altar of a church I had never been to before, I'd be gifted a miracle. One similar to those I'd read about in the bible and seen numerous times in films. My need for a breakthrough made me believe this was my last chance to start living life as I needed it to be---finally presentable to the world. I expected to start feeling free of the soul-crushing pain and inner despair, but all I knew was that my meticulously made up eyes were getting messed up from my hopefully not-so-obvious-attempt to dry the tears that were flowing like the Niagara Falls. I put in a lot of effort to conceal my list of lack and failure from the eyes of others before I left my place, so I became frustrated for being naïve to ever think things would change that instant. I realized my bleeding heart now felt more like a deep, open cut the doctor wouldn't quit fiddling with, with no end to the rough fall into the dark dungeon that was engulfing my very essence.

And there was also that whisper that followed me everywhere: No matter what you are feeling, Omozua, keep on smiling, act like nothing is the matter, and most important, inconvenience nobody with your silly issues. I could even hear my mother saying in her no-nonsense way, "Never wash your dirty linen in public, child." I truly believe this was the silent slogan of my upbringing.

Prior to this moment, life went on swiftly and required me to show up strong to the outside world as the hard worker, loyal buddy, and half-ready girl or woman that I was brought up to be.

113

I had worked in several roles, including as a beauty consultant, a hairdresser, and as a chef. Now I was a pedagogical supervisor and coach, recruiter, teacher, and trainer at work. Many respected me for my abilities and what I was able to achieve with the fake, almost nonexistent resources I had at my disposal to hire new staff. Let's not forget that I had a side hustle, which was gradually growing into something worth noticing and talking about.

Friends were moving on to new phases in their lives. They had children, started relationships or even moved in with partners, got married, bought homes, changed jobs and moved to different countries to pursue new opportunities. The point here being that as much as I truly celebrated the different phases of change and advancement people around me were having, I had this secret grudge against God and the universe.

My big question was when was it going to be my turn? I had done everything I was taught and told to do. All of the written, unwritten formulas and lists were ingrained in my head and heart. I had followed them and fully deserved my badges, which felt like personal medals of honor: *good girl, obedient girl, worthy girl.*

I simply did not see that being a "human" person was more than checking a list of roles and having certain things that were pleasing to the eye.

I carried the badges with pride like a tripled-layered façade, which I continually fortified through the years of my existence. Watching life happen to everyone else but me, these labels were all I had to show. Back then in my time of zero self-awareness, I truly believed this was the only way I could conceal my dark secret, which I'll tell you about later. As far as I was concerned, what was going on inside of me was mine to cover and to overcome alone.

The hidden fact was that I had formulas in place to help mask everything that could possibly show or suggest any kind of weakness within me. I carried this mask of outer strength like an armor and confidently faced life. I was my parents' daughter with all that entailed. This is how I was able to operate through the different snapshot life events and tasks without losing hope that my time would come. I functioned and did very well at showing up for work, family, and friends, but never for my hidden and undiscovered self.

Here I was standing at the church front, being prayed for, having this internal conversation with my inner-mind Chihuahua (my frightened brain), in which I hoped and prayed for my shields to hold up high like a Star Wars ship under fire would do. I prayed that no one would see my heart: *the real weak and exhausted version of myself.* I felt stupid standing there as I realized everything felt just the same and my expectation to walk back home from church, a completely new person, simply left me angry with myself for thinking this possible for a second.

The Mini Break Down (The First One I Ever Acknowledged)

I could not understand why this was happening to me, and I felt lonelier than ever before in my life. I was exhausted to the core of my soul and simply did not know what was wrong with me. I broke down at home and cried my eyes out as I had no idea how I was going to keep going on.

My big questions were:

Who was I?

Why did God create a defective version of me and send it into the world?

Why did everything seem to be falling apart?

Where was I going to get the energy to be or to live another day?

If all I believed myself to be until this moment was faulty or not enough, then what was the purpose of my existence?

Did I have any energy left to actually face the truth that would reveal itself, if it came down to things?

Why was life not happening to me the way I saw it happening to others?

How much longer was I going to be a human doer and not a human being?

My perception of life changed to a certain extent after this church event. My reflections shortly made me ponder about my actions up to that point of aiming for the light at the end of the tunnel, but the next day came, and life rolled on. I continued to show up in my roles that to the outside world looked like I was a fully functioning person that met at least some criteria of the societal requirements.

I told myself that the checklist of labels right in front of me, which a woman in her late 20s or very early 30s should have acquired to a greater extent, although never really within my reach, was simply the only goal my faltering "optimistic me" could keep pushing forward to attain. Even if that meant breaking myself to pieces until things fell in place.

To be honest, I didn't know any better and strongly believed I had no other choice in life. I could not possibly let down my guards or show any weakness, as I did not know who I could be beyond the jolly, strong version of 'Omozua' that I upheld with all my might. Luckily, though, back then and unbeknownst to me, that silent cry for help at church, the daring questions that followed, and the painful reflections I opened up to though not followed up with any action, started my journey to embracing my unseen and unshown self and gaining insights that would turn my life around forever.

The thing I didn't see was that almost all the inner struggle I had was based on how I felt the world saw me, the woman who did not fit in no matter how much she tried and how I understood myself through the perspective of others. I never once looked into the mirror of life to honestly ask myself who I was or how I could show up in the world on my own terms. It took a while for me to understand that the change I could make in my life would only begin by me asking the right questions and basing all action and steps on the findings I made.

Over the years, I had binged on self-help books and motivational videos with a passion. What I learned was that there were thousands of lists spitting out advice about what one should do to excel in life. There was, however, nothing on how or why the biggest barrier to living a fulfilled life that didn't require applauds from the outside lay in running after things that were more trouble pursuing than they were actually worth.

I am a proud and big list-and-formula buff, so those self-help lists sounded awesome and sent sparks down my body but that surge of motivation ended minutes after I closed the book and finished watching the videos. I could never seem to act beyond that point of fire within, so for years, I ended up swimming in my sea of frustration that took on many forms of expression, which varied from time to time.

You may remember the secrets I mentioned earlier. Well, let me share some with you. I did function, socialize, travel, dine out, and spend time with friends and family. Powerful moments, which I tanked up on as those times gave me joy, but when those things were not happening as often as before, I burned all that energy up to deal with my painful reality, which I could not escape as I watched life happen to everyone but me.

1. Locking myself up like a hermit when I had no societal obligations but suffering from loneliness; struggling with dark thoughts. I convinced myself it was better not to display my list of lack and hide indoors like the ancient Greek Medusa fearing to be beheaded. It felt like dying rather than living, as I watched weeks turn into months, and months became years in which I mastered the act of looking fully normal and strong to the outside, but continued breaking inside bit by bit each time.

2. Beating myself up for all of the opportunities that I missed out on by talking myself out of meeting with others and never asking for help.

3. Working out robotic-similar plans to show up at work each day without breaking down. I could by no means let anyone know that when I wasn't in one of the external roles in which I appeared unbreakable. I'd be engulfed by uncontrollable fear which left me feeling deeply sorry for myself to the point of not wanting to exist anymore.

4. Fighting vulnerability as it was not something I had learned to deal with and as such never found myself tempted to fall for its call. I was a stone's throw from losing whatever was left inside me.

5. Delving into being there for everyone and all of the distractions that would simply keep me from thinking about myself and that brain-stabbing hole that was growing at Nano speed.

I was a good aunt, sister, friend, employee, teacher, supervisor, volunteer, and colleague. Externally, I excelled in those roles well and gave from my heart. Those aspects of my life fulfilled me but only to a certain extent, as there was always that nagging voice that reminded me of my secret and all of the other things I hadn't achieved. Not yet I hoped.

I functioned in life as was expected of a good girl, up to the point that left me with no energy to appreciate not to talk about accepting myself. I made an impact in my own small square of the world and was never one to shy away from ensuring that I put a smile on the face of others. Touching the human in others became the focus of my drive in life since doing this did not question my person, and it became the only real thing I had. I listened, helped, and supported whenever and wherever I could, which helped me distract myself from all of the things about me that I was not facing and were wrong in my view. I spent a lot of energy not showing people I needed help and that I was *broken* inside.

Distractions

The achievements I had made in my life were worth admiring, particularly when I was reminded of them by my family and friends. Back then, in my moments of inner-struggle, it was about the only time I took their word for it and allowed myself to see a bit of myself positively. For the rest of the time, although I accomplished all of the things that fulfilled me from an external point of view, I also knew what it felt like to be, or, as I learned later, to feel like a complete waste. It was not uncommon that I erased or forgot about things I had successfully achieved in my life, and unfortunately, I focused more on what had become my invisible scar and power list of lack and failure, based on the checklist of success provided by society of which I met none of the important criteria.

To expand on my dirty secret, despite following all of the rules, my hope, optimism, and my wonderful labels that should have led me to success, I felt like a failure and fraud most of the time. I wondered if there was something wrong with me, which would explain why none of the things that society dictated as normal and a must for a woman were falling in place for me. Interestingly enough, some of the shame and guilt I experienced were triggered by the well-meant, sweet-coated comments from those who worried about me so much, that they would have kind talks to highlight what I may have been doing wrong and what I could try to change things. The more I listened to these talks, the more I was unable to overcome the deep exhaustion that had become an inescapable state in my life.

As I operated through my lens of feeling like a mistake, despite all I could have been happy and grateful for in my life, the more I became my toughest critic and judge. I simultaneously admired and envied all of the people that led normal lives, and moved on in mine with no shades of gray.

The more time that passed by, the more lost I felt and deeply disenchanted with God, life, and the universe. I blindly walked through life with my game face on. For a long time, I didn't know I could feel, and as long as I did not know my underlying blocks, it seemed I was stuck in a rut.

This share is not a sob story nor one of never-ending pain. Rather it is one of stepping up with courage into the greatest gifts I could give myself: Clarity.

I was reliving what seemed to be the end of my trail unless a miracle happened, when my turnaround came with a 2006 diagnosis finally bringing around a thorough and unavoidable operation in 2012, which left me unable to walk for 2 months. For the first time, I had no energy to wear my protective façade or run away from what I considered my hell on earth. Being unable to move forced me to face me, myself, open up my invisible Pandora's Box, and to travel the daring journey of connecting the bridges of my life.

As I writhed in pain on my way to healing, as far back as I could think the movie of my life set itself in motion, and I finally voiced all of those unasked questions and what they revealed. For the first time ever, I experienced what facing and embracing humanity wholeheartedly on one's own term meant.

Formulas and Lists, First Emotions, and My Triple-layered Façade

To understand my love for formulas and lists, challenges with feeling, emotions, and seeing myself for who I was, I have to go back to my childhood and my first encounters with different emotions.

My first conscious encounter with emotions was when I was about 5 years old. My late mother worked as a night shift nurse in a hospital in the United Kingdom, and I remember vividly how I would cry my eyes out each time she would get ready to leave for work. My father was building a home for us to return to in Nigeria. Everything was okay until I started to notice that she would leave after putting me in bed. She left me with her kind neighbor Ms. Gladys who stayed and checked up on me while my mother was away at work. The toys, treats, hugs, and kisses from my mom did nothing to console or reassure me that things were okay.

She always came back from work to play and to spend time with me, but this didn't help at all with the pain I felt when she left again. As early as the age of 5, I became acquainted with fear, anxiety, loss, and feeling lonely. I'm not saying that I knew how to deal with the emotions, but I sure didn't like them, and nothing about this fact changed as I grew older. Feeling these emotions tore my heart apart but worse, I started to notice this deep, sad look on my mother's face each time I used my crying and begging to talk her out of leaving me behind when she had a shift.

The next emotions I became acquainted with were in the form of my two large teddy bears my mother bought me to keep me company when she went off to work called Courage and Confidence. She named them that and said they had super powers to do anything. They became my friends and companions who made me feel good, although I believe somewhere along the line, I must have become tired of crying and having tantrums.

How do I know? Well with time, mom would tell me what a good girl I was, how much I had grown, and was pleased at how I turned into a good girl who didn't misbehave anymore. That was when I realized that I was bad at times.

This was the birth of my first façade, which I chose unconsciously as a little girl. I realized that I was a problem and that by not showing how I felt and keeping my emotions buried down within me, I was able to remove the look of distress from my mother's face. My first formula to live by was created. I realized that by acting a certain way, I made others happy. So, I started to care for how others felt wherever I went and fulfilled what I felt was now my obligation.

This strategy of mine became strengthened by the fact that I saw the trouble those, who did not employ my way of operating, got into with others. I barely complained or spoke about how I felt about things.

121

The relevance of how expressing one's feelings and emotions was to building a healthy picture of oneself and having the resilience to face life as it happens without falling into pieces was simply unknown to me.

Expectations, My Young Girl and Teen Years

My next façade was formed in my early teens. I grew up among strong personalities, carrying my label of what would be considered a good girl. My parents and the elders around were those who I was brought up to respect and imitate as that led to earning a life as it was meant to be. Looking back, I have no idea what that even meant, but with grit and determination, I did everything to uphold my reputation. I was an obedient young lady who trusted everything that came from outside and did not question anything she was told to do.

Life rolled on as I did all the things expected of a good girl and excelled at hiding the fact that I was not the science-loving, super intelligent child they wanted me to be. I never would have told them I loved writing and would have loved to become like Chinua Achebe, Buchi Emecheta, Stephen Biko, or Bernard Binlin Dadié. This dream died, as it fit nowhere. Other family members seemed to carry or to aim for the perfect labels: doctors, accountants, engineers, lawyers, nurses, number-loving, and intelligent. These were the perfect and recognized professions. I couldn't pride myself of having or feeling apt for any of them (I simply did not see or know my own worth), but I worked hard to uphold the only label I had been given and owned. I silently waited for my life to turn out as it had for those grown women before me, living the life phase labelled, "They got married and lived happily forever." I watched films and read books that supported this expectation. Like many others, I had a solid Disney Princess mentality, which required indulging in surface conversations and acts without ever getting deep or admitting how unrealistic the set expectations truly felt.

Stemming from a family and parents who had voiced and unspoken expectations, formulas and lists, I never ceased to see the perfect future others envisioned in front of me. I grew up with an innocent arrogance bred by the talks of my role models who praised my behavior and promised that unlike all those other people with their life challenges and palavering, I would never know a struggle or pain. I was a basket full of unbroken hope. All was going to be well and all I needed to do was wait

Mom Dies

The third façade was created when I was 19 years old. Patience E. Isiramen, my mother, died. My siblings were 21, 11, and 4 years old, respectively. I remember the call as if it were yesterday. A close family friend called us in Germany to tell us that she passed away in the hospital. The last time I saw her, I was saying goodbye to her and my father at the Murtala Airport in Lagos. I can't remember her last words and didn't know that would be the last time I'd see her.

What I do remember is being told vigorously to be strong and not to cry. There was no time for weakness and now we had no mother anymore---we had to be extra tough. Little did I know that it would take another 4 years before I took the liberty to cry and kind-of-mourn my mother. But even this I could never talk about and only do in secret, behind closed doors, as I was so used to not showing any type of weakness---ever.

Pandora's Box

Everything that occurred after my mother died is a wild roller coaster I do not wish on anyone. Life was not all dark but it certainly wasn't easy after being shipped off at 17 years of age, similar to Kunta Kinte in the movie "Roots" but to Germany instead of England, as originally planned by my parents for a "so-called better" future despite thousand reasons that spoke against this plan. However, after she died if there was any hope left in me that life would somehow turn out the way I was brought up to believe it would, it was replaced by anger, shame, guilt, and exasperation.

I had not landed in the land of honey and milk as far as I was concerned. Now with no mother to run back to or ask for help, I feared a bleak future. It was around this time that I unconsciously created my invisible Pandora's Box, which was located on my left shoulder. It accompanied me everywhere and was only opened to dump things into the container. Everything unpleasant, signs of weakness that could make me falter or feel hurt or hinder me from being the jolly good old-functioning Omozua that I usually was. My happy compact family as I knew it, was never to be experienced again after mom left us—for none of us.

Healing and Reflections

Back at home after the operation, helpless, and in my pain that started to unfold in waves, I began to understand what it meant to have friends who were there for me, heart and head. With my body not serving me as it should, my façade melted away like butter on a hot potato, and although difficult, I learned and forced myself how to ask for help. I didn't really have a choice, and I was surprised by the fact the few who visited me and saw me in this vulnerable state had no issue at all.

It was all in my head...

I cried, journaled, slept, spoke out my frustrations and truth (was done hiding this from myself), read poems long forgotten, watched TV, and spent a lot of time reflecting on my life without the influence of external forces. I truly entered a state of peeling back the deep onion layers. The pieces of my life (many which I deemed irrelevant) meandered together to form a recognizable flow of what I came to realize was the war I had been having with myself.

Other companions on my journey of breaking loose of unresourceful ties from what I now identify as nutty beliefs and unreasonable humility were: Journaling, meditation, prayer for nothing else than to be calm, strong in myself and remain in the now, intentionally searching for clarity using power questions, and music. Yes, the lyrics in certain songs that I came across by chance worked magic as I ventured out of my pain zone with more courage each day.

I felt that my physical pain was only decreasing slowly, which left me feeling frustrated. One would have thought with all the lying and staying still, my body would regenerate faster. But something good came of this, I couldn't flee back into old habits nor escape the discovery path I was on. I chose to shamelessly but resourcefully expand my use of distractions and I thank God I did. This is how I happened upon the world of neuroscience, emotional mastery, studies of unleashing one's brain potential, mindset and mindfulness practices. I came across the works of John Assaraf (his teaching showed me the opportunity I could jump on), Srini Pillay, Daniel Friedland, and some others. The brain fascinated me because I finally understood my inner-mind Chihuahua and how not knowing how to navigate it was making me sabotage myself on so many levels. I discovered the calming power, which classic music had on my brain, my inner self-talk, and inner distress.

I remembered something that my parents always told me as a child, *Before you say you do not like something, you must try it out first.* So, I activated a little more of my existing courage and chose to focus on the possibility of living a life outlined by no one else but myself. I saw the shift in my thinking as I shamelessly changed the way I asked questions. No more stewing in any should or could haves. I was simply done with old formulas that hadn't served me so far. I had nothing to lose and simply said adieu to my oldest friend, 'Mr. Waiting' despite my inner-mind Chihuahua screaming a big *No* to this plan. This may sound silly but there were many times, I got so fired up, inspired, and almost possessed to the extent that I sang out loud. I sang, laughed, cried, and even screamed as I went through the emotions and openly exposed myself to the kind of reflection I'd never allowed myself have in the past. I faced my Pandora's Box, and it truly felt like breaking out of hell. I told myself if I was going to die of pain, I may as well do so on my own terms for once. I wanted to know what it truly meant to be free from within. What seems obvious now is that I wasn't only dealing with the physical pain from the operation but the invisible one located deep down inside of my soul.

The song that opened my eyes at this painful stage was Crossroads by Bone, Thugs, and Harmony. It contains a few lines that gave me a strong push out of my pain and my (comfort) zone:

"Now tell me whatcha gonna do

When there ain't nowhere to run (tell me what)

(When judgment comes for you, when judgment comes for you)

And whatcha gonna do

When there ain't nowhere to hide (tell me what)

When judgment comes for you ('cause it's gonna come for you)."

I had big choices to make:

- Keep on hiding behind whatever was left of my façade or seeking self-awareness.

- Clinging on to the mindless 'Shakara' mentality that evaded the society I grew up in or adopting a life in which I made a real difference.

- Opening my invisible Pandora's box or keep on being weighed down and remaining stuck in conscious and unconscious fear and mediocrity.

- Meandering like a proud river to unleash creativity and possibilities, no matter at what rate or remaining stuck like stale water in a glass.

- Holding on to a dead-end job that allowed no room for growth or pursuing my heart's calling.

- Personifying my painful labels: "Queen of Procrastination," "Madame Lazy," "Ms. Unfinished," and "Ms. Wait Forever" or finally losing the unnecessary weight clouding the powerful insights I could tap into in my brain.

Meeting the Emotions and Connecting My Bridges

Opening my Pandora's Box was tough but way overdue, and only by asking non-surface questions was I able to start working through the feelings I had stored away for too long. There are certainly things that will remain sealed (this is a conscious choice, which does not harm me), but I am thankful I had the courage to pull out all I needed to connect the bridges of my life for the future ahead. Shame or not, I had felt stupid, fat, unlovable, unworthy, forever hopeless, invisible, and like a big waste for long enough. Rewriting my life was only going to happen when I stopped swallowing the poisonous pill I carried with me over and over again---like an addict.

Anger at God and the Universe

I remember asking the following questions: God why on earth, have you forgotten me? How much longer did I need to wait?

The guilt that arose from asking this particular question broke me and provoked my free fall into my dark dungeon. I cried and felt deep regret and anger at the same time. Nothing felt fair, and I surely didn't deserve this, but deep down I knew that this was me laying blame again. Things weren't falling in place. Nothing was going well despite doing everything by the book, and then I became angry at my parents for lying and not preparing me for the real world.

Anger at My Parents (Laying Blame)

What would it have taken to say it is absolutely okay to feel, cry, and talk about emotions?

What would it have taken to admit that I'd experience hurt and disappointment at times, but it'd never last if I navigated my way through things as they popped up?

What would life be like if I was not so focused on my lack and inherited checklist, which remained un-ticked to date?

How flexible would I have gone through my early years, if I had been told that everyone has human moments and that sacrificing oneself to be everything for others, being good, humble did not make one immune to life and its lessons?

How empowered would I be if I had not grown up with labels that defined what was worth pursuing and the limitless ceiling of things deemed dangerous though human and bad for my reputation?

Would I have ventured out of my pain zone earlier despite the fear if I had not inherited a bucket full of grit and determination to disallow ever being vulnerable?

Why did they not give me more than the fairy tales that hindered all kinds of progress?

Why was having a perfect reputation to show to the outside world more important than living a fulfilled life from within?

A Different Look at My Life (Being Honest)

Guilt and shame scorched me badly after my rage and anger at God, my parents, and the world subsided.

Then I came across the song "I Apologize" by Five Finger Death Punch, and I was able to get through my favorite movie: Omozua, the hopeless victim.

Here are a few of the lines:

"All these times I simply stepped aside

I watched but never really listened

As the whole world passed me by

All this time I watched from the outside

Never understood what was wrong or what was right."

After going through this painful reflection, I realized there had been so many times in the past when I could have changed things. I simply did nothing with the insights I had. I let fear keep me back. Could I really blame God and my parents for the struggle I was experiencing? I reasoned that this was so wrong and I had to see things for what they were. What was my role in how my life had turned out?

Only when I stopped focusing on the big bang moments, which I grew up with and had treated like the holy grail of living, was I able to start flourishing from within.

I grew up safe, loved and guarded. My mind travels, cautiously observing the trails of my life from Newport to Lüdenscheid to London, then to Lagos and Europe again. From the outside, I am sure anyone would have deemed my life perfect with everything in place. Words like correct, happy, jolly, magnetic fire, power, and unbreakable come to my mind. But frequently I was unsure who they were actually talking about.

My parents gave me all they knew how to, the best way they could. What I know now is you can only teach others what you understand and have learned yourself. My mother was a real woman who lived her roles as they were recognized by society. A mother, sister, aunt, wife, business owner, nurse, humanitarian, and a respected lady. She was definitely not perfect but she taught me a lot that has contributed to who I am today. She showed up as vulnerable as she could allow herself to show or to be, decently loud, and ready to do what was required unconditionally for the 19 years I was blessed to have her in my life. I do however also remember her sitting in our garden, crying and looking worried into the sky. I never dared to ask what was wrong.

My father was the one I approached first if I wanted anything since I felt he was way more lenient and approachable compared to my no-nonsense mother. I remember him being a very warm-hearted but very silent man who told tales through his eyes. He was a man of habit: the same thing year in, year out. I see a lot of him in me, too, but like my mother, talking about feelings and emotions was not something he did. Not even when I had done something wrong would he raise his voice or tell me off but the look in his eyes suggested I was forgetting the rules by which a reputable Isiramen lived and played. That look smacked me back into compliance, carrying my heavy cross with all of its unrealistic labels, silently.

If there was a perfect way to depict how I see my life growing up and becoming a woman on my own terms, bar a few tough moments that taught me lessons, it would be like the loud and active image of the Sistine Chapel Ceiling or the subtle aroma of lavender I imagine spreading in the air, as I experienced looking at Joan Miró's Prades, The Village.

You see, as I maneuvered through life studying, training, working, wearing my façade, labels, and feigned armor of strength though deep down secretly waiting for my life to start, life as such never stopped happening to my "optimistic self."

A labyrinth of life events (which I luckily do not judge or evaluate anymore) were at my disposal that now serve as a source of learning and growth.

Things such as:

- Being cut off from friends, family, love, and everything that defined and formed my identity at 17 years of age.

- Fearfully observing what alcoholism, manipulation, hatred, disgust, and lack could create in relationships (even within blood ties) where communicating about what mattered was forbidden.

- Experiencing life through the lens and stories of women and children who had experienced indescribable violence during my stay at a women's safety shelter.

- Seeing the struggle asylum seekers endured on their search for a better life. This experience made me choose humans first in all I ever did, as I felt this the best way to make a difference in a world where behind the scenes and surface smiles, you could see how nasty humans could get when they deemed you third class citizen.

- My first stint at entrepreneurship as a Mary Kay consultant, where I failed or actually gave up, as I had no sense to ask for help and admit I was struggling.

- Waiting and finding love that only came at 23 years old and heartbreak.

- Feeling constantly disconnected and not fitting in anywhere. These are just a few of the snapshots I choose to remember.

The song "The Light by Disturbed" enabled me to acknowledge this state as my lowest point but also the door to taking responsibility for what was possible, once I got back on my feet. It saved me. Here are a few lines:

"The answer isn't' where you think you'd find it

Prepare yourself for the reckoning

For when your world seems to crumble again

Don't be afraid, don't turn away

You're the one who can redefine it

Don't let hope become a memory."

As I listened to it up and down, I reconsidered my take on the invisible rule I grew up with of never breaking out in distress or showing weakness of any kind, no matter how terrible.

Power Questions to Discover My New Self

- Who can I become if I stopped spending my energy on running away from seeing the true version of myself, flaws and all - the one I loved unconditionally?

- Who could I choose to be if I courageously felt and acted, fully knowing that feeling emotions would never break me?

- Who was I if I simply dropped all the things that was expected of me?

- Who could I allow myself to be if I simply stopped ticking the boxes on that societal, scary list of what defined success?

- How would happiness unfold itself to me if I simply let go of my tie to what was seen as the so-called right way of doing things?

- What inner power could be unleashed if I wrote my story without squeezing it into that of others?

- How about living life daily as myself and nothing else?

- What beauty could I create if I started to define my own terms and direct my own play formula-free?

- Could I dare choose to be nakedly human? Could I be courageous and look within my soul?

Courage

As I explored my mini-ME, I realized another powerful thing. As long as I did not let go of all the things I had been taught, held out for the true and the only way of living, I was never going to be free of the despair within.

My big step of courage: I let go and stopped lying to myself that waiting would allow me to start living. I let go of feeling I was failing my parents, family, and all those who penned my life for me

The truth I courageously embraced included:

- Becoming anything but what I felt in my heart was no more possible

- Taking action to course-correct the way I operated in life was nothing to be ashamed of. Better late than never.

- Emotions, feelings and thoughts didn't break you if you learn how not to allow them.

- Owning one's emotions wasn't a reason for self-doubt or weakness but the road to tapping into my potential as a human and freeing myself of all that did not allow me thrive in my soul.

- Confidently choose to no longer be willing to live life running after other people's dreams.

- It was okay to carve my own way of operating, running my life with my brain and to be more.

- There was more to life than waiting to decoupage it with worldly or mindless labels

Letting My Pain (comfort) Zone Go, Forgiveness, and an Apology

I listened to the song, "I didn't know my own strength and I look to you" by Whitney Houston as I reflected on all of the time I had spent asking unresourceful questions. But now, I'm so grateful this way of being had no more power over me.

Although lessons and teachings came in different shapes, the one thing I didn't know I possessed was choice and only when I learned what this ignorance meant and cost me, did it make the difference I needed to change how I looked at myself and life.

I discovered the power of choice and asking questions. The right questions which allowed me to see myself for who I was. I remember the first time I actually looked into a mirror and said out loud: "Omozua I like you and you are cool." It felt weird but I laughed and this is how I came to understand the resistance I had with affirmations. When affirmations are used to avoid dealing with the inner struggle one has, they simply feel wrong and are as useless as listening to motivational speeches 24/7.

I came to find that a **bleeding heart** couldn't receive, embrace, accept, recognize, see beyond pain, let go, or grow and I wrote this poem, which let it all pour out:

The Apology to My Bleeding Heart

I apologize for not looking beyond what I was taught

For looking past the truth of my mortality

Treading the path still being embarked on by many who rather choose not to see

The one of perfection and acting omniscient which only sounds good in writing

Ignoring the consequences of the labels we humans choose to wear

Underestimating how the stories passed on affect one's ability to breathe and BE

Life is way too short to label one's heart with hate, anger, helplessness, and frustration

Hoping for a breakthrough. Not realizing that rolling up a steep mountain with uneven wheels never happens with ease

I apologize for internalizing my self-talk as the only valid truth

Letting my inner-mind Chihuahua control the reins of my life

Exposing myself to the fake news I allowed in from outside

Dismissing the power of trusting my gut and laying blame

I ran after things I didn't define or outline. I didn't know better. I didn't know how to change

Had no understanding of the power of choice in a world where time is not limitless

I apologize for thinking responsibility was someone else's to take

I apologize for not seeing that if something was to be, it was solely up to me

I apologize for almost giving up and thinking I could throw away a whole barrel for being rotten because of a few bad apples within

I apologize for allowing shame to push me away from wanting more and the unnecessary dance with fear

Now as I step up into courage to embrace my humanity

To you my bleeding heart I say:

I embrace the message of each emotion that comes my way. With no evaluation or judgement, I confidently apply the 'eye for different perspectives' before I act

I pledge to see you through a lens of unconditional love. Human. Robotic no more.

I swear to never shy away from the courage to walk through the temples of my soul and mind. Knowing no human is human alone

With a smile, positive energy and all the resourceful emotions I can summon

I travel this journey of healing with awareness and clarity. The past is where it belongs.

I stem from God and the Universe. My legacy lies in embracing this fact.

All is well, I can now breathe, live and BE

The Courageous Human in me.

New Insights

There is no point expecting an easy life if the way you operate is based on not feeling and avoidance of all kinds. Back in the days when I didn't know how to evaluate things based on who I really was, I believed feelings and emotions were dangerous. My inner-mind Chihuahua, which only sees things in the dark or darker (the amygdala) helped me turn every lizard into a ferocious dinosaur until I started to see this in every single aspect of my life.

My pondering led me to this truth: Life was not happening to me rather I was happening "negatively" to my life and my outcomes. This was the deepest moment of awareness and clarity I had attained to date. Independent of one's upbringing, habits, behavioral patterns, beliefs what you can achieve or change in your life depends solely on what you do once the shackle of blindness is cracked open. Only when I could admit, accept and approach my state and operate through this understanding was I able to start living a free life. One that was not driven by unresourceful emotions and actions.

I have a lot to be grateful for in hindsight. Unknowingly life had been good to me.

- I escaped drowning in an Olympic-sized pool in Lagos, Nigeria after jumping in to prove I could swim without help at the age of 12.

- I survived a dog attack at the age of 13, an electrocution in our kitchen which left me in an induced coma for a few days at 15 and this operation that brought on my life-changing moment.

- My parents gave me the most important "Hs" to enable me to access abundance and all I needed if I chose wisely: Humility, humor, happiness (just because), humanity, head, and heart.

- The true essence of being rich: a smile (no matter what) and a light mind.

- A labyrinth of history, memories, and teachings to draw and create good from.

An Inward Journey Heading Outward

That light at the end of the tunnel took on a whole new meaning. As far back as I can remember I wanted to find myself at a point where all was perfect as planned and prophesied. My journey of self-discovery made the destination less important and rather than dwelling in the land of waiting non-end, I learned new skills to travel life as the happy ball of energy, I deeply knew myself to be, that was a valid part of the universe sent out to learn, grow and expand until it reunited with source one day. Looking back, I see that at each phase and bridge I crossed in my life, I collected various ingredients that formed the "So-So cocktail" that made me get through whatever life was presenting me with as I survived to the next learning spot.

All along I did feel but was simply not processing or expressing it for fear of appearing weak. What a relief to know, I was and am a multifaceted human after all. Courage and confidence that I can now access with unconscious competence, allow me to navigate shame, regret and guilt without beating myself up. The gift of being able to feel my emotions and embrace the lessons and messages they hold in store, by seeing beyond what the ego would usually allow and by operating from my brain's executive seat taught me that the first point of forgiveness must start within.

I had to face the river of my life and believe me, it takes a lot of courage to choose healing and being over appearing presentable to the world. The price of not feeling and facing emotions left me watching years pass by, feeling frustrated and tired but my outburst and breakthrough is what made me choose my new life's path. I made emotions and the brain my hearts work and drive. I finally made my inner connections through the teaching one of my closest friends gave me. Karen van Hout introduced me to the different ways of perceiving oneself with the wooden dummies she uses in her systemic coaching work: the real you - core version which you hide, the rucksack version of you - the one with all your past which influences the "public figure" version of you as shown to and perceived by others. Everything finally made sense. My core version was were my bleeding heart lay.

Losing Weight

I understood losing weight as most people probably do. It meant being thin enough to fit into beautiful outfits, being whistled after, looking attractive, and appealing to others. My somewhat unhealthy relationship with my body started at the age of 11, but I could camouflage it to an extent because girls in my family were naturally curvy and beautiful. Moving to Europe changed that view however, and brought on dehumanizing comments that started a life-long training of different diets and approaches to get rid of the natural, beautiful curves. Looking back, it seems incredible what horror movies we replay and expose our brains to.

With all shame gone, this process of being nakedly open to myself did something powerful—it got me to ask the question.

What good was meeting man-made societal norms of beauty on the outside if the inside was dark, fearful, chaotic, and unable to embrace being human, unconditionally?

I had to start losing the right weight to build the health I needed to thrive in and out.

I broke out of the useless spell of diminishing myself in a punitive manner by redefining health for myself. My new diet which I recommend 100%: healthy brain optimization practices, healthy self-talk, healthy view of one's past, healthy food spiced up with enough hydration and exercise and embracing self-care with no guilt. Simply delicious!

It is so empowering when you no more see life through the lens of other people's should-haves and can show up as you truly are.

Powerful Thoughts and Strategies for Becoming CEO of Your Brain

Being Nakedly Human requires making self-reflection a commonplace, being compassionate in all you do, knowing yourself and being 100% strategic about:

Your conversations - those with yourself and that with others

Your thoughts, feelings and emotions

The formulas and lists you live your life by

The rules you have in place that determine your happiness and success

The actions that promote your personal growth and ability to promote the same in others

The input of information you let in as your body is a temple

The output of information because you are responsible for the ripple effect you send out into the world and the fact whether you like it or not, and independent of your past, is that no one but you are responsible for the legacy you leave behind.

Be super clear and honest with yourself, what it is you are aiming for in all your hustle, being busy and acting happy to the outside. This may feel scary, I know, but life happens and if all you do is go for the fun and surface stuff, ignoring the deep reflection aspects, what will happen when life hits hard? How will you manage, the moment all those material and external pleasures with their short-term sources of satisfaction fade away? I have been down that path and it is not worth it.

Getting help reaching out to get help and insights that can help you does to make you failure

I have come to find that it is so important to ingrain the power in this line, an inner slogan that allows me to release and let go of all that no more serves me.

It puts what has been and can't be changed to rest: *"The past has happened to the past but now, it is up to me if the past will happen to my present and future."*

I do not know what the future holds, but I look forward to it because I am no more walking around blind. Thinking about myself and feeling for one's soul is not a sin or time-stealing effort. It is the best gift you can afford yourself. Many things, good and bad have occurred since my break through but compared to the past, my reaction to adversity and how I respond is way more resourceful and I never stop working on this. I approach change with calm because I have learned to engage my brain to be of service to me in all my moves. I no more need a big bang to start living and I have spoken to many who now share the same thoughts. I am forever grateful that I underwent the journey of discovering my true self no matter how painful it was. I have never looked back and know I owe no one else my personal growth but myself.

Life as I now know it, is no more about some fake dream or static picture that depicts the same perfect but colorless story. It is so much more than living in survival mode if at all. No matter how fast-paced the world gets and talks about how our attention span is getting shorter, you can't swipe humanity into your life and to get what feeds the soul you have to take the time to understand and embrace all that makes you, you.

Life is what you make of it, from what space you operate in your mind and it can be beautiful in all of its colors.

My impact in life is sharing what I have learned and implemented to get as many people as possible to step up into courage by taming their inner-mind Chihuahuas, discovering and unleashing the brain potential they have within for the life they want and being nakedly human on their own terms on any given day.

I will like to end this journey of awakening with the following:

Be compassionate with yourself in all you do. Even when self-reflecting. You are human first.

Know that stepping up into courage and owning your life calls on you to fully integrate and implement being more O.M.O. in your life on your own terms.

Original

Masterful

Optimistic (realistically)

Fireside Reflections

Keywords and Takeaways:

1. Self-awareness

2. Carried mask of outer strength

3. Hidden and undiscovered self

4. Life on my own terms

5. Clarity

6. What is your role?

Omozua goes really deep into trying to understand who she is aside from what others thought she was or the identity that they gave her of WHO she THOUGHT she was. How many of us can identify with that, raise your hand! It wasn't until Omozua discovered having self-awareness that she began doing the work.

A part of us doing the work is taking off the masks that we are carrying around, the masks that makes us feel acceptable in a world where we should be accountable to ourselves and not other's thoughts of us.

When we are able to break free from that bondage we are able to discover our hidden undiscovered selves, and on that journey you'll experience the clarity that will become your compass in life and as you begin to understand, you'll be more courageous to live life on your own terms!

So, I ask you, as Omozua asked herself. What is your role in your own life? How will you break free of being a self-saboteur? What are you holding on to that is holding you captive? Write it down and start to break free from that so that you can discover your own awareness and clarity.

_____
_____
_____
_____
_____
_____
_____
_____
_____
_____
_____
_____
_____

REINVENTING YOUR LIFE
THE POWER!

Cyndilu Miller

Today, I will be taking you on a journey to explore how default decision making became a part of my life. The "day of awakening" occurred when I realized that I did not want to be ruled anymore by old patterns. We will explore in depth the first intentional decision that I remember making about how I treated emotions and how I treated the people around me. There're a few stories behind this, and you may wonder how making solid, conscious decisions could so drastically change not only my life, but the lives of so many to follow. We don't think about making decisions around emotions. Frequently, we believe that emotions *lead* and that we have no choice in our decision making. Unfortunately, this kind of thinking is what led me to give away my decision-making power about my emotions.

I was only 3 years old when I build my first wall. He said, "If you tell anyone, I'll kill you." Again, I was only a 3-year-old toddler, so naturally I believed what I was told. That day, I made the decision that I wouldn't let anyone know, *no one*, that I was afraid, that I was frightened, that I was hurting. *By putting a wall up, I thought I was protecting myself.*

So, when I was sexually abused, a decision was made internally, in my subconscious, without realizing it. Since I was threatened that if I told anybody that I would be hurt or be killed, of course at that point the decision was made to never tell anybody when I'm hurting. However, I never realized that decision would eventually affect and rule my entire life.

By the age of 11, I was perfecting building the architecture of those walls---like the one I built when the kids picked on and laughed at me. I was in the sixth grade, and had I stayed up all night laying out the pattern, cutting the cloth, and sewing the seams to create the most wonderful bright and fun creation!

I made those pants myself and had put my heart and soul into them. I was so proud! I even picked out the cloth. But, this is where the "problem" was. Do you remember the neon colors of the 1970's? You know the solid as well as the mixed patterned fabric with the bright neon pink and green? Those colors and the fabric were amazing to me! Well, those pants were a combination of those colors and fabrics. The right front panel was bright pink, and the right rear panel was the bright neon green- and pink- patterned fabric. The left rear panel was bright green, with the bright pink and green-patterned material on the front. They were simply gorgeous to me!!!

I was so excited to go to school that morning. My heart was full of pride, until the moment I walked into the classroom that is. The laughing, snickers, and hand pointing crushed my spirit. My pants were something to laugh at to everyone. That day, I made another decision. I was never going to show the world what I wanted to make or what I wanted to create. I stopped sharing my creativity freely with the world.

I loved creating things, and during the next years I made many of those same types of decisions. I do think the above two examples help us see that all of us make decisions that are on default. Most of us are unaware of this type of decision making since we we're just making them. After many years of making decisions by default, however, you get to that point where you feel *powerless* and *unable to make decisions.*

Fast forward to when my kids attended grade school through junior high school. I was a married "single mama" raising my children. My husband worked early mornings and I was left alone to wake up the children and get them dressed and ready for the day. Those years were hard for me. We lived in a house with no electricity, we had three propane gas lights in the house and the rest were kerosene lamps or lit by natural sunlight, which was minimal as our house was surrounded by many trees. We lived in what many would call a rustic or even an "underprivileged home," which for sure would be called substandard living.

I did the best that I could and we just made do. I didn't really think about it. This was *his dream* to have this house on that location, and the price seemed right at the time. The stress of living that way was more than I had realized. A well-lit house can go a long way in helping someone spring out of bed in the morning and to get ready for the day. When your home is damp and dark, you can wake up dreary. That and the fact that laundry was only possible by loading the station wagon full ,and I do mean full, to the brim with clothes once every 2-3 weeks. With all this stress, and not much help at home, I found myself reverting back to learned patterns of behavior.

I became the "Screaming Mimi Mama," because I had convinced myself that my kids wouldn't listen to me if I didn't scream. That is the behavior pattern I grew up with. My dad was gone most of the time and my mom was left to fend for herself with four small children---three were rambunctious boys, and I was the only girl. My mom screamed at us kids---as if we never listened---we didn't respond. It was the same old story--- I told myself that my own children would not listen to me so I would tell them to do something six times with no response. It wasn't until I screamed at them that they would respond to my various orders---I mean requests.

At that time, I was working at a retail outlet store, so needed to ensure the shop door was open by 9:00 am. That meant that I had to be at work no later than 8:30 am. This particular day, I had a rough one---every child seemed to be rolling back over to go back to sleep. I probably overslept some, too, so we were rushed. We lived in a house with no electricity and where all of the laundry was washed at the laundromat---if I recall correctly, the night before had been a laundry night, and there had been many late nights. Doing laundry for seven takes a while when you only do the wash every 2 weeks. We had plenty of clothes but there was no energy to lay clothes out the night before. Usually, I would take the children with me to the laundromat since my husband found watching the children to be somewhat of an ordeal.

So, on this one morning, and after I had finished the screaming Mimi Mama routine, every one of my five children, including myself, had tears rolling down our faces as we were walking out the door. The children were late for school and had missed the bus, which meant I had to drive all of them to school. And, of course, that day I was late for work, too. As I walked out the door that morning, I said to myself, "Just forget it." I made a conscious decision that day to never again yell at my children.

Now, as you may or may not know, personal growth takes time. Changing patterns of thinking and the ways in which we interact with the people around us---the issues and things that caused us to be triggered emotionally---they take time to change and to form a new pattern. But on that day, when I made such an intentional and purposeful decision, it stuck! There is only one more time that I yelled in front of---*not at*---them. Here's how that went down...

Five children traveling in a Subaru---a big rig with lots of room for flipping over and moving around in the back seats. We were living in Vermont in which there was a seat belt law. So, when the kids would unbuckle their seat belts, it would make me frustrated since they were also moving around in the car and yelling---as children often do when they are playing or getting excited. But, this frantic automobile playtime can also lead to being a "distracted driver." I was getting more uptight, attempting to quiet them down with no response. Now, in a car we can often not be heard from the back seat when we're sitting in the front seat and speaking. So, as I said we were in the car, driving along, the kids were unbuckling and getting out of their seat belts and doing the things that kids do.

They wouldn't listen to me. I knew that I'd already promised myself that I wasn't going to yell at them again. I just wasn't doing it. Now, normally I would have screamed at them to sit down, and we would have kept going. Instead, I pulled the car over to the side of the road, came to a pretty fast stop, in which the youngest, if I am remembering correctly, who was unbuckled went rolling a little bit. She didn't get hurt. One of the kids said, "Mom, be careful!" I responded very quietly, "I told you that you've got to be buckled. What if we were involved in a car accident"? But, that was after my steering wheel broke. You see, when I pulled over and stopped, I grabbed the steering wheel firmly with both hands and proceeded to pull my head up and down as if I was going to bang my head into the wall. If there had been one there, I probably would have hit my head a few times [I hope you can picture this "Screaming Mimi Mama Bobble Head!"]. I let out a long, loud, "Argh" as loudly as I could!

I sure did yell *in front of them* but not *at them*. I had to release that frustration without yelling at them. That is the day I came to the realization that you can release your emotions without aiming it at someone. A real mindset shift happened for me that day, and that's where the *not treating the people based on our emotional state* comes into play. After I was done with my yell, I very quietly said, "Okay, now, I need you to be quiet, and I need you to buckle up. We're going to drive home the rest of the way, and I don't want to hear any more noise."

You may be wondering about the outcome. Well, they were quiet once I yelled into the steering wheel. To this day they still remind me about that day---they will do the bobbing head thing and pretend to yell. I love laughing at life so I don't mind that they do that! It's a great memory for them that sometimes life doesn't go perfectly, but you don't need to take it out on those you love or those who are all around you.

To this day, I believe that my children learned that I was able to parent differently as I silenced the Screaming Mimi Mama within. The fact that I didn't yell at them anymore was for me a conscious decision. For them, it is now a memory of mommy no longer yelling at them all of the time. It definitely changed our lives, and I believe contributes to the fact that some 30 years later I have such wonderful relationships with my kids.

This conversation was around decision default. When Kim Coles talks about story structure, she talks about challenge, choice, consequence, and conclusion. For sure some of our choices about what happens in our life are not of our own choosing. Sometimes, it's a choice that is made for you. For example, I didn't choose to be molested at age 3. Right? And I didn't choose not to tell when I was hurting or afraid. This occurred under duress---that I even chose to be quiet about it. *It took me years to become aware that I was making decisions based on choices that were made for me.* Once I did that, I was able to take control. We all have the power to go from decisions of default to conscious decision making. It takes being willing to look within at why we react the way we do. When we have behaviors that cause reactions we don't like, such as six people all crying as they left the house to start their day, it was a decision making moment that

I was faced with. I could have chosen on that day to keep going, drop the kids off, wipe my tears, and keep on. I am so grateful that self-awareness was awakened in me during that time when every single person was affected. Usually there's one or two kids crying, but not me, too. But on that particular morning, all five kids, and me, I knew I couldn't keep doing what I was doing------to them or to me.

Yelling and screaming were learned behaviors. However, that is not an excuse to continue the pattern, and we have to break that cycle. We all have opportunities to have a moment of realization and to change the trajectory of our life and the lives of those around us in that moment. We know that frequently people who grow up with a Screaming Mimi Mama often find themselves becoming the parents who yell, too. We all have the opportunity to change and shift the patterns and habits of a whole new generation.

As far as my own children, I don't know them to be the screaming parents, with everything I've seen, anyway. They're actually pretty controlled. I watch my children take their children aside to talk it through. I watch my kids as parents, and I'm in awe. Gratefully, I can say they are amazing!

I know I am not alone in being a Screaming Mimi Mama or in making the same decision to stop yelling. It's huge. I think there's so many parents and people who yell because that's their default. That's what they've been taught. That's what they've seen. That's what's worked for them. You see, that is key here, and it's worked for them, which only reinforces the story that they tell themselves, "My children will not listen to me unless I yell." I want you to know from one rehabilitated Screaming Mimi Mama to another--- if you have already stopped the yelling, I applaud you! If you have yet to stop, I challenge you to take the time to look at what the root is---where this learned behavior is coming from. Is it a learned behavior? Is it a self-protecting habit?

When we yell, frequently it is not necessarily because of the other person, but owing to our own pain in the moment. Or it could just be something that irritated us and doesn't have anything to do with that other person. That's what I have to keep in perspective---Are my children get on my nerves? Is my son's response a little more emotional than I would care for? Maybe it's something that he's dealing with that has absolutely nothing to do with me. So, I need to watch and check both my emotions and response to him. Because if I learned it, who's to say they can't learn it either, and we don't want our children to grow up with this type of behavior as a repetitive cycle.

Take a few moments and think about the decisions that you've made out of your own subconscious reactions to choices that were made for you, or around choices you made based on how you felt about the choices that were made for you. Think about Maya Angelou who made the conscious decision, "I will not talk because if I talk, when I talk, someone dies," because her abuser was killed after she told.

And, so what other default subconscious or conscious decisions have you made?

Here are a few journaling prompts for you to start the journey of more self-awareness to gain back your own power to set intentional decision making as a part of your life from this moment on!

- What are you own default decisions?

- Have you been allowing those default decisions to direct your life?

- Do you want to continue living your own life by default?

I was previously asked, "So, that time you pulled over as the little ones were screaming in your ears---what did you replace your screaming and your yelling with? Because it served a purpose. Everything that we do---the good, bad, and the ugly---serves a purpose, right? So, what did you replace it with"?

I responded, "Getting quiet." I watched what happened when people would talk quieter and quieter--- the room would become quieter, too. That along with my Girl Scouts training helped me to get the room, or in my case, the car quiet. If you wanted to get the room quiet in Girl Scouts, you would raise your hand as you closed your mouth and quietly stand there waiting for those around you to see it and also become quiet. Those two gestures were successful with achieving silence and still still work to this day. Perhaps you have attended a conference and experienced the same type of approach. The leader did not speak one word until everyone was quiet. The key here was that you couldn't raise your hand if you didn't stop talking. It worked every time! So I would just stay quiet and wait...

Now all of you may be wondering how you can shift your mindsets from the questions posed above. Here is the one thing that helped me to continue making shifts and to keep growing. You see, that was the first day that I learned the power in making a decision. I took that first "Aha! Moment" and began to build on it over the years. I would like to provide you with some excellent excerpts from my recently published eBook to help encourage you, too!

Any time we make a new decision to consciously stop or start doing something we are in the "Reinventing Process of Life." I want to encourage you with the 8 Keys to Standing Firm as you journey through the reinvention process.

The 8 Keys to Standing Firm While Journeying Through the ReInvention Process!

As the founder of Be BOLD You, where we help you take life's twists and turns and turn them into something beautiful so that you can live your life out loud and Be BOLD You, welcome! I am so excited that you are walking with us on this journey! This will help if you're trying to figure out the following questions: Who am I? Who do I want to be? What do I want to do? Where do I want to go? What do I love? What don't I love?

Explore your own self-awareness and teach yourself how to make choices about all of those fun things that happen when you're in that reinventing period of your life.

Now on to the condensed version of the 8 Keys to Standing Firm through any transition, including that of reinventing your own self! Along the journey of reinventing our lives, some things will really help you to stand in the face of opposition, as you will certainly face opposition, whether it appears from your own mindset or from others saying, "You can't do that... What are you thinking? You must be out of your mind"!

Key 1 - Stand Firm. Position yourself in a stance of standing with God---Being the person you want to become and stepping into that person to stand strong. Did you know that this is talked about in Scripture? In Philippians 4:1, Paul talks about it. We can stand in the confidence knowing that we have a place to go and that we have somebody we can go to.

Therefore, my beloved and longed-for brethren, my joy and crown, so stand fast in the Lord, beloved. Philippians 4:1

Key 2 - Stand in Unity of Mind. Find people to work with who are of the same mind. Find your tribe, those people you resonate with them and they resonate with you. Search out others who are in agreement with what you're doing, those people who understand you and "get you," all of those things are so important for boldly standing in the person who you are created to be and to boldly stand where you want to go! Unity will take you down the road.

I implore Euodia and I implore Syntyche to be of the same mind in the Lord. Philippians 4:2

Key 3 – Next, we have collaborate and to work together as a team now that you found your peeps. In teams of 3 to 8, and I would start on the lower end of maybe 3 to start, when you collaborate it should be a give and take, where you're all giving and taking from each other in a way that is working together, rather than taking from each other: *you're working to lift each other up.*

And I urge you also, true companion, help these women who labored with me in the gospel, with Clement also, and the rest of my fellow workers, whose names are in the Book of Life. Philippians 4:3

Key 4 - Celebrate (rejoice in the Lord always and again I say rejoice). Yes, this one is about rejoicing in the Lord, however, it is so much more than that. We are to have a life with abundance, and rejoicing in the Lord is simply one way we enter into the goodness of the Lord and learn to rejoice always!

As you study the scripture, you're going to find out that God has a desire for His people to celebrate, a desire for you to have celebrations, to have holy days, to have time set aside to rejoice, to have joy. It is a life with abundance and joy that we're going after. Celebrating the "WINS" along the way. Celebrate the people who are helping you. Celebrate yourself for getting up getting out of bed. Celebrate putting on some makeup and getting on with your day.

Rejoice in the Lord always. Again I will say, rejoice! Philippians 4:4

Key 5 - Be Gentle and Humble Yourself. Be gentle to yourself. Allow yourself to be who you are created to be without beating yourself up. Be imperfect and be okay with it. Be in progress and be okay with it. Progress is perfection. It is the perfect way to be perfect---in progress and *progress itself is enough*. Perfect. You have the gentleness you want to do it a gentleness of spirit when you're being yourself and that is when you are.

Let your gentleness (humility) be known to all men. The Lord is at hand. Philippians 4:5

When you are being yourself in gentleness of spirit, while being unapologetically who you've been created to be, you are being truly humble and authentic. I would challenge you to find that authenticity to find where you feel the most at home with who you are, and it may not be something that you're currently doing. It may be something that you step into at a later date. But in this reinventing yourself journey, you will find that you become more and more authentic because you find out more and more of who you are. And, be humble... Be yourself... Be gentle...

Key 6 - Gratitude. A life full of gratitude is a life that is growing and sustaining growth. The use of gratitude journals for putting your 'sprouts' in, as Dani Johnson calls them, is a great way to begin having a place to go and to remind ourselves of what we have been grateful of along the way of life. Celebrate your little wins without adding in excuses or explaining why it's not a better or bigger win---When you add in any but to your celebration, then you are essentially erasing the value of the WIN.

Be anxious for nothing, but in everything by prayer and supplication, with thanksgiving, let your requests be made known to God; Philippians 4:6

For the quickest road to success, ask God for wisdom, ideas, and strategies in the area where you want to serve. Then set your intentions to stay in that place of gratitude. When you stay in that place of growing and being and stepping into gratefulness and thankfulness, this is a place where you honor and respect yourself, others, and all that has been done for you.

Key 7 - As your life becomes fuller of peace, you will more easily be able enter into and plan your rest. This isn't planning the rest of your life. This is resting for your life! You want to plan your resting times so that you can live from a state of restoration and relaxation. Restoring yourself so that you can grow is something to not be ignored. It is strength given.

And the peace of God, which surpasses all understanding, will guard your hearts and minds through Christ Jesus. Philippians 4:7

There was a scripture that says they that wait upon the Lord will renew their strength. Waiting on the Lord, resting in the Lord, resting for your own life is strength giving. I have actually done more resting this year and accomplished more by working less and resting more. I've worked at resting the last couple of years this year. I'm resting and out of the rest I am finding a path to also be working. It may take you some time to become accustomed to a different type of lifestyle, the same way it did for me. However, that's no reason to not do it! So plan your rest.

Key 8 - ReNew Your Thinking. This one---the eighth one---is renew your mind, which I love since the number 8 in biblical terms translates to that of a new beginning. How fitting for renewing your mind! The choices we make and the things we choose to meditate on are the things that make or break us. They set in motion the direction of our lives to fulfill that which you are focusing and meditating on.

Finally, brethren, whatever things are true, whatever things are noble, whatever things are just, whatever things are pure, whatever things are lovely, whatever things are of good report, if there is any virtue and if there is anything praiseworthy—meditate on these things. Philippians 4:8

This is where I was focused before. I've now realized that in renewing my own mind, I've gone through all the above seven processes to get to the point where I can now look at what my thoughts are. In addition, during that process, I've looked at what my thoughts were along the way, and acknowledge that I was trying to teach this piece without realizing that you have to go back and teach all those other pieces and put all of that into place to put yourself in a position for success when we renew our minds. We want to think on things that are true. We want to think on things that are noble, that are just pure, that are lovely, and that are praiseworthy. This is where we want to place our energy.

The other place where I want to put my personal energy is the fruit of the Spirit of love, joy, peace, patience, kindness, goodness, faithfulness, gentleness, and self-control. These are some of the fruits that I want to take and water in my life and that I want to help you to find and discover in your life. So, please let me help you on this journey.

I would love to walk with you through reinventing yourself. I want to help you turn life's twists and turns into something beautiful so that you can live your life out loud and be boldly who you've been created to be. So Be BOLD You!

Thank you for being a part of our community. I love and appreciate you!

Fireside Reflections

Keywords and Takeaways:

1. Day of awakening

2. Ruled by old patterns

3. Making decisions around emotions

4. Decision making power

5. Personal growth takes time

The reflections around this piece I'm sure are identifiable with many of us. I'll be the first to raise my hand. Let's talk about the day of awakening and what that is. The day of awakening in this case is the day that Cyndilu became self-aware that there was a problem and that problem had an underlying affect and meaning.

It was then that Cyndilu realized that she was being ruled by old patters. Often times we do not realize that these aren't even patterns that we create. They are patterns that we learn, and guess what? We are indirectly teaching them to others.

We also read about default decision making. Cyndilu asked,

What are you own default decisions?

_____

_____

_____

_____

_____

_____

_____

Have you been allowing those default decisions to direct your life?

_____

_____

_____

_____

_____

_____

_____

Do you want to continue living your own life by default?

_____

_____

_____

_____

THE LAST SIN-EATER

Barbara Combs Williams

It is always hard, for me at least, to talk about myself. I believe it is even harder to write the truth. My self-editing or censoring process wants full command of my typing fingers; keeping me from doing irreparable damage to myself. Spoken words can always be denied or misunderstood. You can blame it on the listener's inattention or your own fumbling narrative; but once your thoughts and actions are committed to paper you are locked into your words. It's there in black and white or whatever color you choose to write in. But it is available to anyone who cares to read it, whenever they choose to read it.

I took on this challenge of writing about the "game changing moment" in my life that "dramatically changed the course, strategy, view, trajectory, or perspective for my life." This was the criteria that our Life Skills Coach Kim Coles asked me to think about. First I thought, I'm just regular. No one would write about me or even want to read about me. There's nothing special about me.

But then I thought long and hard about this and realized that in my life there have been so many of these "moments" and that my journey is probably similar to many great women around my age (60ish). If I can talk and write about it, then others may have the courage to put their everyday, regular lives out there. Not being afraid or doubting their worth; realizing that they, too, have a life worth relishing and a story to tell.

Let me go back a few years to January 2007. I was 49 years old and working for the power company. I had been working there for almost 10 years when my body cracked. I not only took on my responsibilities but absorbed the work of some of my coworkers as well. I could never say, "No," to helping anyone in need. I was good at what I did and received praise from everyone. I was an analyst for an upper-level manager. This position itself was very stressful as we were launching a new training program. Not only did I prepare detailed analyses, but I also interviewed and hired these new employees. I was an ear for some and a mouth for others—I was involved in their daily lives much more than I wanted to be.

I remember an old Twilight Zone show about a person who was called a 'sin-eater.' When anyone died the sin-eater arrives at the wake where an extravagant feast was set up around the casket. The sin-eater was paid to eat all of the food that now contained the sins of the deceased so that he or she could get into heaven.

Sounds good right? You get paid and you also get to eat and enjoy great food. But, what happens when the sin-eater dies? What happens if you can't find one single person who is willing to take on the sins of a sin-eater? That's a problem, right? It's just too much! No one can possibly stand under that great burden. Your spirit would go straight to Hell. You're asking now, what does this have to do with me? You see, I feel like that last sin-eater. I take on all of the problems, angst, and emotions of the people who come to me for help. But who shares the burdens of my sins, my problems, and my emotional turmoil? I have my wonderful husband Heyward and our beautiful daughter Nicole who would go to the ends of the earth to help me; but I would never dump that burden on them. So what did I do instead? I suffered and I kept quiet until my mind shattered and my body said enough!

I was in the building's cafeteria when I felt something pop in my head. I stood up and walked to the ladies restroom around the corner. I looked in the mirror and saw that my eyes were blood red. My head was pounding, and I felt dizzy. I ran the cold water and pressed some soaked paper towels to my eyes. I moved to a stall and sat down. I started praying. I asked God to give me strength to do what I needed to do. I think I stayed in that restroom for about an hour. I finally felt better and calmed myself enough to walk back to my little cubicle.

My manager stopped by my cubicle to bring me a report to finish. I looked at his face, and I swear one side of his face was higher than the other. I blinked, then I rubbed my eyes. I couldn't believe what I was seeing. I made some excuse and stumbled back to the restroom. On my way I noticed that more people's faces didn't look right. I stared at them wondering what had happened. Was it me or was it them? By now I really was panicking and I hurried into the restroom. I looked in the mirror again. My eyes weren't red anymore but one side of my face was higher than the other. How could this be possible? And it was only my face. No other part of the body was affected.

Somehow, I lasted through the rest of the day until it was time to go home. I carpooled with my husband Heyward, who also worked for the power company, but at another location. He arrived to pick me up and I looked at his face as I got into the car. His face was lopsided, too, just like my face and everybody else. I didn't mention what had happened. I sat through a 45-minute drive home and never told Heyward what I had experienced. Once the car pulled into the garage, I got out, rushed into the house, and immediately went to the bathroom again. I don't know why I expected things to have changed, but I cried when my face looked just as distorted as it did before.

Watching the news before we went to bed, I finally said something to Heyward. The newscaster's faces were lopsided. I asked him, "Do you notice their faces? They don't look right?" He looked at me strangely. He asked what I meant and I said, "Well, one side of their face is higher than the other. In fact, yours looks like that too. Mine does also when I look in the mirror." He shrugged, but only because he didn't understand what I meant. I made some excuse and said, "Well, I think I got soap in my eyes from earlier." And my sinuses were a mess, so bad that I had continuous sinus infections. My head was always stuffed up and achy. "Antibiotic" was my middle name. Yes, that must be the answer; that explained it. Too much pressure on my eyes from a sinus infection was causing the eye distortion. I prayed to God that was the answer but I knew it wasn't. I wanted to believe anything other than the truth.

The lopsided faces disappeared after a couple of days. I knew what had happened, but I didn't want to believe it—I had experienced a mini stroke. I read up on it, and I had all the signs and symptoms. I never went to the doctor; choosing to bury it deep, hoping that it would go away and never happen again. I hid my fears and worries in the back of my mind and retreated behind a smiling façade.

By March 2007, I couldn't take another day at work. My health was terrible. I was overweight, tired, angry, and just downright disgusted with myself. Not talking it over enough or even thinking everything through, I wrote up my resignation and handed it to my manager. He shook his head but said, "I understand." Of course, he did. In my mind, he and everyone else at the job were the source of all of my pain.

You would think that this is the game changer, right? No, I am too stubborn and too smart to let these little things change my life; or so I thought. I was still not being proactive. I was allowing things to happen to me and then responding. I didn't think things through. I panicked and reacted; not a good combination. I had so much to learn, and God was going to teach me some lessons.

It was now the end of May, and I was a total mess. I had resigned from my job. I had a saving's account that I cashed out and had almost run through, by being frivolous to the extreme. I was helping one of my sisters take our father to the doctor. He was 93 at the time and not doing well. Our 81-year-old mother was overwhelmed and on the verge of a nervous breakdown, trying to deal with his stubbornness in not wanting to visit the doctor.

My life was more stressful than ever! I had thought working was hurting me physically, and now I was declining mentally as well. I thought I was praying successfully. I kept asking God to fix me. What and how, I had no idea. I was vague in my prayers, and I thought unhappily that God wasn't hearing me. I didn't realize that God was steadily helping me, otherwise I wouldn't have made it through the first mini stroke.

Things were not going well, and my husband Heyward was trying to help me deal with all the changes going on. Emotionally, I was clinically depressed. It just wasn't going the way I thought it should have. Money was starting to become an issue. I gave up a $70,000 annual salary, with nothing now coming in on my part. We lived a good life and had all of the bills to show for it. Huge house and huge mortgage, car notes, helping our adult daughter, expensive trips; you name it, we did it! My physical health was suffering, and I didn't know where to turn. I became withdrawn and uncommunicative. Exasperated with my sullenness, Heyward said, "If you can't say what's bothering you out loud, then write it down."

I slowly took Heyward's advice, and I start writing. I had never written before. Maybe in school for an essay or something; so why did my wonderful husband think I could write? First, it was poetry that I start writing. I always loved the poetry of Maya Angelou, she's my muse. But my poetry was dark and unhappy; more like Edgar Allen Poe, who is another one of my favorite authors. My poetry was filled with regrets, sorrow, and hurt. I blamed everyone around me (especially my spouse) for my miserable existence. I joined on-line groups, sharing my writing and expressing myself there. A game changer has occurred, you think? Well, like I said, I am too stubborn for my own good. God wasn't through with me yet!

It was a cloudy morning in June, and I visited my gynecologist for my annual checkup and mammogram. I had been feeling angry, sad, disoriented, tired, and listless, and spots were dancing before my eyes. I experienced a headache every day (sinuses, right?). My gynecologist asked me what was going on in my life and how did I feel in general. I didn't reveal to her any of the things that had taken place--- not the eye problems, not the headaches, not the joblessness, nor the depression---nothing. I told her that I was fine. I don't know why I withheld such critical information. I guess I was embarrassed and I wasn't "holding it together too well." It never occurred to me that I would not be able to receive the correct treatment if I withheld information, but I stubbornly persisted with my denials. I was still letting things happen to me and responding in panic.

Finally, one of the nurses walked into the room to take my stats, with one being blood pressure. I was feeling pretty unconcerned until she shook her head, as if she wasn't seeing something correctly, and said, "I'll just take your blood pressure on the other arm." She took the right arm's blood pressure and told me that she was going to get the doctor. My doctor comes in after about 5 minutes, with my file in her hands. She told me, "The blood pressure reading is pretty high." She took it again and looked at me hesitantly. "How do you feel right now," she asks, "any headaches, blurred vision?" I told her I felt a little disoriented and see a couple of spots in front of my eyes. She says that we'll go ahead and get that Pap smear done, get a little blood and then I want you to go to another doctor and have them take a look at you. "Don't worry, he's a good doctor and will take good care of you."

It's now about 2:30 pm and I really didn't feel well. I followed a new nurse back to an examination room, where they proceeded to take my vitals again. She asked, "Why are you here today?" I responded, "I don't really know. My gynecologist instructed me to come up here and see you guys because of my blood pressure." I was still in denial, downplaying the entire situation. After taking my blood pressure, the nurse frowned and shook her head. She said, "I think we need to get the doctor in here right now." Okay, so now I'm starting to worry! What exactly is going on?

The doctor walked in and said, "all right, what's going on with you, Mrs. Williams?" I respond, "I really don't know," and explain again why I think I'm sitting in his overcrowded doctor's office. Denial, thy name is ME. The doctor retakes my blood pressure for what seems like the fifteenth time. He says, "Your blood pressure is off the scale! You're at stroke level, and we need to get you to the emergency room right now. I can't believe they sent you here and not straight to the emergency room." I started to cry. I didn't want to go to the emergency room! I hated hospitals in general, still do, and under no certain terms wanted to be sent to the emergency room. The doctor told me to calm down, emphasizing that this wasn't going to help my blood pressure. I cried even harder. He said, "Okay, okay, let's get you fixed up here," and then they start to work on me.

It had been about a couple of hours, and somehow I had fallen asleep. I don't know if it was owing to the pills they were giving me or just my general state. I was able to reach my husband after they hooked me up to a heart monitor but he was 3 hours away in a meeting. Eventually, the nurse walked into my room and said, "We have someone here who wants to see you." My daughter walked in, looking like someone had died. She has on her uniform, because she is also a nurse. She walked over to the table with tears in her eyes and said, "Daddy called me and told me what happened. I had just started my shift at the center when he called." She was of course babbling and saying things that I already knew, but I figured she was just distraught over the whole situation. I wondered how I would feel in her place. Was I to be the last Sin-Eater? I finally looked at the machine, which gave a reading of 200/180. I figured that had to be an improvement.

The doctor returned and says, "We are trying to get your blood pressure down to at least 170/80 before letting you go." I reply, "Oh, I guess I better get to working on that!" I got jokes, right? I was so nervous that I really didn't know what to say. Later, I glanced at the machine and the stats for my BP are now 165/80. I think, finally I can get out of here. It was about 6:30 pm and the office was closed for the day. I felt guilty because I was making everyone stay past their scheduled working hours.

They finally unhook everything allowing me to sit up while the doctor is going over the list of things for me to do. He tells my daughter also and advises her to make sure I do everything as outlined, including returning for a visit to see him in 2 days. Now we can leave.

After a couple of days I returned to the doctor's office along with my husband. The nurse takes my blood pressure today and it's 154/75. The doctor comes in presently and asks how I'm feeling. He reviewed my charts and said, "You sure look better than you did the other day. I was really concerned about getting that blood pressure down. You know they should have sent you straight to the emergency room and not have wasted that much time." I agreed with him somewhat and ask, "What now?" He informed me that they had the results back from the lab and that they were not seeing too much damage to my heart, which is a good thing… but, there were still a couple of things he wanted to talk to me about. One was my cholesterol. He said that my numbers were unreal. The really bad one, the LDL, was 300, which meant that I probably had a clogged artery. We also discussed the diet changes and medication he was going to give me to help bring it down.

The doctor then said, "This other level concerns me also. Your creatinine level is way too high." I have never heard of this before and had no idea what it meant. He wanted me to go to the Nephrologist, a kidney doctor. I was a little speechless because I was suddenly thinking about my mother and brother. My only brother had renal (kidney) cancer and died in 1999, within 1 year of being diagnosed. He was only 51 years old. I shuddered. I was now 49. My mother had been diagnosed with kidney failure a couple of years earlier and had been fitted with a stint for dialysis. These thoughts were whirling around in my head as the doctor went over the rest of the results from the lab tests. Again, I did nothing but mutely go along with whatever I was told.

I was sitting in the kidney doctor's office with my husband discussing why I was given a referral to see her. I explained about the blood pressure incident and we discussed any previous problems.

The doctor gave me a huge jug and stated, "We are going to need a 24-hour urine sample." She goes on to explain the what's and why's and so forth. I sort of understand and shake my head up and down in understanding. My husband looks on and shakes his head up and down as well. I don't know if he understood any more than I did or if he just did this for my benefit.

It's now time to return to the Nephrologist. I am alone today, as everyone seems to think I'm able to get myself in and out without too much hysterics. I had a short wait in the reception area before the nurse called me back. Today, I greeted the doctor with a smile. I wasn't feeling too badly and just wanted to get this over with. The doctor took my blood pressure and listened to my chest, then she took up my chart and started reading.

"Mrs. Williams, the results are back from the lab and you have 30% kidney functioning. You are in the third stage of kidney failure." She put it out there so bluntly that I just looked at her in mute denial. I didn't know what the third stage of kidney failure meant, but I was positive it wasn't a good thing. The tears started to fall again. The doctor rushed over to my side and gave me a tissue. She patted me on my arm, saying that wasn't that bad, and to let her explain. She went on to say that there are five stages of kidney disease and where I was wasn't that bad. She informed me that as of right now I didn't need dialysis and that people could stay at the third stage for the rest of their lives, never needing to go on dialysis or requiring transplants. I cried even louder and harder. The doctor tried to calm me down, and I let her.

I went from taking zero prescribed medications to taking six. I went from thinking I was sort of okay to knowing that I was now pretty sick. So here I am, weak and tired. All of the medications I now have to take have side effects. I am listless and have no energy whatsoever. I can't even walk into the grocery store without a cart to lean on. And to add to the misery, we were behind on our mortgage. I was embarrassed and disappointed in myself. I was paranoid, looking around corners and imagining the worst in every situation. I did not want any of my sisters or my mother to know how bad the situation had become. Honestly, I don't think they would have believe me even if I told them. They always thought Heyward and I were the golden couple. They had no idea that I felt like the biggest failure ever.

In the meantime, my father passed away, and the family was in turmoil. I could barely get myself from one place to another without passing out, but they expected me to help out with all of the arrangements and comforting of each other. But no one was really comforting me. Heyward tried but I pushed him away, feeling as if it was only pity on his part---I don't deserve it.

Again, I also felt as if my wide shoulders had to carry the heavy load. To say my life sucked is being way too generous. But no one saw just how depressed I really was. I hid it too well and to my family. I was the solid rock on which everyone else stood. I was always labeled the "strong and the cautious one" who was dependable, no matter what the situation was. I presumed with my wide shoulders that I was supposed to support the world. Unfortunately, I always tried to do just that.

I wrote about my misery, I cried. I wrote some more and cried. I put every emotion I was feeling into writing dark and dreary poetry and short stories. It was so depressing that no one even wanted to read what I had written. Frequently, I tried to show Heyward when came home from work, but he would say, "So who died or who did you kill off this time?" They knew me by now. I was the very last sin-eater. A game changer? Yes, it was and about time.

I'm going to jump ahead a few years. It's now January 2008. I was busy trying to pull my weight in the family. I asked God to help me. I needed some type of income coming in and asked for a job, any job. God heard me. So, I worked various part-time jobs up until August 2010, and we got our finances back on track. It came at a cost (bad credit rating, had to borrow from Heyward's 401k, etc.) but it was worth it. I worked jobs that I hated at times, that were not to my liking, but we made it work. I had been on antidepressants for a while and they also helped.

In November of 2010, I returned to work at that same power company. Through the grace of God, I pulled through all of my struggles and emotional breakdowns. I took better care of myself than ever. I still had kidney failure, but it was stable, and I even managed to lose some weight.

So now I was back where it all started. I was able to get my time earned from before to continue and stay vested in the company. I didn't get my $70,000 a year job back---mainly because I didn't want the stress that went along with it---but it paid well enough for what I was doing. I was trying to take control of my life and stop letting things just happen to me. I felt I had learned a few lessons and that maybe God was finished experimenting with me. In general, everything was all right; not jump over the moon in glee, but all right.

It was a Monday morning, and my first day back. I was walking into the building that I had promised myself I would never return to in life or death. Well, here I was again, walking right into that building, that prison, that isolation. Of course it wasn't a prison but that is how I felt. My office was an interior one with no windows. It was dark and gloomy down the hallways. I had my first breakdown in that building working under a very stern manager. He was a nice guy otherwise, but the stress I allowed was devastating.

I had an okay job, and I was very good at what I did but I wasn't challenged or even put much effort into what my work. In fact, some of those same co-workers wondered aloud why I came back into "this position." One even said, "Why are you slumming? You know you are working way below your level of expertise." I laughingly told those people that everything was fine, and that I didn't return to work to take their job.

The only problem that I had now was that I was always extremely tired. My lunch time usually found me sound asleep in my office covered with a light blanket. I had medical problems. I know I wasn't unique or the only one, but when it happens to you, you are the only one in your head. I was still suffering from kidney failure that was brought on several years ago by that mini stroke. Here, I was overweight with heart disease and because of the very-low-kidney functioning (around 30%-40%), I was also anemic. Now let's throw some sleep apnea into the mix, and you can see that I was pretty messed up.

Yes, sleep apnea. I had trouble sleeping at night. I would wake up in a panic from some horrible dream. My heart would be racing and I couldn't breathe. Demons and monsters were chasing me, and murderers were committing heinous crimes. I called them "Murder, Death, Kill" dreams. Every night I prayed for no dreams whatsoever. I asked God over and over to spare me. I wanted to wake up in the mornings without a headache. I wanted to be normal. This time I had learned a lesson. I asked God to help me end these horrible dreams by leading me to whom and what I needed to get better. I didn't want to be a Sin-Eater, and certainly not the last one.

During one of my visits to my kidney doctor, I told her about my night terrors. I wasn't going to swim in the waters of "denial" any longer. I didn't want to die in my sleep; I wanted to live. I wasn't going to wait until the unspeakable happened again. I was going to do something about my own life.

My doctor jumped on it and set me up with several appointments. She had me return to my heart doctor and also scheduled me for a sleep study. Heyward was right there holding my hand. We talked about what had been going on with me. We discussed his fears as well as my own. And when the results came back, we met them head on.

First, based on my history, the heart doctor set me up for a heart catheterization. The procedure is not painful but extremely dangerous. A catheter filled with dye is inserted through an artery in the groin. The doctor follows the path looking for clots or clogs all the way to the heart. If any are found, then a stint is placed inside of the artery to open up the clog. The main danger of this procedure is that you can bleed out in seconds if the wound is not closed correctly. Fortunately for me, my clog wasn't that extensive and thank you, God, I didn't bleed out.

Second, my sleep study turned up some interesting things. It turned out I have several sleep disorders. We learned that I completely stopped breathing more than 60 times in an hour. Next, we were informed that my oxygen levels dropped below 75, which means I wasn't receiving any oxygen to my brain and organs. Then, I found out that my horrible dreams were another type of sleep disorder that caused me to wake up in a panic. Because of all of these various things going on in my system, I also had respiratory problems. It was a miracle that I hadn't died in my sleep or upon waking up a long time ago.

I did everything the doctor told me to do. He put me on medication and a CPAP machine. I can't say I loved the machine because a mask over your nose and mouth takes a while to get used to. But the medication made my sleep terrors go away. For the first time in years, I could sleep without being scared out of my mind. I could sleep without my breathing stopping. I could sleep without the fear of my heart stopping. Thank you, God!

Remember I told you about those terrible sinus problems? Well, guess what? They were still with me and it seemed the CPAP therapy only brought it out more. I was constantly on antibiotics for sinus infections. My primary doctor finally sent me to an ear, nose, and throat (ENT) doctor to find out exactly what my problem was. After more tests, x-rays, MRIs, etc., I was diagnosed with a deviated septum and totally blocked sinuses that were filled up with awful gunk. I was scheduled for surgery.

February 2014 found me sitting in the out-patient wing of my local hospital. I had been here lots of times before for various procedures so I wasn't nervous. I was scheduled for 8:00 am, and they called me back right on time. The nurses set up an IV and the anesthesiologist came in to talk with me and Heyward. Since I was on a CPAP machine, they put a special tag on me; denoting my breathing conditions. I was given a mild sedative and told to relax for my procedure.

They wheeled me back around at 8:45 am on February 26th.

I knew I was dreaming or at least I knew that what was happening was really not happening in real life. I looked around and saw beautiful blue skies overhead. The sun was shining so brightly that I had to try hard to focus on my surroundings. There was no sound, no birds chirping, no wind blowing, no traffic noise---nothing. I was alone as I walked up the sidewalk to a big brick house. Beautiful flowers were blooming along the walkway.

There were vibrant yellows and cool blues. Purple-headed exotic flowers competed with brilliant white hues. I wanted to reach out and touch them, but I knew I needed to get to the front door just ahead. As I continued walking, I saw there were terra cotta-designed tiles placed strategically in the bricks beside the door. The tiles were a burnt-orange color with blue lapis designs running around the edges. The front door was a dark-brown wooden door with a round, dark-metal doorknob. I knew without being told that I needed to go through that door. Something wonderful awaited me on the other side. Just as I reached out to grasp the round, metal knob in my hand, I heard someone call, "Mrs. Williams, Mrs. Williams, please, you have to wake up!"

I thought there was a mirror over my face because I was looking down on myself. There was a tube taped in my mouth, my nose was bloody, and a greenish cap was on my head---the weirdest thing, though, was that my eyes were closed. So how could I see myself? I was snatched back so abruptly that I jerked awake and looked around. I was still in the operating room. The room was crowded. I saw people with masks covering their faces and caps on their heads running around grabbing different types of equipment. I heard someone say, "she looks terrible." Someone else said, "she's spastic, she's spastic." I passed out again and when I came to, the doctor was holding my hand. "Mrs. Williams, if you hear me, squeeze my hand. Please squeeze my hand if you can hear me." The doctor was asking me this question over and over. I finally squeezed his hand.

Hours later, back in my room with Heyward looking scared, the doctor came to talk to us. The doctor said that I stopped breathing twice and they had to aspirate me. He said that I had some sort of seizure and that the breathing tube was stuck in my throat, so they had to go in beside it with another tube. They couldn't get me breathing and every time they thought I came to; my eyes would roll up in my head and I would be out again. He said this continued, over and over, but he didn't give up. He told us that I was too young and too lovely to leave this life now.

Recovery was slow. My throat was raw for over a week due to the trauma. What should have been a routine nasal surgery almost killed me because of my respiratory problems. The doctor who saved me was the emergency room doctor that my ENT had to call on. I never even knew his name, but GOD put that man there to save me, and I will always be eternally grateful for that.

I needed to tell everyone what I had seen and been through. A lot of people looked at me a little skeptically but I had to tell them anyway. When I told my pastor and my church family, everyone was overjoyed. They told me I was back with them for a reason and God wasn't finished with me yet.

Unfortunately, that trauma was not the end, more was still to come. My nose didn't heal. After 3 days, I returned to the ENT and things seemed to be healing normally. I followed his instructions, but 1 week later a foul smell was in my nose and I was dredging up disgusting black clots. I ended up with the mother of infections. If I hadn't caught it when I did, my nose would have rotted.

After a session with the strongest antibiotic, Levofloxacin, I ended up with damage to my tendons, which was the major side effect from the antibiotic. Weeks of physical therapy and a steroid treatment later I was able to walk without too much difficulty, but my joints and tendons would never be the same again.

Let's jump ahead some more. It was January 2018 and I wasn't unhappy but I wasn't double up dog-gone happy, happy either.

I was still working for the power company, processing timesheets and creating invoices that paid our contract labor force. No small feat. I and one other lady invoiced over $100 million in contractual labor costs. Like I said, I was very good at what I did. In fact, I could produce enough invoices, talk with our coordinators who oversaw the contractors, deal with and resolve incorrect data received from the contractors, and paint my fingernails all before noon!

I had time on my hands. So I fell back to my real joy. I wrote. I wrote poetry. I wrote short stories. I wrote a novel and even started on the sequel. I would come to work around 6:30 am and start my regular job. After I finished that, I would ease my thumb drive into my computer and pull up my files. It was easy. I had my own office with a door instead of a cubicle and lots of time on my hands.

You would think that all of these problems would have caused lots of "aha moments" and believe me they did, but it didn't add up enough for me to do something about it. I was content to wallow along in my paid job while doing my dream job on the sly. I used my coworkers and family as my audiences. I would write and slip my work to my friends at work, hungering for a good review. And I got them. In fact, I received, "why are you here wasting all this talent? Why don't you do something with it? Do you realize how many people would love to hear what you have to say?" All I could do was drop my shoulders in defeat. I kind of figured that if I didn't start it, then I couldn't fail at it.

I was scared. I was so afraid of failure that I wouldn't pursue my dreams. I did nothing to further my writing career. As one comedian joked to their less-than-successful adult child when they couldn't find a job, "what do you think? A job gonna come knocking on the door? You got to get up and do something." So I was waiting for a big time publisher to come knocking on my door.

And we all know that wasn't going to happen.

Well you know eventually all good things come to an end. The paid job that is. Our department merged with a larger group. The plan was to move my little group out of our comfy offices into cubicles at a location further away from our current one. Now you know this was going to just tear apart my routine. Nobody can write in a cubicle with a new supervisor crawling all over your back!

I was going to be old and 60 in November (obviously I had age problems as well). That's somebody's "old" grandmother (I do have two beautiful granddaughters) because in my mind that's how I thought. But I had choices. I was vested in the company and was eligible for a small pension. My husband Heyward of 40 years (yes, I said 40) also worked for the same power company as a manager in a technical group. He had been there for more than 35 years and had an excellent salary. I had options. I was going to be 59 and a half on May 22nd. I could take my pension, take my savings with no penalty, and retire. I could rely on my husband's medical insurance for all of my ailments and live quite happily. Or so I thought.

Now, you say hey, this must be the "game changer." No, it wasn't. My husband and I worked out the details forward and backwards. It was doable. So, I made up my mind to retire but nothing really had changed for me in the way I thought. I allowed a little retirement party to be thrown for me where I told everyone that now I could finally write to my heart's content. Well-meaning coworkers and friends piled me high with journals to write in and well wishes. I walked out of the working world on May 25, 2018 and didn't write another word for 5 months.

So what exactly was I doing? I was sleeping in. I needed the rest. Years of getting up at 5 am had taken a toll on me. The worst thing possible for my sleep apnea was not getting enough sleep. After I woke up around 8:30 am, I would start my day with a light breakfast, thinking about what I wanted to do today. Writing never entered my head.

I had plenty of other things to do. One, I promised my husband that I would cook a hearty dinner at least twice a week. Check, did that. Two, I did my hair. I wasn't a beautician but I had a process that could change hair styles overnight. So I played with my hair at least once a week. I also did my daughter's and granddaughters' hair sometimes. Three, I went shopping, really I mean looking. I loved looking at all the stuff in the stores. I didn't need anything but it was fun to look. Four, I read quite a lot. I love reading. Fiction, romance, fantasy, paranormal, you name it, I read it. Did it as much as I could. Five, I played online games and puzzles and posted on Instagram. See, I was very busy. Too busy to write anything. So how did I end up writing again? That's another long story.

One day in early October 2018, I was scrolling through Instagram and saw a story posted by Kim Coles, who I follow. She was coming to Atlanta at the end of the month with a seminar on "Loving Your Story." I repeatedly looked at the information. Something was just pushing me to look at this in a different light. Finally, I took the plunge and signed up to attend.

When Heyward came home, I showed him the information and told him I had signed up. If you ask me why, I couldn't tell you. All I can say is that God put the information there for me to do something with it. I only purchased a ticket, but already I was dreading what I had done.

As October 28th approached, I was apprehensive. I was like, love your story. I don't even have a story and loving it was never on the top of my to-do list. A couple of days before "the day," something whispered in my ear to look at my writing. Furthermore, it said print some of your writing and take it to the seminar. The class was on a Sunday afternoon and to tell the truth, I wanted to chicken out. I started making excuses. I told Heyward that I didn't know where the place was in downtown Atlanta. He said, "I'll take you." I said, "I don't feel well." He said, Take some Tylenol." I said, "I don't have anything to wear." He directed me to my closet and helped me choose something. I had no choice but to go. Game changer, finally!

So, I'm sitting in the lobby of the event space waiting for the seminar to start. There are a group of women sitting on one side of the lobby. I take myself to the opposite side where no one is sitting and plant myself there. Already I am hating every minute of this. Contrary to how I look (happy, friendly, and open) I am not; I am really shy and withdrawn. Suddenly, another woman comes in and stops to chat with the women on the opposite wall. After she chats for a few minutes, she then comes my way.

I'm thinking, Oh no. Now I have to talk to this lady. She says, "Hi, mind if I sit here?" I nod and mumble, "Sure." Well, she starts talking to me and she is very friendly. She tells me about herself, that her name is Candice Davis, that she is a coach, and an author among other things. She then asks me my name and why I'm here today.

I tell her that I retired in June from the Power Company and now I can write more. I even have some of my work if she wants to read it. Candice takes my folder and starts reading some of it. She says, "You are a very good writer," then asks about my work and what I'm doing with it now that I'm retired. I tell her, "Actually nothing. I haven't written anything since June."

She asks me why and seriously I didn't know. I think I had given up or possibly I didn't want to be hurt by the 'no's' that I knew were coming.

Candice is very easy to talk to and we pal around for the entire program. We received some wonderful information from Kim Coles. Kim has several guest speakers who really enlighten me with their true heartfelt stories about their careers and lives. Several people in the audience also talk about their lives, what they have been through, and where they are now.

I personally felt out of my league. These people, these women have suffered life-changing hardships and difficulties. They have had their spirits broken but have rebuilt themselves and come back stronger than ever. Again, I say to myself, you have no story worth telling, you don't belong in this group of survivors.

Candice and I part ways after the program is over. I give her my folder containing my writing and she promises to get back to me. We exchange our contact information and go our separate ways. After a few days, I hadn't heard anything from Candice, and my shadowy, sometimes confidence drops to zero. It had now been over a week, and I started to doubt anything good about what I am doing. It seems I have not come as far as I thought. I get depressed and hate that I told my family what had happened at the seminar. Heyward tells me to contact Candice and see what is going on. I reluctantly send Candice an email.

Candice responds and apologizes for not getting back to me. She had some unexpected work come up and had to finish it before she could follow up. She goes on to tell me how impressed she is with my work. Then, she tells me she is there if I need help getting my story out there, but that it's up to me to do something about it. I'm so embarrassed at my own negative feelings that I continue to downplay everything she tells me. I retreat to my usual "don't do anything" mode of operation.

It is now the middle of November 2018. The Lord moves in mysterious and exalted ways as they say, and places an email from Kim Coles in front of me. This one is on figuring out your passion and your purpose. It's a seven-day challenge called "Choosing Y.O.U." I take the challenge and dare myself to find my passion. One of the challenges is setting goals. I don't know why but I respond publicly that I will publish my book The Color of Your Tears in January 2019. This is the story about Jackie who is hiding a shameful secret. She is at a pivotal point in her life and like me she doesn't know what to do or how to go about it. Next, I vow to finish the second book in this family saga, Chrystal Clear in March of 2019. These are bold promises coming from me, but I contact Candice and ask her for her help.

Now here I sit with two of my books published. I published the first one, an epic fantasy poem called Soul Catcher. I did all the editing and formatting on Amazon. This one went live on January 29, 2019. It wasn't the novel that I promised but for once I had created something I was proud of. I had kept my word. I had published something.

My novel, The Color of Your Tears, took a lot more doing but it went live on Amazon on February 28th. This story developed from a poem I wrote of the same title. I did the artwork for the cover and Candice did the editing. I had a book signing in March that was a wonderful success. And now you are reading my testimony, my truth; included in this anthology. Another amazing gift that God placed in front of me. And the second novel Chrystal Clear, a story about Jackie's daughter is coming along more than halfway finished, tentatively scheduled for release in July 2019.

No, my work has not pushed me into another income bracket, but it has been a source of delight and fascination for me and my family. I have learned so much about writing, storytelling and publishing by being receptive to what is given me. Our daughter Nicole has been my right hand with suggestions that lighten my burdens. It has brought me closer to my sisters as they get to help me; something I didn't even have to ask for. My sisters are my beta readers and as they say, "this is a family journey." My husband Heyward stands proudly beside, behind and all around me. He encourages me each and every day to push ahead just a little bit more.

So, what does all this really mean? Well for one thing I am not the same person I was in early October 2018, nor 2010, or 2007, etc. You get the idea. I have opened up to all my family members and allowed them to see me for me. Not this super woman without a care that I pretended to be. I'm another creation and still evolving.

Yes, I am 60ish, but I am so thankful to be a big beautiful curvy woman and in my right mind. Sixty turns out to be a beginning, not an ending. No, I don't have all the confidence in the world at my fingertips, but I do have a lot more than I started with. I was given a talent to write and I mean to use it; to tell you the story I didn't even know I had. I can say that I did it, and beautiful lady, you can, too.

This journey, this path that I am traveling, has even surprised me with all the twists and turns. I think it all comes down to this. Anywhere along this path we're given free will to keep on traveling it, discovering something new every day. Or, we can step off the path, lay down beside the road and blend into nothingness. My path wasn't straight with wide sidewalks. Rather it bent, twisted and even turned back upon itself. And yours probably will too if hasn't already. But you see, I am still here. I'm going to raise my head high and keep on pushing on. Living and experiencing what I can along the way.

I am so happy that God directed my steps and I decided to keep on. Yes, I bring my doubts, questions and fear with me. But I am not the last Sin-Eater. God has led me to so much more and believe me it's not over yet; because you never know what might be waiting for you. All you need sometimes is to heed that little voice and believe. Your story just might be the gift, the Game Changer who encourages the next woman down her path.

Fireside Reflections

Keywords and Takeaways:

1. There's nothing special about me

2. Doubting your worth

3. Having a story to tell

4. Age is just a number

It is not uncommon that we think there's nothing special about me that someone else has not experienced or have gone through. It is the false story that we tell ourselves in order to push us away from sharing a piece of us with the world. You have to stop doubting your worth, because your story is unique to you for the fact that no one else has dealt with it in the way that you have and no one ever will. No matter how common you think your story is, there is someone who it can impact.

Here Barbara speaks about her journeys of taking on everyone else's problems but realizing that she held onto her own and no one was there for her to share her own burdens with. She identified this with being the "Sin-Eater". It wasn't until she got very sick and had to rely on the caretaking from her husband and daughter that she began to open up and do more writing.

By Barbara sharing this story, she is encouraging her peers who are 60 plus to still live and find your joy, the same way that she did and still does with writing. It's not about age, a lucrative income or status. It is about realizing through self-awareness what *YOUR* joy really is. And you have been encouraged through all of these stories to take the pieces that you've learned and create life on your own terms as well.

What is the one thing you find unique about you that others should know about? What is your gift to the world? Remember we are *all* connected through story? Tell us…

_____

_____

_____

_____

_____

_____

_____

_____

_____

_____

A LETTER TO MY FATHER

Bri Cooper

Dear Father,

Father I never really knew.

From the daughter you barely know.

I'm begging to have that innocent little girl back.

But at the end, all of the words fell flat.

When I was 12, when you went away, or the age of 6.

Or when I thought your love began and ended with a fist.

Pieces of me I suppressed but they surfaced as a child while playing house with my cousins.

Unaware I am now the predator who hurt me.

But I am my father's daughter right?

You took away any trust I could possibly have for a man.

Dysfunction became my reality and the destruction of myself became my goal.

Muzzled as a child how could I break free.

Do you love your children? Was a real question for my mother obviously blinded by his false love unable to see.

My sisters were supposed to be a reflection of her, so how dare they speak?

I guess it was all just a dream, a nightmare, a figment of our imagination

Growing up I envied what my friends had: A DAD!

Someone to look up to, a hero, not a villain.

Years of anger and resentment for my mother because your abuse became our pain and her neglect.

If you were the hero in my dreams you would have protect.

Protected us from the monster and his bottle or the people who were convinced we were nothing

Bastard children that came from dirt.

So, we didn't deserve love, respect, or even allowed to hurt.

See, our innocence wasn't just taken by you. It was also the people my mother leaned on to take up her slack.

But they were battling their own demons. They could not handle that.

How can I forgive you when pain is rooted to my core?

I'm not so sure I'm willing to forgive you.

I'm so full of hate not willing to love you again.

Missing Pages from Steele Butterfly

After my father left, I grew up believing that I had to be beautiful... that I had to be somebody... that I had to be successful. In my house, my mother only invested in material things, things that made you beautiful. She would primp and press, although I watched my father abuse her while admiring her strength for making lemonade out of lemons. Deep down I think changing her looks made her feel powerful after being weak for so long. I remember my dad making my mom wear unappealing clothes. I think she forgot we experienced the same abuse at an early age when we were most vulnerable. Children are supposed to feel safe and secure when they are with their parents. Unfortunately, we never knew what would happen next and lived in constant fear. I remember dreading going home because I knew my mother wouldn't be there and we were going to be left with my father. Although my little brothers thought it was fun being his target, I didn't! I was afraid to run around in the house, fearful of the pellets from his gun that may or may not hit and hurt me. He would turn off all of the lights and pretend that we were playing hide and seek. In reality, though, I was experiencing mental and physical child abuse from a broken man with malice intent.

When I was 9 years old, we moved to Dallas, Texas, from Texarkana, Texas, away from my grandmother, which at the time was difficult for me. We would spend every summer at her house, and although I hated it at that time, vacationing at my grandmothers was all that I had ever known. My dad decided to take us to visit his family---the family we barely knew---for Christmas. Although we were strangers, I was excited for the opportunity to become better acquainted with all of my relatives. My half-brother on my dad's side was a part of the family who accepted him. Eventually, they accepted my little brother and my sister but not me since I was dark-skinned. So, it was hard to believe I was his child. When we arrived to open presents, we looked for our gifts. But the only child who received anything was our half-brother. I know that gifts shouldn't be important but that wasn't what broke my spirit. What hurt me was that we have always been treated "less than" because of who our mother was, and we didn't deserve that. Children never forget how they feel during unforgettable times, and that moment I hated those people. I never wanted to see them again. Even after my dad went to prison, they never attempted to contact us. They treated us as if *we* were the problem---that we lived in dysfunction. No one came to save us. No one believed we were worthy, which had a profound effect on my adult relationships. I would push people away, always waiting for the ball to drop. Nothing good was mine for long. I became a pain freak. Pain made me feel love. Pain made me feel safe. I loved the comfort that pain brought since real, devastating pain was a defining part of me.

I was jealous of my older half-brother because they accepted him, and I hated him for the lies he rooted in my head. He told me that my father's family would never accept me, and that they hated me because he wasn't my father. A part of me loved that idea that I had a new father---I could start all over---but I was already broken. Finding out the truth would devastate me. Although he was a monster, it wasn't all bad. He had taught me to play the guitar, and music became a great escape from all the pain I had endured, all the things I had lost. I spent most of my life trying to be accepted, but that never happened. So, I took comfort in being the "weird girl" who distanced herself from others who created depth within me. Most of the people around me were shallow---they saw life through different lenses. Bonded by life's pollution, I never wanted to live in bondage. Soon, I became a free spirit and a rebel. At an early age I knew that was how I wanted to live, but I couldn't unshackle the chains from the suppressed hurt and anger that wouldn't allow me to heal.

When I woke up on March 29, 2013, it was a normal day. I wasn't working so I decided to get a facial and to get my nails done. Although my sister was going to the hospital to have a C-section, I knew I should have been there, but I felt I needed to be beautiful. One week prior to my sister's surgery, we fought over my vanity and constant need to be in the mirror. My sister would repeatedly tell me,

"Vanity is a sin! Learn to love yourself for who you are. You are beautiful." I never felt like she understood how I had blossomed into a beautiful flight attendant from being that "ugly duckling" who had no friends, as I was constantly made fun of throughout school. My mother would tell me all of the time, "You would be pretty if you would just lose weight!"

And, with those words of wisdom, I spent most of my life proving I could be anything, even with my weight. In school, people took pride in humiliating me, and for many years afterward I let others validate who I was. I realized being different wasn't a bad thing. People feared what they didn't understand. It just took me a long time to get it.

As I sat in the nail shop waiting for my nails to be done, my mother called frantically saying there was a Code Red at the hospital. I quickly jumped into my car and drove nervously to the hospital. As I walked into the waiting room, I saw everyone in tears and asked in a timid voice, "What's going on?" I repeated in a much louder voice, "What's going on?" My uncle stood up and told me that my sister was gone. Everything stopped. I couldn't believe it. I stood in disbelief and shock. Then, my uncle said it again. I took off running down the hallway screaming, "Where is she"! My mother ran after me and tried to console me, but what could she do? My sister---my best friend---was gone. I walked to the other end of the hall and saw my grandmother holding my sister's hand telling her to wake up. My heart dropped as I saw my sister's lifeless body lying in the bed. I was angry with myself that I was getting my nails done---that I wasn't there for my sister in her final moments. How selfish could I have been not to be there for her when she spent most of her life being my cheerleader and protector. I knew at that moment that I would regret my selfish decision-making for the rest of my life.

After about 10 minutes, every one gathered to pray but I was done. I couldn't believe in someone who would destroy my nephew's chance at growing up without a mother. She was the glue that held our family together. I knew we wouldn't be the same after that. I walked out of the hospital with my brother, and we drove to my sister's house. I could remember listening to Tracy Chapman and the smell of stale cigarettes. I would never forget how close all of us were and everything that we experienced together. My sister was the oldest, so she felt as if it was her duty to protect us; however, she couldn't protect us from everything. I could remember my sister getting beat for no apparent reason and we would all bond together against him. Then, he threw us all into "the dungeon." It was pitch black, but the beauty in these moments was that we felt good, we stood together, and we fought for one another.

Later that evening, we all slept on my sister's living room floor. When I woke up in the middle of the night, I saw my mother crying hysterically. I got up and held her because losing a sister is tough, but losing your child and having so much guilt about not being able to protect her was a totally different thing. Once my mother dozed off, I got up and started looking through my sisters things. I began thinking about our argument, how it was so small, and that I would give anything to argue with her again. It still didn't seem real and that she was going to walk through that door with my nephew at any time. Unfortunately, instead of us celebrating his life, we were mourning hers.

As I snapped out of my dormant state, I walked into my sister and husband's bedroom and spotted a notebook sticking out of her dresser. It was her diary. I knew at that moment it was wrong to read it, but I needed closure and believed that was what would give me the healing I was desperately looking for. I instantly noticed that there were missing pages. I quickly learned that her marriage wasn't as loving as I thought it was, but none of us are perfect so I didn't judge him. After discovering her husband's infidelity, I learned that she was raped as a child, around the age of 12. I knew that he was in jail for molestation, but I never knew he did that. At that moment, I was hurt that my mother kept that from me for all of those years. I guess she thought that she was protecting me, but that ship sailed when he would turn off all the lights and shoot us with pellet guns. This was by far the worst news. I didn't approach my mother about it because at that point I would have been adding insult to injury. The truth is that my grandma told me--- the real reason my dad was locked up---my second year in college. When I was in the seventh grade, my mom told me a different reason. My dad was never a positive force in my life, so I didn't feel anything, but I was hurt my mom had lied to me for all of those years. I quickly closed her diary and fell back asleep.

The following week we planned her funeral with our good friend who was my other sister's friend---she was like family, as we knew both her and her kids for a long time, so she was like a sister. We decided to have purple shirts made, which were my sister's favorite color, and to also feature her beautiful face. That's one of the saddest days I've ever encountered but I stayed busy doing for others and stayed strong. After the funeral, I returned to work as a flight attendant. But, how could I? The one person who encouraged me to follow my dreams was gone. My heart turned cold, and I became angry. I didn't know how to handle my grief. People say that scars are lessons learned and sometimes you just have to rip off the Band Aid. The thing about ripping off Bands Aids, though, is that they never stick the same again, and you can't ever predict how bad the lesion truly is underneath or if the wound is fully healed.

Six months after my sister died, I left my job to help my family. But, I was no use to them because I was headed for destruction. I stayed in the bar where they knew me by name. I would get so drunk that I would flirt with every man I saw and used my new-found sex appeal to get what I wanted. I deceived men---I felt no man deserved the real me. I was 26 and no man could control me. I didn't want to be married, I dated who I wanted and I slept with who I wanted even if that meant hurting someone else in the process. The old saying "hurt people hurt people" became a pattern of mine. I knew that I was self-destructing but I didn't care as long as it felt good to suppress all of those bad memories that surfaced when I read my sister's diary.

Although I tried my best to forget, they surfaced through my actions, my words, and my relationships. My sister's death was a constant reminder of the pain I endured as a child. The truth was supposed to give me closure of some kind---a type of peace. Instead, I lost myself. Remembering the times when my dad would pick us up from school and play the game hide and seek, I never knew my dad used those games to sexually abuse us. When my grandmother would ask, "Did he touch you?" I couldn't answer. How could I explain something that I just never knew about? My mother never asked such questions, but caught me several times doing unspeakable acts as a child---was she really that blind?

When I was in college, I had a huge crush on this guy I would do lots of things to get him to notice me---but he never did. One night after a party, I was in my dorm room about to pass out, and I heard a loud knock on my window. I jumped up, looked out of the window, and saw that it was him. I was excited but naive. Shortly after I snuck him into my dorm, we began to kiss right away. I could tell he was a little more inebriated than I was. He started trying to take off my dress. I was either too inexperienced or uncomfortable, so I kept moving his hands off of me. The third time he became extremely upset and started forcing himself on me. He ripped my clothes off while his hand was over my mouth. My screams were muzzled so I knew no one heard me. As he tore off the remainder of my underwear off, he jammed his fingers inside of me. I screamed loudly, then he slapped me---hard. There was a knock at the door, which spooked him. He jumped up and said, "If you tell anyone, I will kill you," then he climbed out the window. I cried very quietly so that the person at the door would leave. Although I was hurt, experiencing trauma wasn't new. So, I was numb. At an early age, I learned to sweep shit under the rug and to downplay situations. After the rape, I avoided people and I stayed in my dorm room until I couldn't take it anymore---I left the school for good. I couldn't stay there. It was too much for me to handle and I never spoke of what happened---ever. When I played back all of the things that happened to me, this made me want to further numb the pain.

One night after binge drinking, the phone rang. It was my brother-in-law waking me up asking for help with my nephews. I had just gotten a job so that we could help each other. Although I was afraid and I didn't know the first thing about children, I knew that my sister would do the same for me. Admittedly, the incident written in my sister's journal affected the way that I looked at him, but I didn't say anything because most men would have walked away. Although I had turned my back on God because I believed no weapons applied to me because every weapon formed to destroy me had prospered, I knew that God had me there for a reason. Those boys changed me, and I loved taking care of them.

About 2 months later, I had just finished working an overnight shift and spotted a Black and Mild with a certain shade of lipstick. I instantly knew who it belonged to. My mind was wondering *why she would do that that since she attended my sister's wedding and funeral?*---She was damn-near family. There were things I didn't like about her. Although she was a moocher, she had no goals or ambition. She was never my friend, but I accepted her because that was my sister's best friend. I could remember going out for my birthday and buying her drinks. But this was low even for her. I didn't say anything to my brother-in-law and I also didn't put anything past him. He had slept with everyone. The fact that I was mourning my sister and had to watch him behave that way was a slap in my sister's face. She had given her life to bare his child, and he showed no respect. Although he would disappear for days at a time, I understood that he lost his wife.

Whenever I walked into the house, my nephews were up running around. My brother-in- law would quickly leave for work, so I barely slept and those two were always hungry. Later that day I just couldn't get that Black & Mild off my mind, when I was the only one who smoked those things and wore that lipstick. But I was just like my mother---I investigated. I drove to her house that weekend just to hang out and waited until she went to the bathroom. I looked at her Facebook where he was messaging her. I jumped up in a rage and asked her, "What in the hell is going on"? She replied, "Nothing"! "Liar"! I screamed and ran out the door. She ran behind me with tears in her eyes. "I would never do that! Your sister was like a sister to me"! I let it go and left. I didn't want to start nothing if it indeed was nothing. The respect I had for this man was already nonexistent. In my eyes, he was not a man of dignity. He created more chaos in our lives, and I would never forgive him for that.

After several more weeks, I decided to move out. I knew that they were sneaking around, and with the simmering anger I had toward both of them, I knew that it would be best if I went stay with my mother---I would visit or retrieve the boys whenever I could. They had saved me from my destructive behavior. I quickly returned to that dark place and would go to my other sister's house. She always had alcohol and playing cards, but I didn't tell her about her so-called best friend. From my experience, people shoot the messenger and I knew the truth would reveal itself. Plus, I was too busy getting drunk, again numbing the pain.

Almost a year later in February, when my sister's so-called best friend texted me asking for our blessing to date him, I laughed because she was making it appear that she was asking us if it was approved by the family for her to go out on their first date. "Is she still your sister?" was my response. That was a valid question because a year prior that's what she had said to me. But I knew better--that girl lacked morals and values. She saw a ton of dollar signs. Since my sister left money for both her kids and husband, he was well off. This opened the door for her to leave her mother's house and to jump on his coat tale. I was angry because I was the only one who would voice how uncomfortable that made our entire family. It was so disrespectful for them to show up at our family functions together---he was no longer a part of our family---drop the kids off and leave. Until I could make peace with my sister's death, I just couldn't be around him or her. Eventually, she began to control when we were able to see the kids. When I called to see my nephews, my brother-in-law never answered the phone. Regardless of how I felt about their relationship, my nephews were precious, and the only treasures left from my sister, but she wanted me to have a conversation with her---I never would and I never will. They both know that their actions were wrong and that there was no justification for that type of behavior. These were all trigger points. I had never dealt with so much turmoil in my life. So, all I knew was to act out in violence and to be combative. I stopped going to church and lacked ambition. I was just working at the hotel and partying. I knew there was more to life, but I didn't see any way out.

What changed me for the second time was an older gentleman who I worked with and in whom I gradually opened up to. One day he asked me, "What is your definition of beautiful"? "I don't know," was my response. He then said to me, "No matter how much makeup you put on, beauty isn't broken. To be truly beautiful you need to heal the part of you that's rotting away." For the first time, I didn't get offended by someone's "pearls." I would listen to his wisdom and tell him my problems. Then, he invited me to church. Although I had different beliefs, I knew I needed change if someone could easily pick up on the pain I attempted to hide for so long. When Sunday finally came around, I was joyful for the first time in 3 years. My grandma would always talk to me about God and there's no doubt in my mind that her prayers saved me growing up. I always thought my grandmother had special powers. She always knew things that I never told her. I couldn't help but think that her prayers had something to do with me meeting that man at my job. When I attended his church, I felt something I had never felt before. I didn't feel hatred anymore, and I wanted to pray for those people who had wronged me. From that day forward, I started praying. I stopped hanging out at the bar, and I enrolled into law school---I wanted better for myself. The problem that I had was condemning people for their sins. Who was I to judge people for their mistakes? No matter how big or how small, it just wasn't my place. I had to learn that God heals and fixes everything. I wasn't completely healed because I was still on my journey to becoming a better person. Everything starts within. My grandmother always said every tub has to set on its own bottom, meaning everyone must be responsible for their own wrong doings. I forgave those people who hurt me and my sister because they have to live with the betrayals. I was finally ready to free myself from the pain and self-destruction.

One year later, my paternal grandmother died, and my father asked us to attend the service. So, me, my sister, and my mom decided to go, although my little brother, who despised my dad and his whole family, wasn't interested in attending. He felt abandoned since our dad or for that matter, anyone in his family, wasn't around when we had no lights or simply attended school events to show support. However, after all that family did to my mother, she still supported them and I admire her for that because all I felt was hurt, anger, and resentment. I didn't know her. She spent her life in the same state, living less than 1 hour away from us. Yet, I'm supposed to celebrate and remember a life who never wanted to be in mine. I could remember sitting in the church and listening to them speak about her as me and my sister sat in the back pew not even sitting with the family. We were just there to send our condolences. Then, I started crying---not for a lost life---but for a lost childhood, for a lost relationship that I would never experience or have. I got up and ran out. I wanted to leave but I had to wait on my mother and my sister. So, I waited in the common area. As tears fell from my eyes, I looked up at a table where pictures of the family were placed. Of course, none of our pictures were on the table---I didn't see them anywhere. Why couldn't we be a part of this beloved family? As the family walked behind the casket, I saw my sister and my mom hugging everyone, offering her condolences. But, I couldn't. I walked away. I was in too much pain to talk to people who never wanted to be a part of my life in the first place. I remember trying to add my Auntie on Facebook. She blocked me, and I never understood why. My grandma used to tell me all the time to forgive people. After all I went through, I learned to forgive them and to move on, but that hole still remains in my heart.

As a child we should never know the pain of our father's presence and absence.

When he left, emotionally my mother left, too. But who could blame her, he was all she knew.

How can I shake being afraid to walk alone in the dark?

How can a monster be real, if he never leaves a mark?

Being broken isn't beautiful, but the journey to healing can be radiant.

Self-love.

Can love heal me or hold my hand and teach me to love

Myself again?

I'm no longer resentful because what I've lost I've gained.

Fireside Reflections

Keywords and Takeaways:

A huge part of this story is about facing abuse and abandonment from those who are supposed to have our backs, *family.* During the course of her childhood and even into her adulthood, Bri suffered from the losses in her life. She experienced the loss of her Mom's identity to be a protective Mom. She also experienced the loss of her Dad who wasn't a loving Dad, and the physical loss of her sister and later a Grandmother who lived within an hour away, yet whose love she didn't feel, or from the others on that side of the family for that matter. But what do you do? Like Bri's Grandma said, you have to *forgive them and move on.*

Who is *your* letter to? Write a letter to that person who needs to hear your voice. It doesn't matter if they are here or not. This healing journey is for *you...get it out.*

_____

_____

_____

_____

_____

_____

_____

_____

_____

_____

_____

PURPOSEFUL SHIFT

La'Tia Reed

Nothing that occurs in your life is a coincidence. As I look back over the past 8, maybe 10 years of my life, I laugh at the fact that I had convinced myself that I was living *purposefully* and needed to do nothing more, when in actuality I knew that I wasn't and I knew that I needed to. Here I was living my usual life and doing my usual thing in being a wife, a hands-on mother, and a best friend to everyone who I knew. I was working at a job that I loved, with a boss who I absolutely adored, and colleagues who I thought were the best things since sliced bread and spray butter!

Although things seemed good and I appeared to be happy, but I was only partially happy, and even that wasn't always the case. Inside, I was lost, confused, unfulfilled, disconnected, desperately looking for a greater sense of purpose. I couldn't quite understand how each day I went out into this big, beautiful world full of living, breathing things and beings, all of which had a purpose and made perfect sense that somehow, I felt that I didn't. At the time, I felt that my only job and purpose was to be this supportive wife, great mother, best friend, and dependable employee. Although I loved being all those things, all of those things weren't my soul's only purpose.

As time went on, I became less happy and for the life of me, could not understand why. I had frequently heard that once you find your purpose, that's when true happiness would manifest. If that was indeed true, then I should have been living in bliss because I kind of knew my purpose. I was born knowing it! I would often wonder, how on earth could this be? How could I be aware of my purpose, but still feel like there had to be more to this thing called life? How could I still have this burning desire for something greater, for something higher, and for something more?

I thought to myself, *Oprah lives a purposeful life. Even though she isn't a wife, she has a pretty solid relationship. Even though she isn't a mom biologically, she has taken in all of those beautiful girls from South Africa who so eloquently call her Mama O. She is also a great friend to "everyone on the planet," and works harder than any individual I'd ever heard of.* She made this purpose thing look so easy, and I felt that because I had all of those things and was charitable beyond measure, that just like Mama O, that I, too, automatically lived from a space of purpose.

Come on! I watched most of Mama O's talk shows in the past, transitioning to her Super Soul Sunday's and Masterclasses. Yes, honey, I thought that I was doing it. I thought that I was evolving in the best way! I was doing and being all of those things that she and her guests were teaching about, on top of being born, and knowing my purpose. In my mind, that qualified me as this purpose-filled super woman and then some. Mama O wasn't the only one pouring into people. I've poured into more misguided individuals than I've poured into myself and on top of that, I fostered youth for God's sake! I figured you couldn't get any more super than that. No matter how tired I was or what was going on, I was going to keep that superwoman status by any means necessary.

But oh, baby! I soon found that I wasn't as super as I thought. It was time to get schooled for real. It was about time that I go through some things, lose some people, get beat down by the ebb and flow of life then grow up. As I was trying to keep it all together, like us super women have been programmed to do, my cape slowly started to unravel, and Mama O had not prepared me for that at all, honey. The cape unraveling happened so fast that it would make your head spin. Everything that started to happen even before this point was so weird, so intense, so surreal, and just simply unexplainable. The feeling of pain, misery, and discontent became so great that in a strange kind of way, I felt as though I was drowning. I felt as if my life would soon be over, not realizing that there was more to that than what met the eye. My life as I knew it really was coming to an end, both literally and figuratively. I was dying! The first life changing thread to unravel my cape was my health.

In 2014, I kissed death in the face for the first time. I remember it as if it was yesterday. I walked into my place of employment feeling like my normal self that day. I say *that day* because a little over a month prior, my health was so off. I began noticing that I was getting sick and visiting the doctor's office more so than usual. After more than three visits with no diagnosis, my self-diagnosis was that maybe I was just pushing myself entirely too hard. If you are a parent and a wife who is experiencing marriage struggles, then throw in a full-time career to boot, burnout was a definitely a possibility.

That morning, I went about my usual tasks, including stopping by the company's kitchen to visit with my favorite people before starting my work-day. After about 20 minutes, I walked down to my office, spoke to other colleagues, got my morning coffee, then I sat down at my desk. All of a sudden, I began to cough uncontrollably, with chills running through my body, and my skin beginning to visibly become damp and gray. I remember telling my coworkers who were in the office that I was freezing cold. I always kept a space heater on the floor by my desk since I was generally cold anyway, so of course I turned it on. That left everyone in eye shot of me very confused because it was a sunny 80-degree day outside. At that point, they all turned up their noses, shook their heads, and let me be.

I began working, making a short pile of all the things that needed to be copied and filed. I grabbed the first sheet, got up from my desk, and copied it. I pulled the second sheet, got up, and copied it as well but noticed that I was dizzy, and that my equilibrium seemed to be a bit off. Although dizziness was one of my primary complaints on my third visit to the doctor, I had been given anti-vertigo meds, and to experience this type of dizziness again was alarming. The more I moved, preparing to make copy number three, the more I began to go from really cold to really hot, turning the space heater off and unzipping my favorite fleece sweater.

I waited for a few minutes, then decided to attempt to walk to the printer one last time. At this moment, I was thinking, *Man, oh, man, I'm really having a hard time getting to a printer that's literally three steps away from my desk*! In my own state of confusion, I sat back down and leaned forward, placed my head in my hands, and closed my eyes. My thoughts began to wonder as I prayed and questioned God, "Lord, what is this?" I had never felt so bad in my life! Continuing to hold my head down, I opened my eyes to find that my yellow paper was soaking wet from what my sweat. It was so bad that my hair had begun to curl out of the ponytail and was plastered to my forehead as if I had just participated in the infamous Ice Bucket Challenge.

As my coworker walked back into the office, she sat down with the same confused look that she had earlier. She told me that I looked awful and suggested I should go home. Me being who I am, a person who must see a task through until the end, I would not even think about leaving. A few seconds had passed, and another colleague walked into the office. He looked at me as if he had seen a ghost and proceeded to tell me flat out, "You look like shit!" I recall trying to laugh it off, and responded, "Gee, thanks!" He, too, suggested that I go home. You shook his head and said with concern in his voice that *I really didn't look like myself.* He was so concerned that he left to get our boss. He then returned, informing me that she wasn't in the building, so he talked to the next best person. After a bit, she stopped by. Knowing full well that I was feeling worse by the second, I continued to plead my case, asking that they not make a big deal out of my condition and to just give me a little time to pull it together.

The next person through the door was my next in command. She took one look at me and said, "Oh, yes, something is visibly wrong." Sticking with the theme, she stated that *I needed to go home as well.* I had no choice but to wave the white flag and to agree. It seemed that it would take more energy to fight them on this than it would to just leave. I got up, moving like a baby trying to take its first step. Attempting to pack up my things, it looked like everyone in the room was anticipating my fall. I began to fade in and out, vaguely hearing the chitter chatter of whomever was in the room at that point; I can't recall. What I do recall is someone telling me that I couldn't drive home. My supervisor at the time began asking me for the contact numbers for my family. I am not sure what happened in between that time and the time that my friend arrived. I had started having black outs. I remember saying to her that I would not leave my car there, and that I was determined to drive it home. I told her that she could just follow me. Hard head, right? I made it home with my friend close behind. With a sigh of relief and a thought of home sweet home, my friend, who was also my childcare provider, proceeded to pick my children up from school. As I transitioned from the car to the house, I instructed her to tell the kids that the door would be open when they got here and to come on in. I went inside, sat down on the first piece of furniture I could get to, then the madness began, and the struggle became real!

The door opened and in walked my babies. It was clear as day that I saw my son and heard his voice. I remember him asking me, "What's going on?" and telling me that he was going to call his dad. That was the last thing I heard. My mind could not comprehend another thing. I knew nothing, I could hear nothing, and I could see absolutely nothing. I didn't know the time, day, month, or year. Then, POP! The lights in my head came back on again. I still wasn't sure if I was home though, if you know what I mean. I remember one of my daughters on one side of me trying to pull me up the stairs, and my son behind, trying to push me. My youngest little one was standing in confusion, which clearly was the going theme here. All I know in that moment is that midway up the stairs, I was on my hands and knees. Then, lights out again. My mind was shot! My energy was shot! My life compass was shot! I was literally not present in this world. I was a shell.

Here we are, somehow, at a different day. What day? I don't know, as previously stated, because I wasn't there for the "in between." I didn't mention that this was the second time in that same week that I had left work not feeling well. All I know is that one day, I woke up and called the doctor's office telling them that I had a horrible case of the flu. I expressed that I had been coughing terribly and that my fever had to be high because you could feel the steam coming from my body. At the time that I called the office, I had no clear recollection of each step in the episode I just explained. As I spoke with the secretary at the doctor's office, I remember her saying *they could get me in on Monday*. I don't know what reply was coming from me. I imagine I borderline blacked out again. Whatever I said, she had a change of heart and thought that it would be best to go ahead and squeeze me in that evening at 5 pm. Then, I blacked out again.

The next time I came to, I was soaking wet; my hair, my face, my back, my legs, my feet, literally everything. You could squeeze my clothes out. How crazy is that? I remember telling the kids to call a girlfriend of mine who lived close by and to tell her that I didn't feel good. I am guessing this all of this took place during the morning because that evening is when I drove myself to the doctor's office, then to the hospital. I had my kids with me the entire time. I refused to alarm anyone until I knew exactly what was happening. I also used them as a cover up. My kids went everywhere with me, including work sometimes. I knew that if I left the kids at home with their dad, then that would send red flags, especially to him. He was often gone but on this particular day, he was there monitoring the new hot water tank that being installed. So, he would definitely wonder why I left the kids at home during the repair.

Fast-forwarding past many details, I got to the hospital just in time. My skin had already started to dull, my voice was down to a whisper, my entire body was ice cold, and everything around me was spinning. I felt like I had just run a marathon in Antarctica. That would be the last time that I would see my young children. After multiple tests and scans, I remember the last one. I was taken to a room where I was laid out in the dark. It was cold, quiet, and very eerie. I felt closer and closer to my final hour on earth. Shortly after, I was taken to another room. It was full of equipment and a few nurses. When I looked up and saw my personal doctor in tears that is when I knew *it was serious*. My nerves were officially shot to shingles at that point, and I knew it was time to notify people. That was first on the agenda once this test was over. I could sense at that point that this would not be a turnaround trip, and that I would be there at least overnight. The good thing is that my friend, who had my kids call that day, had already shown up and was waiting for me in the hospital's waiting room.

As the doctors began to set up the room and explain the process, I started to feel worse by the second. I recall the nurse asking if I was ok. I continued to say, *yes*, when I knew I wasn't. I definitely wasn't ok because I thought that I heard the nurse tell my doctor that they could not perform the standard test because I wouldn't make it through. That was unnerving but in good LaTia fashion, I had somehow convinced myself that I was hallucinating and that wasn't what I actually heard. The test began, and I started to feel outside of my body. Then, that was it. I died. I literally died. By the grace of

God, that was not how the story ended. I remember opening my eyes, seeing a room full of doctors, nurses, an allied team, and what I now know was a crash unit. I recall some lady shoving something down my throat, my doctors back turned saying how sorry and how unfortunate this was, and someone shouting that *they had lost me*. I was in a frustrating state of confusion because I couldn't speak. I only had the energy to look around the room in complete fear. Once things calmed down, I could do nothing but sleep. Still unsure what happened or what I was even thinking or feeling, at some point I was moved to a room on the cardiac unit where I coded again.

This was the start of an uphill battle. A battle that had threatened my whole entire life. It was a battle that had me calculating every single move that I made. I had prayed and promised God that if He would grant me more time with my kids, that I would stop doing just enough to get by and eat, sleep, and live out my purpose. I told Him that I would make the shift wherever I needed to and go through whatever He wanted me to *as long as He would have mercy*.

This health issue turned into an extended stay in the hospital. Talk about stir crazy. After being there for weeks, I begged the doctors to release me so that I could go home to my family. Although I was told that I probably would not live to see the end of the week, I continued to beg and plead to go home to my babies that I had not seen and to allow me to die there. On May 27th, I was released with a heart machine. As fearful as I was that night, I was elated to wake up the next day to my daughter saying with fear and uncertainty in her voice, "Mommy? Happy Birthday!" Yes, it was my birthday. The first day in a new year that I was told that I would never see. God granted me the grace and mercy that I prayed for, but not with ease.

As the days continued, things finally started to get back to normal. My life-threatening heart condition never repaired itself, but it had become stable and I was able to return to many of the things that I was told by doctors that I would never do again. Although life wasn't perfect, it was good. I was back to being superwoman; of course, on a more purposeful level but still not fully.

Next thing you know, BOOM! Life happens. Another thread in my cape had come unraveled and I began to fall fast. I tried my best to hang on, but I lost my grip. My life was crumbling in every way imaginable. I had finally come to the realization that I was hitting my rock bottom. First, it was my health, which affected my job and my money, then here we go with my personal life issues. My relationships started to randomly shift, and I became more and more quiet and withdrawn. I typically stayed to myself anyway, but this was a little more than usual.

Even though I was going through hell, I had still been running my charity, which was still considered new. This caused my family to say things such as. "You have your little charity now, so you think you are better than everyone else. You are too good to come around and talk to your people." Yes. I was called antisocial and all of that. You name it, I've heard it! Of course, I took issue with that because I was none of those things and could not understand why or even how they came to that conclusion. Just by me staying to myself. This was crazy.

It was so crazy that I was ridiculed for not continuing to reach out to one of my relatives who I had reached out to for months. There was absolutely no response of any type, yet I was told that *I should have never stopped trying and that because I was so funny acting, it was all my fault*. How was that even logical when I was the one reaching out, even in my funk? What's funny, is that everyone must have forgotten that the phone works both ways. Not once did anyone call to see if I was okay or if I was even living, as if my heart condition wasn't a real thing. I was hurt, confused, and irritated---I could not do anything right. You know, that whole *damned if you do and damned if you don't* thing. So, I decided that I would just go with the *don't* and be damned for that! Why not? My thought was this: *If the end result would be the same, then I should just go with the one that would cause me the least amount of stress*. Some of my folks have the takeover spirit. They are the people who wanted to dictate what I did, where I went, how I lived, how I should think, and even who I should support. I had always lived my life according to everyone else's terms and demands, and I was over it. I tired of being the one who showed up in spaces that didn't fit me. I was over being the dependable person who showed up for everyone, even when they didn't show up for me. Most of all, I was sick of trying to explain those feelings to a family that just didn't get it.

I figured that I had my friends, so to hell with the family foes. But then, those "friends!" Lord, some of those friends! They were more of a dead weight than death itself. Trust me, I know. Remember, I experienced death. I only had very few friends because as far as I could see, the more friends that you had, the more problems you'd definitely have! Well, I soon found out that the problem was never in the number of friends but in the quality of the friendships. I didn't have either. I found that in the few friendships I had, I was the giver in all of them.

I was the counselor, the spiritual advisor, the problem solver, the nurturer, the savior so to speak, and the healer. They only needed me to be the sounding board for their drama and self-inflicted pain, so all I knew at the time was to be just that. Not only to them but to everyone. Eventually, I arrived at a place where I didn't want to be around them either; family or friends. I was just tired and borderline miserable.

Even though I lived life on other people's terms, it wasn't all on them. It was on me, too. Remember that I stated that I *sort of knew my purpose*? Well, loving, supporting, and showing up is very much a part of that. Although it was a part of my purpose, I was unhappy doing it most of the time. I felt like I had to. I didn't want to be known as that person who didn't show love and support to my family nor did I want to be crowned as the friend who didn't show up to everything. I found that I was so busy (no matter whose fault it was) trying to save and heal the world when I was the one who truly needed to be saved and healed first.

I needed to be healed from the loss of my biological mother who died when I was young, and healed from my oldest sister who also died. I had to be healed from relatives who all fought over me and wanted to care for me, until they actually had to. I needed to be healed from a broken relationship with my father who I loved to life and who loved me. I needed to be healed from the separation from some of my siblings. I needed to be healed from the devastating loss of my first-born child. The list of losses could go on and on. Isn't it funny how we are a collection of our experiences? I was to everyone else all the things I needed for my younger self. I took on the burden and carried the cross of other people in dire need like myself. As if the pain of my relationships shifting wasn't enough, there was something else shifting, too. It was something internal. For so long I had functioned in dysfunction, and I did it so well, that it was not only the norm, it was a form of comfort for me and all that I knew.

During the internal shift, those spaces that I once functioned in began to make me uncomfortable. The things that I loved, I seemed to love less. The people I cherished and adored, I didn't seem to be as connected as I once was. Every single thing in and around my life was shifting and starting to look and feel different. You would think the shifting that happened after the whole health scare, and my promise to live a more meaningful life would be enough, but it wasn't. There was still more shifting that needing to take place; perhaps because I was still playing with my purpose.

All I know is that I had this indescribable feeling that was frustrating beyond measure. There was this sense of urgency for something. I felt as though butterflies were having a party in my stomach. You know, the unsettled feeling you get that doesn't ever seem to want to go away? It reminded me of that weird childhood feeling that signaled you were in trouble the minute you got home from school. That nervous type of energy. It was so baffling. I literally started to wonder if I was crazy! I couldn't quite understand how I wanted to be around people but at the same time *steal away*, as the older folks used to say. I felt like I didn't know myself but was somehow becoming more in tune with my true nature. I had this strong desire to go on some form of an exploration and journey through self. As the days continued , the nervous energy became greater and greater. It was like a volcano preparing to erupt, and eventually the hot lava poured out all over!

The walls started crumbling so fast that I was not fast enough to gather the bricks needed to rebuild the broken foundation. At that moment, that was it! Everything had fallen apart. I could not swallow the tears anymore, I could not suppress whatever that thing was that had been trying to rise in me. All I could do was throw myself in the middle of my bed and scream. I kicked, and I punched. I did everything under the sun but go into convulsions and throw up. All I could do was cry out to God. I had so many questions. I wanted to know *what else, Lord*! *Why me, Lord*! How did I get here? How am I going to get out of this indescribable rut? At that point, I was in a place where I wanted to throw out the never-ending hamster wheel I was riding.

After my 10-minute knockdown, drag-out with myself and God, I was exhausted and now laying lifeless. I looked and felt all kinds of crazy! Then, I slid to the edge of the bed, down to my knees, and flat on the floor. I just laid there in silence. That silence then transitioned to anger. It was the anger that made me pissed enough to *say to hell with barely existing, to hell with meeting the demands of others, to hell with living a mundane life, and to hell with living with limits because some doctor told me that I had to*.

It was at that exact moment when I accepted the fact that ***I was responsible for my peace, happiness, and success***. It was my job to live from a place of authenticity, abundance, and purpose. It was in that moment when the game had officially changed, and I was introduced to my higher self.

I now live a life of authenticity, abundance, and purpose. I get to wake up every day and do my life's work as a change agent. I get to mentor underserved youth and coach women who want to find their purpose. Here is the best part! I get to live free from the demands of others, affording me with the opportunity to dance to the beat of my own drum.

When I die, I want to die empty and I want you to do the same. There are entirely too many people living and leaving this world unfulfilled, having yet to even scratch the surface of who they were designed to be.

So, if you are in a space of discontent, a space where everything in your life is shifting and falling, and you are tired of trying to hold it together, just **STOP**! You don't have to be "Superwoman." Go ahead and let life fall apart. Only then can you collect yourself, pick up the pieces that are in alignment with who you are, and begin to live from your space of authenticity and abundance. Not one thing in your life is happening by coincidence. ***The shift is on purpose.***

Fireside Reflections

Keywords and Takeaways:

1. Superwoman

2. Taking on the burdens of others

3. Responsible for your own peace, happiness, and success

The infamous Superwoman story… the one many of us know very well and own up to or are in denial about because we are either naïve or oblivious to the fact that that's what it is. Throughout her story, LaTia references moments in her life where her capes is unraveling. This depicts a woman of strength who is becoming more self-aware as this cape continues to unravel and the mask is being taken off, while she is left there to discover her naked truth!

LaTia for as long as she could remember, has been taking of the burden of others. I can tell you right now that, *that will BURN YOU OUT!#jotthatdown*

It is important to be conscious of how you are expending your energy, especially for and towards other people and things, because at the end of the day, YOU are responsible for your own peace, happiness, well-being, and success.

Here's an exercise.

Do you often feel fatigued from being the "go to" person for everyone else?

□Yes_____   □ No _____   □ Sometimes _____

Do you set healthy boundaries?

□Yes_____   □ No _____   □ Sometimes _____

If you answered either, "No" or "Sometimes" to the above answers, we've got some work to do. It is to your own wellness that you are giving to yourself more than you give to others. Why? Foe one, it keeps you sane. Two, you should only give what you have in excess of so that you do not feel depleted. Know when to stop and reset and understand that it is okay to not feel accountable to everyone's urgency of you. Here, it's this simple... If it feels more of a burden and doesn't feel good, rethink it. If necessary, get out of it and don't own it, because folks will run you in the ground dry and once you're no longer good for their use of you, they'll move on while you're left there to figure *you* out.

UNMASKING CONFIDENCE
WHAT HAVE YOU GOT TO LOSE?

Denise Newsome

In many ways, I had the most "normal" childhood you could imagine. I lived with my mother and father in a house in the suburbs. I had siblings. I had friends. I went to school. I went to church. Eventually I became old enough to work and explore the world all on my own.

That was the first mask I ever wore---the mask of normalcy. My whole family wore it, to tell the truth. But for me, it was like a security blanket---and I held on real tight!

I laughed loudly. I made jokes (often at the expense of others). I played games and tricks. I wore a smile, but anyone with a basic understanding of psychology would know that it was all an act. My actions spoke louder than any of my laugh or any of my words.

I struggled in school---I hated it. I had a hard time and didn't receive the support I needed, so I just gave up. I often cut classes.

And home wasn't much better. I was always worried about the dysfunction of our household. We were constantly walking on eggshells.

It's hard to talk about because the truth is that parents are far from perfect. Not only that, but mine are from a generation when society's beliefs about family were quite different from what we understand today. I love my father, who passed away 3 years ago, and I love my mother, who I'm blessed to still have with me. But it was rough. *He* was rough.

His entrance always woke me up from my sleep when he returned home from work late at night. I waited with bated breath for him to settle in, and I couldn't get back to sleep until he did. Would there be an explosion? Or would the night end in peace?

I never knew...

And, verbally, she sometimes took that uncertainty out on me (in my mind)---but not unjustly. Of all of my siblings, I was---by far---the least well-behaved. I was a troublemaker, and she tried to reign me in the best way that she knew how.

But at a time when I was supposed to be concerned with what I'd get for Christmas, I was receiving messages that I wasn't "smart enough" and I didn't always feel safe in my own home.

On top of all of that, I was also hearing loudly and clearly that I wasn't attractive enough either. As a child, the pain of being compared with your siblings in any way is unimaginable. But when you grow up with sisters who have more "acceptable" features, you get treated differently. Adults think that children can't understand favoritism, but we do---all of us do. And it hurts. For a long time, I didn't even feel pretty.

Messaging about not being "good enough" was coming from all sides, but I kept on smiling. I kept on laughing. I kept on bullying...

...*to mask* my own confusion, *to mask* my own anger, *to mask* my own shame, and *to mask* my own pain.

Storytelling was the only outlet I had to escape. I started writing early. Eventually I aspired to act as well. I mean, wasn't my life proof that I was good at wearing masks and pretending?

As I got older, things didn't get any better, especially in school. Finally, at 15 years of age, I was expelled. My mother told me that if I was grown enough not to go to school, I was old enough to work.

So, I did---I got my first job.

As I worked various odd jobs over the years, my potential for leadership shone brightly. Even as a teenager, I progressed quickly through the ranks with various employers. I was reliable, trustworthy, hardworking, and bright. But I couldn't see my own light. In my mind, it had been dimmed by a lifetime of negativity.

Despite my own self-doubt, I was living proof that anything you put your mind to, *you* have the ability to learn it, through hands-on experience. Degrees are a blessing and take hard work, but my life is evidence that they aren't required to be great and to have greatness in you. God is in control of that!

But He isn't only in control of the good things. God helps guide us through the bad things as well. Sometimes He even leads us there Himself. I'm just glad that I met Him when I did; if I hadn't, this next part of my life probably would have led to a nervous breakdown---or worse.

I was on my way to work when sirens went off behind me. When you're driving, sirens just become another type of background noise. *"Oh, an accident must have happened." "They're probably just using that to drive faster."* You don't usually imagine that it's for you.

But, to my surprise, I was pulled over. So, you imagine that it's for speeding or making an unlawful turn. You're aggravated, but ready to deal with it. Then they tell you that you have to accompany them for questioning at their precinct. You have to leave your car.

If you've never been in police custody, let me tell you: it's indescribable. They kept me in there for hours, interrogating me, asking me things that made no sense, and trying to get me to say what they wanted to hear. I didn't ask for a lawyer or anything like that, although I should've at my age then, but I didn't know any better. I didn't know that I had rights.

Before I knew it, they were writing up a statement of confession--- and I was expected to sign the document. I was tired, and I just wanted to go home. So, I did just that.

Of course, I didn't get to return home. As I waited for my family to faithfully post my bail, I sat in the local jail. I don't know which was darker---the cell I was in or what I was feeling inside. All I knew was that life was over for me.

Out on bail, I started going to church with my mother. I grew up in the church but, like many, I strayed away. I figured, what could it hurt to go? I was at the lowest point of my life. Anything that could help was more than welcome.

After deep reflection, I decided to give my life to Christ. I am a witness today that the living word of Philippians 4:13---"I can do all things through Christ, who strengthens me."---is a powerful truth. I held onto God. He was my strength during that time. I would not have made it (at least, not with a sound mind) without His grace and mercy, combined with my family's support

I refused to take a plea but, at the time, I was pretty uninformed about how the judicial system worked. I was found guilty. My entire insides felt like they dropped down to my feet. My family was devastated. So was I.

217

I spent about 3 months in the county jail before being shipped off to my first of 3 prisons. Initially sentenced to 5-15 years, I ended up serving a total of 9 years.

It was hard but, once again, I put on a mask. I was strong. I'd get through this. I had God on my side. The truth, however, was that I was terrified. Although I didn't know a lot about how the system worked, I was aware of the many horror stories---and that most people don't go there voluntarily.

The day I was transferred, there were two other black women being transferred with me. They were inconsolable and unashamed to show it. I, on the other hand, put on my mask. "We gon' be alright."

They say you gotta fake it 'til you make it,' and I was certainly faking it! Prison was no cake walk, but I was determined to make the best of it. It was a daily struggle for my mind. Your life is controlled in ways that most people probably can't even imagine unless you've been there yourself. It's even harder when you don't have outside support. I'm so incredibly grateful every day that my family was there for me, to see me through. I don't know if I would have made it without their love and care. They sent packages, they put money in my account, they visited, and they prayed for my safety and for my mind. Their presence in my life reminded me of what was waiting for me on the other side, if I just held on to God's promises.

I resolved that *this* moment would be the lowest point in my life. I took every program and class that was offered to us. I attended therapy. I even got my GED. Even in prison I excelled. I went from taking classes to teaching classes. Once transferred to a different prison for a most coveted DMV job, I progressed from a customer service representative to supervising the entire department all the way up to serving as a trainer---the highest position available.

Of course, this didn't make doing hard time any less trying, painful, or demoralizing. However, I knew that, upon my release, I wanted a different life for myself. A better life.

I was sincere in that desire, but the road to hell is paved with good intentions, and I was on my way there with gasoline drawers on!

Once released, I worked in fast food, determined to turn things around. I even started my own cleaning business, which, once it took off, allowed me to quit my position as a manager at White Castle. But my struggle wasn't over just yet.

You see, I was never the type to drink or do drugs, but prison left me with *one* vice: an addiction to women. I even attended Narcotics Anonymous during my stay in prison to help stave off my desires. But clearly, the lessons I learned there didn't take.

On multiple occasions, I got myself into trouble for women. Violating parole, in 2004 I was sent back to prison to serve another year.

Despite the setbacks of my own creation, Mr. Clark, a high-ranking employee at the SUNY Long Island Educational Opportunity Center, believed in me. When I'd visit him, he would tell me "You got a book in you, Nisi! You got a book in you!" I listened to him, nodding my head, but it would take quite a few years for me to actually *hear* him.

Eventually, I found myself in Georgia... and I was miserable. I wasn't getting into trouble, but my life was going nowhere fast. I wasn't happy. I wasn't doing anything that mattered to me. I was in a relationship that felt hollow. My life didn't make any sense. *How did I get to this point?* I thought.

You got a book in you, Nisi!

For the first time, I truly heard Mr. Clark's words---and they made perfect sense. I'd always been a storyteller, but it somehow got lost in the fog of a hard life. I wasn't completely in the clear, but the fog was finally starting to lift. My legs creaked and cracked as I made my way back to New York. I knew I couldn't write anything in the environment I was in.

In 2009, I published that first book, "Misty's Blood". At that point, I was using a pseudonym. That ghost of unworthiness hadn't left me yet. Despite the potential that I'd shown over the years, decades had gone by and the foundation of my self-esteem was still rocky.

You may wonder why, after all of those years, I couldn't shake the demon of low self-worth. The great abolitionist Frederick Douglass is often believed to have said, "It is easier to build strong children than to repair broken men." Whoever actually said those words was right on the money! What's planted in your childhood has deep roots that are hard to unearth, especially if you aren't willing to work with the soil. And when you're working with damaged roots, any injury to the plant above ground just makes things that much worse.

When I wrote "Misty's Blood," I knew something needed to change. It was why I left Georgia, and also why I was determined to make "Misty's Blood" work. But I just couldn't shake the clouds of self-doubt, anger, self-pity, pain, and shame. They followed me home to New York. And there were quite a few people in my life who were more than happy to remind me that the clouds were there---and that they deserved to be there.

When I returned to New York, I stayed with an aunt, one of my mother's older sisters. I didn't have any place of my own nor the money to procure one. I knew that Georgia was no place for me to write my book---the environment was toxic. So, I left one toxic environment and fell right into another one. My aunt, God rest her soul, seemed to have a crusade against me. I couldn't do anything right and nothing good could ever come to me. I was no good---the same message that I'd been hearing my entire life. I depended on her charity, and she wouldn't let me forget it.

When she fell ill, my giving soul wouldn't let her flounder by herself though. I took care of her. Doctor appointments, medications, hospital visits---whatever she needed I was there, despite her many injuries to me. Although I didn't deserve her wrath, I knew I hadn't been perfect either. And I was always grateful to her for opening up her home to me.

To pay for costs related to self-publishing and help sustain myself while I lived with her, I hustled by driving cabs in my neighborhood. I took the dangerous night shift. I was making good money, but not enough to live on my own. Once my aunt passed away in 2010, I found myself--- once again---with no place to go. My sister was gracious enough to let me move in with her for the second time in my life.

I learned that when the circumstances of life require you to depend on others, when you don't have your own, people treat you differently. You're looked down upon, disrespected, and pitied. No matter how hard you work to change things, you're never enough.

Not long after moving in with my sister, I had to leave my job driving cabs. They were becoming stricter: drug testing, proper licensing, and my worst nightmare---background checks. Even after giving my life to Christ all those years ago, I just couldn't believe that God had my back in all things. I was convinced that my time in prison would be too large of a strike against me. Rather than being found out and embarrassed, I left.

"Oh ye of little faith."

At that point, I was at the mercy of social services. My book wasn't selling nearly enough to support myself. My only steady income was through food stamps and rental assistance. I leaned and depended on them---and my sister---for survival.

One night, about 2:00 or 3:00 am in the morning, I was lying on my sister's floor---I didn't have my own bed---attempting to quietly eat a bag of potato chips. My sister got up early every morning to work in Manhattan. In hindsight, I imagine that my midnight cravings weren't too welcome.

Suddenly, I heard my sister's exasperated sigh, "Nisi, I'm sorry, but you got to go."

I was devastated, and I felt betrayed. I couldn't even depend on my own family for compassion. So I got up and left. I didn't even bother to gather my things. As tears streamed down my face, I rode the bus from Long Island into Queens and hopped on the subway.

I sat there all the way into Manhattan and back again---back and forth, back and forth. What was I to do? I had nowhere else to go.

Eventually, I decided on settling into Penn Station. Cops routinely make rounds there, so sometimes I had to leave and wander around outside. After about a day, I started to smell. I didn't have any toiletries or even money for food.

I was hungry, I felt gross, but most important I felt defeated. I felt like *nothing*, like garbage. Hopelessness, rejection, anger, hurt, and disappointment enveloped my soul. I asked myself, *"Why should I continue to live like this?" "Is it better to just die?"* Living the way I was felt like suffocating; getting it over with *had* to be better than what I was enduring. My sister's words echoed in my head. I couldn't stop crying. I felt like a burden, so empty and all alone.

By some God-orchestrated miracle, my sister had a change of heart. After about a day, she called me and apologized. I returned, beyond grateful, in part because I know that so many homeless people aren't nearly as blessed.

For a long while, my sister encouraged me to attend church with her. Even in the misery I was living, I was always convinced that I had better things to do.

One day, she'd had enough.

As she scurried around the apartment preparing to leave, she walked up to my little corner and jolted me awake.

"You goin' to CHURCH this morning! You goin' to CHURCH!"

Up to this point, it had always been a gentle coaxing, but something in her voice and demeanor had changed.

Much to my surprise, I enjoyed myself, so I kept going back. The music was jumping, the pastor was passionate, and the people were more or less friendly. As I stuck around, I began to feel a slow burn rising up inside me; something was changing. I listened to my now-Bishop preach, and the word of God flowed from his lips like a river of fire. He and his sister, Executive Pastor Dr. Jacqueline R. Gates, had a tag-team ministry that was like a one-two punch to me. Over the next few months, I felt convicted. I could feel God working on me---and I wanted it. But I wasn't quite ready to truly commit.

In the beginning of 2012, the church hosted a series of New Year's revival services: 10 Days Ablaze. Like the name suggests, the fire that had been started in me over the last few months took on a life of its own. The fire grew hotter and hotter. It got so hot in there that I just wanted to rip off my clothes---men's clothes---right where I was.

Layers started sloughing off of me: depression, defeat, shame, blame, anger. All of it. It was a powerful unburdening. I was hooked from there. That was the best feeling I'd felt in a decade, and I didn't want it to go away.

I was changed forever. I rededicated my life to Christ that week and, although far from perfect, my life hasn't been the same since.

Although there had always been a part of me that cared about people, as my new life with Christ developed, I began to look inwardly like I never had before. I prayed for God to show me *me*---in all of my ugliness and truth. And boy did He!

As my former self started to die, I began to realize just how often I blamed others for my circumstances, and how often I shirked responsibility for my choices. As I acknowledged the ways in which I contributed to my own pitfalls, my capacity for compassion began to grow. I could think of nothing else but my desire to lead people to healing and deliverance. With God's help, I wanted to lead people out of their darkness---a darkness I knew all too well. I can't even watch a commercial about abuse---even of animals---without my empathy rising up from the depths of my soul. I automatically start praying. I just want to help people get *unstuck*, and get them to dig deeper to understand what's keeping them from prospering, from accessing God's promises.

And a funny thing happened along the way: as I began to be honest about who I really was, and as my love for God's people began to grow exponentially, my ability to finally see my own worth also grew. I *am* somebody---and I finally believed it!

From that point on, I was on a mission. My life's experiences, combined with my newfound dedication to Christ, helped me uncover my deep love for and commitment to the downtrodden, the brokenhearted, the abused, the confused, and the lonely. I took my mission seriously, and I already knew how it would manifest: through storytelling.

My first project post-game changing moment, was adapting my novel "Misty's Blood" into a stage play. I produced it, while recruiting others to both write the script and to direct. Following in the footsteps of my Bishop, I decided to *dream big*: I aimed for an off-Broadway production. Although I wasn't where I wanted or needed to be when I wrote it, I knew that the core themes of "Misty's Blood" were the center of my ministry: trauma, abuse, self-esteem, and striving for something better, for God's promises. I knew that I could turn it into something that would give God the glory and make my biological and church families Godly proud of me.

Tapping into the skills that I'd developed when I started working, as a teenager---the skills that helped propel me toward promotions in every job I worked---I took it upon myself to do the research needed to get my production off the ground. I was now confident enough in my abilities---and trusted God enough to see me through---that I wasn't afraid of what some people might perceive as "shortcomings." I knew what I was passionate about, what God had entrusted me with, and I gained the knowledge needed to move forward. I learned that that's all it takes.

I began reaching out to my networks. It was like the resources I needed just *came* to me. The people I needed to be connected to appeared in my life. The money I needed to produce a high-quality theatrical experience fell into my life like manna from Heaven, in spite of my own personal financial struggles. It was no picnic though; collaborative efforts always come with their own stresses. Everyone has different personalities, different priorities, and there are many obstacles and situations outside of your control.

But I know Who has the *ultimate* control---and that's what carried me through, as it always does.

So lo and behold, in 2013, I presented "Misty's Blood the Stage Play" for three nights in a row, one weekend in September. All three nights were sold out---a completely packed house! Beyond the numbers, it was also critically well received. I felt blessed beyond measure but, most important, I knew it was only the *beginning* of God's work in and through me!

Next I wrote my own original play, called "The Birth." It follows a couple who learns the importance of understanding your purpose in life---and the sacrifices that get made along the way. Premiering in 2016, it has been performed multiple times and more productions are in the works even as I write this! It's been the source of both laughter and tears for the audiences who've seen it. As God continues to enlarge my literal and metaphorical territory, I know that the healing power of "The Birth" can only grow.

Perhaps my most powerful, anointed work to date has been "ARISE! My Message Is in My Mess," a book of essays written by 13 authors, including yours truly, that highlights the triumph and tragedy, and the power and pain of life. It reveals God's mercy and grace and the ability of God's people to "get back up again," as Pastor Donnie McClurkin once wrote.

It was a transformative experience that reaffirmed my dedication to God's people; it was confirmation that I was on the right path. I felt honored that the authors trusted me enough to put their vulnerable stories in my care: stories about cancer, suicide attempts, domestic violence, school struggles, prison, and failed relationships. *This is the work*, I thought. *This is God's work through me.*

Finally, my most recent endeavor is my six-section online course "Heal Your Relationships by Healing Your Past" on teachable.com. Through my own experiences, God revealed to me how often our past dictates our present. That's certainly *my* life story. For years, I allowed what I'd been through and what had been done to me to define who I was. I let it determine how far I was able to go in life. It wasn't until God reminded me that I was *His* child, until He began breaking the chains of my past, that I realized how powerful I was. And that breakthrough has paved the way for the works I've done since returning to Him. I wanted to pass those lessons on to others, and God said, "This is how you do it."

Although I certainly still have a ways to go, I've come a long way since my self-conscious, self-pitying, bullying days. Allowing God to truly do a work in you---to transform your entire being---is the ultimate game-changer. Nothing can top it.

But my journey to get to that point was a rollercoaster of a ride, and this one chapter can only scratch the surface.

And what I've learned on this journey is that the possibilities of life are limitless. We aren't bound to fail because of the obstacles that life throws at us (abuse, racism, poverty, etc.) We have the power to *make a choice*. God reigns over all, but He also gave us free will. We have as much of a say in what happens in our lives as the hand that we're dealt; you just have to have enough faith to play the game.

So go forth with a Godly boldness: dream big, make plans, and execute them, imagine a future without struggle, and then work toward it, one day at a time. And no matter what you do, take it to God in prayer. Believe and trust in Him and take that step. What have you got to lose?

Fireside Reflections

Keywords and Takeaways:

1. Don't allow your past to hold you hostage

2. Let go of the mask

3. Limitless possibilities in life

4. Imagine the future *without struggle*

"Imagine a future without struggle". That's what's possible when you *believe.* When you Denise found the Lord and her place in this world as a writer, she was able to imagine herself being freed from the labels that she held onto behind her mask. She began to discover ways to not let her past define who she was and the many gifts that she's been born with to share.

She began *believing* in the limitless possibilities in life, knowing that if God brought her to it, that he'll surely bring her *through* it!

However, Denise is not alone. We all have some part of our life that we are not too proud of but know this. Everything we have gone through was necessary to develop who we've *become today* or who we are on the path of *becoming.* #jotthatdown

It's time to let those chains fall. Break free from the mental bondage of shame, hurt, fear, doubt, and anger. It's *necessary.* Give yourself permission to *WIN!*

What are you breaking free from today?

_____

_____

_____

_

A WONDERFUL CHANGE IN MY LIFE

Candace Nelson

It's funny how you envision what your adult life will look like when you are a child. You are filled with hopes, dreams, excitement, and know exactly how you want things to fall into place. When you are a child, it seems that the world is your oyster. The sky is the limit. You think about what you want to be and what you are going to do ...when you grow up.

I had big dreams as I was growing up. I just knew I would be a journalist. Initially, I wanted to work as a television reporter. Eventually, I realized I wanted to write for a newspaper. I still remember being chosen as "Author of the Week" as a second-grade student. I had written a poem and my teacher selected me for the upcoming week. I was so proud of myself. My poem was displayed on a bulletin board for any and all to see and during the awards ceremony. I received a beautiful certificate with my name on it. (I kept it for years. I am not quite sure where it is now.) Those were the days.

I also dreamt of being married, living in a nice house, and having children (at least two), in that order. Overall, I was a happy child and I had a great childhood. I grew up with a loving mother and a father, and three siblings: two sisters and one brother. We have always been a very close family. My parents worked hard and provided over and beyond for our family. My mother was an elementary school principal, who is retired now, and my father was the first African-American Executive Director of the Atlanta Housing Authority and ended his career as Vice President of the National Institute of Community Empowerment. Both of my parents were huge advocates for education. It was important to my parents that you always do your best and take advantage of the education being provided. My father used to say, "If you are going to be a ditch digger, you be the best darn ditch digger there is." My mother had this awesome poem that she taught to the students at her elementary school titled, **"We Are The Best."** Needless to say, the expectations for my siblings and I was high. I never wanted to let my parents down, although I made a lot of mistakes growing up. I am the oldest of my siblings and I felt a little bit of pressure to set the "right" example. I knew right from wrong, but I don't know that I knew enough to be an example for my siblings.

I moved out on my own at 25 years of age. Excited to be moving into my own apartment and experiencing the world on my own. Overall, *I was happy*. Of course, I had some ups and downs along the way but God had His hand on me. I remember my brother being a little sad when I moved out but he has always been right there whenever I needed him. There is only a two-year age difference between me and my brother. If I needed my mom or dad for anything, they were always there. I tried not to bother them much since I was trying to be an independent young lady. My parents were married for a little over 37 years. This was what I wanted my life to look like. *A happy family.* A loving husband. *Two children to love and watch grow into productive adults.* My family was not perfect by any means but we had each other, which is why we are so close to this day. My reality was very different.

Living life as a single woman was good but I was not where I wanted to be and I was not living the life I had dreamed about for myself. I finally made the decision to return to school and complete the degree that I had started August 1983 at 18 years old. I applied and was accepted into Mercer University in August 2000. I enrolled in school and took evening classes to work towards completing my BA degree in Public Relations and Organizational Communication. It was an accelerated program; however, I made a commitment to myself and wanted to make my parents proud! I graduated May 12, 2002. My father passed away before I graduated but I know he was more than proud of me that I had gone back to complete what I had started so many years ago. Three months later, I found myself pregnant at 36 years of age, living in a nice, one-bedroom apartment, and NOT married.

I had so many thoughts and emotions running through my mind and body. I was not sure what I was going to do. I was happy, sad, excited, confused, curious, afraid, and filled with wonder; all at the same time! I always knew that I would be married before having children. God's plan was different. Don't get me wrong, I am certainly not the first person to be an unwed mother and certainly will not be the last. I just knew for my life and the plans that I had that this was not the way this was supposed to go. I thought I wanted to marry my daughter's biological father. But I quickly discovered that was not going to happen, and it was painfully clear that I was going to be a single mother. Once this became more real to me, I started doing everything I could to prepare for this new life that was going to be my responsibility. I read to my daughter while she was still in the womb. I talked to her every day. I prayed for her every day. I kept each appointment I had to make sure things were on the right track. I delivered my daughter April 24, 2003 at 11:59 pm and became a new mother. I never envisioned that I would be a single mother at any point in my life. God knew the plans HE had for my life. I just did not know what HIS plans were at that point.

Sometimes life is like a game of chess. When you are playing the game, you may not be able to see all of the moves. However, someone else who walks to the table and looks at it from a distance may be able to see something you don't. One of my aunts shared with me something she told my mother when she learned that I was pregnant. I had a degree from college, a good position with my employer, my own place, a car, and this may (or may not) have been my only opportunity to have a child. I had not considered any of these things. *I was focused on what I didn't have.* Even at 36 years of age, I realized that I was still more concerned with what other people thought about and how they viewed me than being happy and content in the skin that I was born in. I was worried about what other people thought about me as though *they* were in control of my life. I was full of emotions (some of it was hormones) but I knew one thing for sure. I loved my baby girl.

It was just the two of us for the first five years of her life. Yes, I was a single mother, but I was not alone. My daughter's biological father chose not to be a consistent part of our lives. My family that I love so dearly, came through then as they always do. When I needed them for anything to help me with my new daughter, they were there. Without question. I thank God for my family, each and every one of them, but especially my mother. My mother was with me every day for the first two weeks after leaving the hospital to help me with this new life. My sisters came by to help with cleaning so that I could take naps and just hold the baby so I could get a break. I remember once, my brother offered to watch my new baby so I could go to the movies with my sisters. When I tell you I love this group I call my family, I really mean it!

I was so nervous about raising this little girl. I was afraid to leave the hospital. As you already know, no manual exists on how to raise a baby. I had been given the book, "What to Expect When You're

Expecting," by Heidi Murkoff and Sharon Mazel but... what was I supposed to do now that my baby was actually here? Again, God knew the plans HE had for both me and my little one. I had been given the sole responsibility of raising one of GOD's angels and I did not take the task lightly.

My sweet baby girl is one of my biggest blessings in my entire life. My daughter's name has different meanings based on the various origins. In French, her name means May, in Roman mythology, her name means goddess of spring, and in Greek, it means mother. I didn't really look at these meanings initially when choosing her name. However, once the decision was made, these definitions just solidified my decision. My daughter is one of the kindest and dearest people I know. She is consistently looking for the good in others, and it didn't take long for me to see her loving spirit as a child. Her compassion is easy to detect after spending a little time with her.

As she journeyed through her middle school years, I was amazed as I watched her grow and begin to blossom into a young pre-teen. During her seventh-grade year, her history teacher said "She has a kind soul that shines brightly for her peers as well as all younger students. She truly lives out her faith in her actions and example. We are blessed to have her in our school." You can't imagine what joy I felt to read these words about my child. The thing is, she received similar comments from all of her teachers and almost anyone else who came in contact with her.

Now, by no means is she perfect (or is anyone else) but she is a good girl! I continue to watch her as she lives out her life and begin to handle accomplishments as well as disappointments and learn those all-important life lessons. I know that she is watching me too, looking to see how I handle my life. This was one of the first reasons I realized that by becoming a mother, this was my huge game changer. This little person was looking at me, looking to see if she should follow my lead. It became crystal clear to me that I had to be very conscientious about the way I carried myself and the way I handled situations. Good or bad, this child was looking to see how to live her own life.

My daughter became the absolute most important person in the world to me once she was born. My family teased me about how protective I was of her and how she was so attached to me. I remember falling on my knees one night, praying, crying, and telling GOD, *Thank you for trusting me, ME, with this life. One of HIS precious gifts.* I promised to do all I could to take care of her and to nurture her as she grew into a young adult. I now knew this child was not only depending on me, she was watching me because she loves me just as much as I love her.

Even though I thought my child's biological father was supposed to be in her life, GOD knew that was not the case and HE already had chosen the person to be her dad. God knows the plans HE has for each of us (even when we don't). Even through the pain and hurt, all I had to do was put my trust in HIM. As I have prayed and meditated throughout this process, I have been reminded that when things don't go the way you like or think they should go, instead of being upset or angry (like I was), *you must change your perspective.* There is always a reason things *happen* or *don't happen* to or for us. We may not understand it at the time but we must put our trust in GOD and know that at the end of the day, HE knows what's best for us. My mother helped me to realize this as well. As a mother, I now know that it hurts to see your child going through anything painful. My mother's love and her faith in God never wavered and I am certain that her prayers helped me to listen to God speak to my heart. I had to let go and trust that The Almighty knew what was best for not only me, but for my newborn child.

A friend of mine wanted to introduce me to a guy, but I needed time to bond with my new daughter. I did meet the guy sometime later and we dated for almost one year. He was a nice guy but this was not the guy God had intended for me. When the relationship ended, I made a decision to not date anyone and I asked God to heal my heart and allow me to give my very best to my baby girl. I needed to get back to the essence of me. For a full year-and-a-half, I loved my child, created and participated in wonderful mommy-daughter activities, prayed every day, and spent time with my family to feel the unconditional love that comes each time we are together. "Grace brings you back to who you really are."

Life was good but I knew there was more out there for us. My daughter became my life. I only wanted to give her the very best. Even if it meant I had to go without, she would not. I believed God had trusted me with the task of raising one of His children and I did not take that task lightly. I wanted to show Him, that even though I was nervous and excited at the news of being pregnant, I had been reminded that my baby was a blessing, and I had every intention of honoring HIM and showing my gratitude.

As I am writing this, I am participating in a 21-day Meditation Experience with Oprah and Deepak Chopra. The series is centered around Manifesting Grace through Gratitude. This was timely for a number of reasons. These lessons are reminders of who we are how we use various tools to keep us connected to the Almighty and remind us to appreciate the wonderful gift of life. One of the first messages during the meditation experience was "All good things bring gratitude." Truer words have never been spoken.

"Love is like a butterfly. It goes where it pleases and it pleases where it goes." I met my husband, Norris, in February 2006. Two months before my daughter's third birthday. We were introduced to each other by my baby sister and one of my husband's nephews. I now know, that God was right there in this orchestration as HE used the two of them as the vessels to bring my husband into my life. In 2006, Norris called me from the fire station on Valentine's Day. He is now retired after 30 years of service. I didn't recognize the number, so I didn't answer the phone. I called him back once I listened to the message and got his voicemail. He called again, and we finally connected for our very first conversation. We weren't able to talk long since he cut me off in mid-sentence when the fire alarm went off for a call. (I was not used to that. I am not sure that I ever got used to it. Even after our wedding.) We talked on the phone for an entire month before we ever saw each other. Once he asked me out, I was nervous about saying yes because I had been single for the past year-and-a-half, and I wasn't sure if I was really ready. It was easy to talk on the phone and have great conversations. There was no pressure. I finally said *yes* and agreed to meet him for a movie and dinner. He was the perfect gentleman and we had a nice evening. At the end of the night, he asked if he would ever see me again. My response was a definitive yes.

From that point on we dated each other exclusively for an entire year. Norris had planned a trip for us during the President's Day weekend to travel to Beau Rivage in Biloxi, Mississippi. It was a weekend getaway and we had a great time! We returned to Atlanta, Monday, February 19, 2007, and went to my mother's house to pick up my daughter. We were in the family room and my mom was in the kitchen, talking about the trip and having a good visit. All of a sudden, out of nowhere, he comes up to me and looks me in my eye and asks, "Will you marry me?" I was speechless. Then, I shouted, "YES!!!!!!!" My mother was in on the whole thing. The plan was to propose in Biloxi; however, the jewelers were not done with sizing the ring by the time we were scheduled to fly out.

We were married September 28, 2008. God sent me this awesome blessing to allow me to see just how much HE loves me and my daughter and HE knew the path HE had was the one I never thought of for my life with raising my daughter. I still miss my father to this very day. I was very close to him, and it ate me up inside at the thought that my child would not be able to experience that love and that relationship that I had been so blessed to have. Jeremiah 29:11 tells us, "For I know the plans I have for you, declares the Lord, plans to prosper you and not to harm you, plans to give you hope and a future." I shout with joy each time I read or hear this scripture. I am so grateful for God's grace and mercy. I learned that God has a plan for each of us and that it is only through HIS grace, mercy, and will that we take time to see the lessons for the paths that we must take. My steps are ordered, and as long as I stay connected and always ask for HIS guidance, HE will never steer me wrong. Even though I thought my child's biological father was supposed to be in her life, GOD knew that was not the case and HE already had made plans for what we both needed. Even through the pain and hurt, all I had to do was put my trust in HIM.

We have all heard the adage, "Any man can create a baby, but it takes a real man to be a father." My husband stepped in and showed love and respect for my daughter just as he did for me while we were dating. He has shown nothing but continued support to both of us with each and every endeavor we take on. He loves our daughter as if she is his biological child. From the father-daughter dances, to cheering her on during her basketball and volleyball games, to taking her to or picking her up from school, to just spending time together to talk. He is doing what a dad does and doing it with a loving spirit. He is one of the most giving people on this planet. Whatever he has to give to make our lives better, he offers without question. The love and care that flow from his heart each and every day he breathes, shows both me and our daughter who and what a father should be. Everything Norris does, he does with love. Love for me, love for our daughter, love for himself, and love for our family. I thank GOD every day for him and I thank Norris for always listening, for the selfless acts he gives and mostly for the endless amount of love he shows each day to me and our daughter. My husband is a reflection of God's love for me. I continue to be grateful for this blessing that I did not know was waiting just for me.

Our daughter is now 16 years old and looking forward to her junior year in high school. She is growing into a beautiful young lady. Yes, I say "our" because we are a family. My husband loves her as though she is his biological child. She is one of the most genuine people I know. She has a caring heart and is full of compassion. She cares about people and is an advocate for those who can't or are afraid to speak for themselves. She has a gentle nature and a humble spirit. She tries to find the good in all people. Her favorite scripture is Philippians 4:13 "I can do all things through Christ who strengthens me." She has the scripture posted on her two walls in her room. I remind her of this when she begins to have doubts as she grows and experiences life.

Before my daughter was born, I remember traveling to Washington, DC for my baby sister's graduation from Howard University. We were walking down the street, and I was looking rather good (if I do say so myself), and this guy was just hanging on the street and he looked at me and said, "Girl…...you are the Natural Truth!!" I smiled from ear to ear. Interestingly enough, this is how I would describe my daughter. She…...is the natural truth!

Becoming a mother has become one of the biggest blessings in my life. Even as I was learning what to do how to care for and how to teach my daughter the things that she needed to learn, she was teaching me as well. I learned patience, humility, determination and how to be grateful as a result of becoming the mother of my daughter. Her heart is so big and full of love. She only wants to see the very best in people and never wants to hurt anyone. I see the love of Christ through my daughter and I will be eternally grateful to God for choosing me to share this part of my life with this person HE sent to me.

I honestly did not know how I was going to raise a child by myself (although I was never alone), even at 36 years of age. Being solely responsible for my sweet baby girl was unexpected and not part of my plans and although my dream was to have my husband first, the delay was not a denial. Things didn't happen in the order I had initially so desired, in a nice and neat fashion, but they happened the way God intended and it was part of the plan to lift me and allow me to grow into the woman I am today. I love my daughter with every breath of my body and everything I do is for her. She is my WHY!!!!! Because of my desire to honor GOD and keep my promise to HIM regarding my daughter, I was recently offered a position that I applied for, which was a promotion for me. My daughter has been able to watch what perseverance looks like. Even when I applied for other positions and didn't get them, I was able to show and teach her not to give up. She is now enjoying a ring side seat as I launch my voiceover business, CJN Voiceovers. I work hard and live to be a shining example of what hard work and dedication will yield. She has watched my dedication, my persistence, and the hard work that goes into starting something and seeing it to fruition, One of my absolute favorite songs (and I have plenty) is "Closer" by Goapele. I do what I do for me and at the same time, I do what I do to show my daughter to never give up on your dreams.

After completing the 21-Day Meditation Experience with Oprah and Deepak, I learned that to experience complete freedom, you must be free within yourself. At 53 years of age, I can honestly say that I am free to live the life within me out loud. My daughter reminds me through her spirit, to always be true to myself. I have always been a sensitive soul and my daughter has this same trait. Earlier this year, a friend of mine did an exercise with me that allowed me to see what my essence is. It was so eye-opening and humbling to learn what my true friends think about me. What shows up when I do and what qualities do I bring into the room? This was the question I asked seven to 10 different very close people in my life. Their responses brought tears of happiness and joy---a level of sunshine, authentic, nurturing, beauty, glowing personality, and charismatic. These were some of the responses I received and I acknowledge them all. This is who I am. I am a daughter, a sister, a wife, a mother, a niece, a cousin, a friend, an aunt, but most important, *I am a child of GOD!* I don't have to be ashamed, afraid, disappointed, or frustrated about anything that has happened or that will happen. I believe God sent my daughter and my husband to me to show me once again, all of the traits He had given to me when He created me.

Delight yourself in the Lord, and He will give you the desires of your heart. (Psalm 37:4) I have received exactly what I dreamed of as a child. Maybe not in the order I expected, nevertheless, God sent the things to me in the order that HE wanted me to have them. God knows exactly what HE is doing. I am married. I live in a nice house, and I have a child. I am a work in progress. I take each day one day at a time. I give my best, and I continue to dream and work to improve who I am each day. My life is not perfect, but my life is good. As I work to build my brand and my business, I know that I am being prepared for outstanding blessings. My inner light is guiding me. I am succeeding no matter what it takes because I am working and preparing each day to make the rest of my dreams come true. I had the awesome opportunity to hear Fabian Cousteau, the grandson of the legend, Jacques-Yves Cousteau, at a conference last year. He shared with the audience some profound words from his grandfather. "When one person, for whatever reason, has the chance to lead an extraordinary life, he has no right to keep it to himself." My story isn't over. My life is not my own, as I work and stay committed, it is my responsibility to share with others along the way.

Oprah Winfrey shared a conversation she had with Maya Angelou once. "God has put a rainbow in every cloud and the rainbow is coming. Say thank you even when you can't see it. Say thank you. Prepare yourself, so you can be a rainbow to someone else." The message is to always be grateful. Even when you don't understand why. Be grateful. As I continue to live my life, my goal is to be a rainbow to those that may need it during a cloudy day.

It is a beautiful sight to see a rainbow in the sky after a cleansing rain. It is a reminder of the fullness and greatness of the Lord Almighty. I smile when I see a rainbow, I smile when I see the sun rise, I smile each time I see a butterfly, I smile when I see the clouds in the sky from an airplane window. I smile each morning when I look at the blessings God bestowed upon me. He keeps his promises and for this I am grateful. I smile when I see my husband and I smile with all the joy in my heart when I see my beautiful baby girl as I watch her growing each day into a beautiful young woman. I say, THANK YOU!

Fireside Reflections

Keywords and Takeaways:

1. Sometimes life is like a game of chess. When you are playing the game, you may not be able to see all of the moves.

2. Being more concerned with what other people think

Life will happen and things may not go according to plan, however they will unfold according to God's plan. That is what was learned from Candace's story. Much like Omozua, Candace had the image of her life being revealed one way, when it actually revealed itself in another, but with the same result she desired. She married and found love with a husband who stepped in and became the father to her daughter that she wanted in their life.

Being more concerned with what other people think rather than being focused on your own fulfillment in life is a recipe for anxiety, low self-esteem, and a negative competitiveness with yourself and with others.

What are the desires of your heart? The Bible says in Habakkuk 2:2, to write the vision and make it plain. Remember, the path to get there may look different that you planned, but eventually you'll get there with the faith of a mustard seed!

_____

_____

_____

_____

BUILDING MY FAITH IN GOD

J Hill

Understand there are situations and adversities that will unexpectedly occur in your life that can possibly overtake you like a world wind. But wait! Whatever situation is going on now, that is a part of the process and you will either be overtaken or find yourself repeating the same struggle repeatedly. When this happens, you leave many who are looking at your life as hopeless. It is paramount that we glory in tribulations, knowing that tribulation produces patience; patience, experience; and experience, hope. (Rom 5:3-5; KJV). I discovered long ago that people are looking at my life and how I handle adversity. I'm going to share with you pieces of my process. It was my turn to go through hardship and adversity in a manner that I never imagined or even thought I could endure. But who knows you better than you know yourself, the strength that you possess, and the gift of resilience that lies dormant? You never know what or how much you can endure until you are faced with difficulty or adversity. I will share with you what I did to allow the process to help me build stamina, patience, endurance, character, resiliency, and ultimately, my faith in God. The advice and steps outlined below will show you how I learned how to *wait* during the process.

Have you even wondered what sort of things could have transpired during the waiting process? Allow me to share with you what my beginning or wait looked like. I was a normal 7-year-old little girl who loved life and my little gold cat named Blimmie. My home life was fueled with domestic violence owing to my alcoholic father. I used to be so frightened when my father would come home, because he would frequently start an argument with my mother, which would lead to a huge fight. The kids would often be left with the older siblings and my aunt. This particular day, my mother decided we would go into town to visit my grandmother's house. Everyone, including me, was super excited. What I didn't know was that this visit would change the course of my life forever. I never felt I would have anything to be concerned about since everyone we were around during these visits were family members. But at the tender age of 7 wearing a plaid red- and-white checker top and denim skirt, I was molested for the first time by a female relative who I admired. This event was so traumatizing that I became withdrawn, oftentimes isolating myself from my 7 other siblings.

No one except for my eldest brother noticed my isolation because there was always some type of confusion in the home. Everyone was in their own world dealing with the turmoil the best that they could. Several months had past and we were celebrating my 8th birthday with cake and ice cream. Ironically, I was pulled aside by my aunt, who asked, "Did you enjoy me touching you?" I said, "No!" and she never touched me again. I thought things were going to get better for me but they didn't. This roller coaster of mine starts up again but, unfortunately, I'm the only one still on the ride. Shortly after my 8th birthday celebration, I was molested by my eldest brother. My reason for not saying anything was because my mother was already going through enough, dealing with my abusive father and his drinking, and I did not want to add extra stress or to be a problem. I tried my hardest to stay out of the way and never be around him alone, but he would always find me or come in the room when everyone was sound asleep. I would just lie there and not say a word, but in my heart I was screaming, "I HATE YOU"!

I felt like a garbage can that would only be used when someone needed to bump their trash after being molested I didn't feel like I was enough or that I deserved love, and I felt that defeat was my destiny and that abundance wasn't for a girl like me. After all, I'm am ugly girl with short, red hair and nobody paid any attention to me anyways. The molestation traumatized me in that I started bed-wetting and sometimes having bowel movements on myself, especially at night because I was terrified to leave the bed. It was during this time I started getting burned on my bottom with the head of an ironing-comb as punishment for using it on myself. This continued but still I never said one word about being molested because I was afraid. Why? To this day, I don't know. Then, I started hearing that I would never be nothing because I was fast. Actually, I was a very quiet and shy kid, and there was still so much I didn't understand. I started believing that I DID NOT DESERVE LOVE OR ANYTHING GOOD HAPPENING FOR OR TO ME. Unfortunately, I still cannot recall ever feeling loved.

I believe his dislike for me is what motivated him to allow two of his friends to molest me in the fields while he watched. I recall him telling the two brothers, "Man it's okay, she won't say nothing because I always do it to her." I became depressed and miserable but nobody noticed. Again, I never said anything because I didn't want to cause confusion, and at this time, I really didn't think anyone would believe me because who would molest his own sister? This would have to be a very sick individual. He and his two friends molested and raped me until I was 11 years old. At this time in my life I was a very angry pre-teen. I remember family members constantly saying that I had a nasty attitude and poor hygiene. I purposely neglected my hygiene hoping that would deter them from raping me, but they didn't care. Prior to my 12th birthday my mother and father had the worst fight ever, so my uncle sent for us to come and live with him in another state to get away from the drama. I was so excited because I was tired of those brothers raping me and hoping my brother would finally stop molesting me. We arrived at our new address on my 12th birthday. The family got settled in good and mother found a job. All was well. I found a church that I liked that had a lot of young people my age.

Going to church was my escape from my childhood traumas. A couple months living at the new home, my brother started molested me again. I didn't have the courage to say anything, and I felt worthless because of it. I resolved in my heart that I would continue to deal with my brother molesting me and that I would never tell a soul. I chose to use the church as my safe haven because every time I went I felt so much better afterward. Home was the place I feared and never feel protected or loved. I continued with my life as usual until one day I was invited to attend a revival. I accepted the invite with no expectations of anything miraculous happening to me or for me. But I was sadly mistaken. As I sat in the service, the words from the revivalist began to prick my heart so much so that uncontrollable tears flowed from my eyes. A presence that I had never felt before pierced my heart, and I felt these amazing warm arms engulf my entire body. Although I was raised in the church and witnessed many of those I loved being made free from the obstacles and weights that would so easily beset them or otherwise keep them bound and entangled with the harsh reality of life's issues.

Unfortunately, I believed that I was undeserving of anything good because of the type of adversities I had endured growing up. Somehow I knew this presence didn't care what I had experienced but rather wanted to make things better for me. This took place in April 1979. I know this date clearly because when I came to myself, I had a measure of confidence that was unbeknownst even to me. I left service that night with a high that I cannot explain in the English language. All I know is that later that night when my brother walked into that room, I was going to give him a word and I did. Unfortunately, I was unprepared for the response I would receive the following day, when I would finally divulge to my mother what had been happening to me. Of course, she did not believe me and felt as though I just wanted attention because at this particular time one of my older sisters was receiving all of the attention because of her accomplishments. Thankfully, she proceeded to take me to the emergency room for a checkup and they in fact validated that I was not a virgin. But still nobody believed me and although my brother never touched me again, he made my life miserable every opportunity he got. I can recall when dating as teenagers, my husband (now) and I were sitting at the table talking and my brother walked in. He immediately became angry and smashed a whole pie in my face.

I never explained to him why my brother did that, but I knew it was jealousy. For years I wanted my family to believe what he had done to me and as time progressed I left it alone. That is until one evening when I was 19 years old. I saw my brother's face flash across the news for doing to someone else what he and his two buddies had done to me for 4 years.

NOTE: If you have someone in your life who you truly care about and they're acting out and you cannot seem to put a finger on it or have a reason why this person is behaving in such an odd manner, ask the hard questions that many of us won't ask or are just afraid to ask or don't even want to acknowledge because I thought all was well and there was no reason for my daughter to be acting and making the type of decisions that she was making. And all the time there was indeed a reason but unfortunately that reason was beyond my wildest dreams and devastating to the core. We must provide a safe environment for our loved ones to comfortable in when talking to us about difficult subjects and hurtful things. We must have an ear to hear and recognize their body language is speaking to us louder than their facial expressions that are speaking louder than words could ever say. Most important, their behaviors are speaking louder than words can ever express. It is so important that our intuitive mind is functioning at its highest so that we can see and hear the unsaid and the unseen.

The things I suffered as a child shaped my perception, beliefs, and acceptance of a life that consisted of lack, mediocrity, and constant desire. Becoming a young adult was not easy for me because I found myself looking for love in all the wrong places. This time I believe I found real love because he and I shared everything. I finally opened up to him about my childhood and the dreaded pie in the face incident comes up. I could not believe he remembered that incident because it was so many years ago. He asked, "Hey, why did your brother smashed that pie in your face"? I shared with him the horrors of my childhood, including the molestation, and he understood. Hence, that conversation was never spoken of again. This young man came from a great family and I would often wonder what he saw in a girl like me. As a matter of fact, he was the first person who I ever met who lived with both biological parents. As our friendship grew, he literally became my best friend.

I was always happiest when I was around him because I could be myself and he never pressured me for sex. We often talked about getting married and having children after graduation. Everyone knew us as Bonnie and Clyde because when you saw one you always saw the other! It was a relationship that one could say was too good to be true. Well, it was too good to be true because during our senior year he was busted during a drug sting and sent to a boy's camp unbeknownst to me. Those old feelings of being unworthy and alone resurfaced because my best friend was gone and I didn't know what happened. You see, because he was from a well-to-do family, they were embarrassed by his conduct. After being sent to the boy's camp, his mother decided I didn't need no man like this in my life because she perceived me as a good church going girl. She never would divulge to me where he was and how long he would be gone. So, I wrote him letters every week and would give them to her, hoping that he would receive them and explain to me what happened. I concluded that he wanted to break things off with me but didn't have the courage to do so face-to-face.

So, my actions moved on but my heart never did. In my attempt to fill the void of missing my best friend, I got into another relationship and ended up getting pregnant. Rod and I would see each other through the years, but we never discussed what happened and why there was never closure with our relationship when we were teenagers. I was unhappily married to my children's father, dealing with infidelity, adultery, and emotional abuse from both him and his family. No matter what I did, it was never good enough and he could not stop cheating on me. I started getting tired emotionally and desperately wanted more for my children. I continued to perform my wifely duties while he continued to cheat and do his own thing. Have you ever had an unction in your spirit so that you would actually dream about the person your spouse is committing adultery with? Well I have! I starting having these dreams about my brother's girlfriend. Only, in the dream she looked like me, dressed like me, and acted like me. Except, I would perceive her as being naked and I would say, "Doesn't she know that she's naked"? I didn't understand what the dream meant. So, I continued to pray and deal with the foolishness from my husband at the time.

Several years later, I was sitting in a church and the spirit of God began to move. The preacher started to prophecy, called me out, and said, "I need to tell you something, it will hurt but God will bring you through this." Of course, I was nervous as I listened attentively. He proceeded to say, "A sister you befriended is having your husband in your house and in your bed." I almost fainted because prior to going to service, we had just had an argument about condoms being in his work bag. I was devastated, and the old feelings of worthlessness resurfaced. Then, it dawned on me that the person he referenced my ex-husband was having an affair with was the same person I was seeing in my dreams. I had to really seek God to get my mind right because my first reactions were to kill him and her. However, I thought about who would raise my children if I went to prison for murder?

When I confronted him about the affair, all he could say was, "Oh! Well sorry you had to find out like that." Blood boiling and rage was about to take me over, and a voice even told me to run him over. I told God that He needed to help me because I was going to do bodily harm to my husband with his car. I finally drove off with tears flowing so heavily I could hardly see the road. Y'all, I had to dry fast, read my bible, and stay in constant prayer just to maintain my sanity because the person he was cheating with was a close friend of the family. After several months of fasting, meditating, reading my bible, and biblical affirmations, God freed me to go visit her. I showed up at her door, bubbly and happy like usual so that I would not alarm her. As we joked around, I said, "Oh! Sister, I know about your affair with my husband but I wanted you to know I'm not angry with you and that you have a soul and I'm praying for you." Then, I left and haven't spoken with her since. That was 25 years ago. There's no need to get revenge or be spiteful because vengeance is mine said the Lord. (Romans 12:9) "Dearly beloved, avenge not yourselves, but rather give place unto wrath: for it is written, Vengeance is mine; I will repay, saith the Lord."

I am divorced and have learned how to love me and accept me as I am with all of my flaws. It would be 15 years later that I would finally get the opportunity to speak with my best friend from high school. We ran into each other at the neighborhood store. Our eyes meet and his smile brightened up the store as he said, "Hey, stranger"! We have small talk about how things are going. I tell him that, "Everything is going great"! When in fact it was not but I was happily divorced for 4 years. Being the gentleman that he is, he says, "Oh! That's good, and you still look like the teenager I called my best friend." I smiled as he talked more, and then I took his number with no intentions of calling him, as I'd actually become content with being alone. I didn't want to risk being hurt again. A couple of weeks passed, and I felt an urge to call him. I called and he was just as nervous as I was. We talked for almost one hour and decided to meet each other at a local Starbuck's. Mind you, I do not drink coffee so whatever possessed me to say Starbuck's I don't know. We met at 10 pm and ended up talking –until 6 am the next morning.

Y'all we talked about everything that happened in each of our lives and most important, we discussed how I felt when he dropped off the planet and I never heard from him again. He explained to me what happened about getting busted in a drug sting at school and going to a boy's camp in Spring Mountain. His mother didn't give him any of my letters until his release. He stated that as soon as he was released he read all of my letters. Then, he came straight to my house, only to see me from a distance standing on my porch, pregnant. He said that he immediately made a U-turn and headed back to his house crying and brokenhearted because he knew I had moved on. Of course, this was a very emotional night and all those feelings that I thought were gone had literally resurfaced, it literally felt like we had never split up 15 years earlier. He told me that he knew I was married but that didn't stop him from loving me and that he told God he would never marry anyone else but me. Although I had been married twice before, he didn't care because he loved me and had never stopped. Would you believe he asked me to marry him that night after I divulged to him that I was divorced?

He told me that if I said "Yes" that he would make up for every day of hurt and rejection I had ever experienced because he felt a level of responsibility after he was sent away and I didn't know why. Initially, I said no, because I was concerned about what people would say. But at the end of the day, people didn't know our history or story. After several months of secretly dating, and after being asked to marry him for a third time, I thought it would be best if I said yes.

Joshua

Do you think my testimony could be any greater than this? Do you think my process could be any more devastating than this?

Unfortunately, Joshua was an angry juvenile, an angry teenager, and now he was an angry young man because he longed for a relationship with his father that was never there for him. Although he had the support of so many amazing men in his life; like any son he still longed for a father-son relationship with his natural father. He was a great kid but had a temper that was out of this world. He didn't bother anybody but if you brought the foolishness to him he would surely shut it down. I can't even begin to count the times he got in trouble at school through no fault of his own. Unfortunately, it was always the other child bothering him because he was quiet, but once that temper got stirred up, you could literally hang it up because it was going to get ugly. He had always been a no-nonsense type of kid, but a kid, nonetheless, who loved and adored his mother, who was a jokester, and who could sing. Have you ever been told or had a feeling in your gut and soul that your child was going to suffer and suffer greatly because of the commission on his life. This is how I felt about Joshua and I never understood why. But in the midst of that suffering God promised he would not kill him.

The Spirit of God spoke to me and told me that he was going to suffer greatly but that he was not going to kill him because he has a special calling on his life that required great suffering. I can recall him being a toddler going into his adolescent years and my mother used to say, "That little boy is too good to be true, he's going to give you hell when he becomes a teenager." I would ask my mother, "Why do you say that, that's mean." She said, "I'm telling you he is too good to be true and when he gets older he is going to break your heart." Well, my mother is resting in heaven and she was surely right, because her words have come to fruition. What she was saying is that as a toddler and adolescent he was the most well-mannered and behaved child any of us had ever seen. Therefore, she was confident that his negative behaviors or acting out would start when he would become a teenager. She did not believe that a child could just be a great kid forever. He was surrounded by several strong men in the church. However, they were no substitute for his natural father, and this made him very angry. I longed for him to be a part of his son's life. But unfortunately, it just didn't work out that way. As he became older, we noticed his ability to sing and dance. He got really involved in crumping, street dancing, and he even won a few dance contests.

On one occasion, I allowed him to stay in California with his dad for what I thought was going to be an entire summer. But it didn't work out that way. He ended up returning home about a month-and-a-half after leaving. I believe he was 8 or 9 years old then. When they brought him back to me, I was informed they had to put him on Ritalin because he had ADHD. This did not sit well with me at all and in fact it made me very angry. I felt like they disregarded me as his parent and main support system and to place him put on medication without my knowledge and consent was wrong. Unfortunately, I was not privy to this until I picked him up from the airport. He was no longer the happy, bubbly kid who left. When he returned, he arrived resembling a zombie. So, that also caused a rift between his father and me. I promptly took him off the medication and he was fine. He was no longer hyperactive, in fact the only time he got into any type of trouble was when someone did something to him that caused his temper to flare. His outbursts always stemmed from lack of a close relationship with his father.

Although Josh had severe anger issues, I can honestly say he has never been disrespectful to me or to his stepfather. As a matter of fact, on several occasions he's told my husband, "He was truly the best father that me and my siblings could ever have had. And the thing that I respect the most about you, is that you treat my mama like a queen. You love us and we can feel your love for us. Thank you for helping my mom take care of us." Joshua acknowledged that he has a temper, saying it has nothing to do with us but everything to do with him just being angry. Not understanding why and longing for that relationship with his father. He got himself in trouble when he was about 12 years old. Vandalizing an abandoned house, we had to go to court. I watched my husband stick by his side during the entire process. I believe that showed Joshua how much my husband loves and respected him as his son. His journey in becoming a teenager was all about his singing and dancing. He participated in the church plays during Christmas and Easter. He gained a large following because he was such an amazing dancer. The neighborhood even began to call him Psycho.

Shortly after this he started implementing more of the singing with his dancing and was putting together his own routines forming at local schools and other talent shows in the city---and winning. When he saw the notoriety that he was getting from his singing and dancing, he began to obsess over becoming an R&B singer. I used to affectionately tell him, "Son that voice is not for R&B that voice that God gave you is for the church." And of course, he would say, "Mom I can sing gospel and sing R&B, too." Of course, I agreed with him, and he asked to me if I would agree to manage him and help him get out there in the media. Of course, I said, "I don't know anything about helping nobody become no singer." But as a mother you don't want to tell your child "no" when they express such passion for something that they love doing. I found myself getting busy on the Internet searching for Wendy Williams or anyone (Ellen, Oprah) who promoted talent on their shows. Even 106 and Park had a competition where you could compete on the spot; there would be four rounds, and in each round you must progress to the next round until there's only one person that would go to the live show.

I sent tapes of Josh singing and dancing to all the places I could possibly think of. Two months later, I received an email from the producers of 106 and Park and to New York to audition. Wow! I could not believe that my son got a spot to audition for 106 and Park, Everybody was happy. God has blessed him with an amazing voice and the ability to dance, but there is one thing about him that annoyed family members and many of his friends. Joshua was very arrogant and very cocky in his ability to sing and dance, not to mention tall, dark, and handsome, standing at 6'4" and weighing in at 230 pounds. Yes, was handsome and the tallest out of all my children, including me and his father. Joshua was so excited this was his big break. At

18 years old, his dream to be on television was coming true so of course everyone was excited for him. I set him down because I knew that he was arrogant and cocky and I said, "Son, do not go around bragging about going on 106 and Park, do not discuss this with anyone outside of the family." Of course, his response was, "Yes, ma'am." He always says that but Josh couldn't do it because it was exciting news, and he wanted to tell everybody that he encountered.

I have made up in my mind that I am more than a conqueror through Him that loves me and most importantly I can do all things through Christ which strengthens me. So, I'm getting stronger spiritually, mentally, emotionally, and I am getting glad in my heart for the opportunity to be a witness of what God can do and what anyone can do if they would just embrace the trial instead of fighting against it. Embrace it, love it, woo it, and before you know it, you are out of it.

I am strong enough to receive this call two months after my baby boy Joshua turned 18 on August 21st. On October 1st at 1 am, I hear, "Clark County detention Center on the line, "Yes, you have a collect call from Joshua." My heart was already prepared, I calmly said, "Yes, I will accept the call." On the other end was my 18-year-old crying. I looked over at my husband and said, "Baby, Joshua is in jail." My husband's first response was, "Are you kidding me? How much more can you bear? How much more can one person take? Baby are you alright?" I calmly said, "Yes, I am fine." I began to talk to him and he began to tell me what he was charged with. Burglary and robbery. I asked him who was with him. He named the individuals who were with him. I told him, "Okay, well there's nothing I can do right now. We will just have to wait until the morning to see what can be done." My son began crying hysterically. I could not recognize or understand his words. He began to apologize to me and saying that I didn't deserve what happened because he knew what I had already been going through during the last 4 years.

He began to show some remorse and empathy for what he did, and empathy and concern for me, his mother. And then he proceeded to say, "I know pops is going to be so mad with me right now." I responded with, "Yes, but that's nothing that you need to worry about right now, we just have to see how we're going to get through this." He asked me if I still loved him and whether we were still best friends. With tears in my eyes I said, "Yes, son I love you, and we are still best friends." I proceeded to ask him if he truly understood what this means. He was silent for a moment and then he said, "Yes, ma'am." I asked, "What does this mean?" He said, "I won't get to be on 106 and Park and my dream to be a singer is going down the tubes." I agreed with him in that he wouldn't be on 106 and Park, but I did not agree with the fact that his dreams were going down the tubes.

I began to remind him of some things that I said to him about his gift to sing, his gift to encourage young people and to inspire them, and I reminded him how God had let me know when he was a toddler that he would suffer but that his suffering won't kill him. His suffering would in fact help him with maturity---he would gain experience, patience, character, and stamina. This was hard for me because this is my youngest son at the time. But even in this moment, I could encourage him and let him know that this is a situation that he would have to endure. He now must prepare himself mentally for it. Then I said to him, "I'm just in disbelief that you are literally heading to the same place where you and I would visit your brother." A couple of months passed and they finally had his arraignment after several rescheduled court appearances. Joshua pled guilty to the charge an accepted a 5-year deal.

If he did his 5 years with all good time, he would have only 12 months of probation once he is released. Unfortunately, during this whole year, going to court, accepting all the collect calls, going down to the detention Center to visit him, not once has his natural father gone to visit or shown up at a court hearing. He never even helped by putting money on his books. This made him angrier because he said to me, "Mom, I know that he's never been there for me, but out of anytime I need his support, it would be right now." While I am going through this, I assured him that I reached out to him many times, but unfortunately, there was always an excuse about why he couldn't do this or could not do that and finally my son said to me, "Just leave him alone." He knows where I am going and he knows where I will be. He said to me, "I have made it this far without him, and I will continue to make it. As long as I have you and my pops, I will be just fine." Today, I have grown to see that God is the same God I witnessed as a child and is the same God who is blessing, healing, and delivering in the 21st Century.

A declaration by which I wait until my change comes.

"I can do all things through Christ which strengthens me." Philippians 4:13 (KJV).

I've resolved to build stamina so I can go through my struggles with grace and ease as so to encourage and be the gift of hope to someone else in their time of struggle. Faith is built exponentially when we embrace our struggles rather than expending energy complaining, murmuring, and idle wishing for the struggle to be removed from you. There have been times in my life when I simply didn't have the mental strength or the courage to embrace my struggles. Negative thoughts and feelings about my situation would bombard my mind constantly. But I am reminded of a scripture in the Bible that says:

"And we know that all things work together for the good of those that love God, to them who are the called according to his purpose." Romans 8:28 (KJV). As I matured, my faith and belief in God's ability to meet my every need grew also. Well-developed faith helped me to quickly turn my breakdowns into *breakthroughs and opportunities* to inspire someone else to stand therefore. Embracing the process, whatever life throws at you, opens the floodgates to peace and assurance that everything will be alright. This is my written testament of the benefits that waiting change will come, such as assurance in knowing beyond a doubt that you can embrace whatever betides you, no matter how difficult or tumultuous the situation may be. After all, if I can do it, after all that I've been through, so can you.

Fireside Reflections

Keywords and Takeaways:

"I can do all things through Christ which strengthens me." Philippians 4:13 (KJV).

These are the words of LIFE! What I know for sue is that although everyone has not encountered being sexually violated, experienced infidelity, failed marriage, or to have a child in prison, but one thing for certain, we have all encountered adversity. J Hill was no different, however her steadfast faith kept her going and allowed her to also be the strength that her son needed in his time of need. She stated that well-developed faith helped her to quickly turn her breakdowns into breakthroughs and opportunities to inspire others.

What is your go-to scripture of choice when times are challenging, and you need reassurance or a good word that will inspire you to press forward? What is that for you?

_____

_____

_____

_____

_____

_____

_____

_____

_____

_____

HOLD ON TO YOUR DREAMS
Juanita Grant

My mom was 17 and my dad was 18 when I was born. They were recent graduates from high school. I am the oldest of four children from my mother and four from my father. The oldest in this family's generation and the first grandchild on either side. Parenting isn't easy and it does not come with instructions. I call myself "the test baby, the baby doll."

As a child, I remember walking hand-in-hand with my father. Always a fashionable dresser, one of his trademarks was his long, black leather trench coat. He reminded me of John Shaft, who was an incredibly handsome man. I was proud of my father because of the man he represented in my life. He was strong, and I felt comfortable and secure—just holding his hand I felt a sense of pride walking down the street. The main reason I remembered my father however was because of his light complexion, like mine. When I was 3 years old, I remember watching my father walk down the street, and the scream that emanated in my belly that day was, "I want my daddy to come back"! Was he leaving me for good? He kept walking, and I kept standing in the hallway watching. I cried and cried and watched him until I couldn't see him anymore. My father had had enough! He wanted to go into the service to make a better life for himself and his family. He expected to have the support of his mother and stepfather---and followed the lead of his stepdad who he loved so much. The Army stationed him far away from me and my mom, initially in California. It was difficult grasping that I couldn't talk with him all the time, and that the only way we could talk was on the phone. I missed him so much and cried whenever I thought about him. I often wondered if I would ever see him again---I really needed my dad, but my "daddy" was gone, and it hurt deeply.

Growing up was not always easy. Sometimes, parents make decisions that really affect the lives of their children— not realizing how much those choices can hurt or traumatize them. As adults, we sometimes make decisions that will either help someone children to grow or that will stifle their growth. We grew up in a nice area of Dorchester in a three-family home. When I was a kid, I always had premonitions or dreams and never understood why. I would dream things and they would happen 1 week later or sometimes the very next day---it was really scary at times. I would remember that I had been there before and I would know exactly what was going to happen next. This was so incredibly unnerving as a child.

I had an aunt and an uncle, both of whom were 1 year younger than me. Both of my grandmas decided to get pregnant around the same time! How about that?

My love was purchased. I had such a lonely childhood---my mom worked 20-hour days to pay the bills and to keep her mind off the nightly "thumpings." I had a big, canopy bed in my own room and nice things. But, I didn't like the style of clothes that my mom chose for me because they were old-fashioned and just ugly! I preferred the hand-me-downs from my Auntie J. I remember always being with one of my aunties or with my grandmother growing up where we always had to sit down and eat together. This was the etiquette followed on both sides of the family. We would have our lunch with a snack had to wait for our drinks until our food was complete. We would also do certain things together like play outside, make dirt pies using dried worms as candles, or play tag or hide & seek.

I was always an honor roll student in school and academically performed very well. But no matter what, it just seemed that the kids never liked me. I was skinny and frequently wore the hand-me-downs from my Aunty J. who worked at a hair salon, so I always looked pretty decent.

In order to attend the local school, I took an exam and aced it! All of the students who I enjoyed hanging around were older than me—I didn't care for the kids who were my own age, as they were "childish." I started out doing very well, and I would always do my work, which at times was intense. My mom would help me as much as she could so that I could meet my deadlines. Although she would yell from time to time, when she helped me with my work, that was "our time" together, so I took what I could get!

Sometimes when we rode home on the bus, I noticed a dark-skinned guy from the football team staring at me who would have girls who fought over him all the time. His stare, which pierced right through me, made me nervous, so I always tried to stay away from him. I never knew what his intentions were, and I really got bad vibes from him.

One day, when I was walking down the hall between classes, the bell rang and I ran to the locker room because I needed my books for class. I walked inside of the locker room as the other students started leaving and began struggling with the combination to my locker as always! Frustrated, I found myself alone, "Man, open up"! Still no success. Hearing the locker room door lock in the background, my lock finally opened! I grabbed my books and started heading off to class, I will be late. I thought I saw someone, but didn't care I reached to open the door and oddly enough, it wouldn't open. I thought, "Now, my teachers are really going to kill me! I'll try the other door."

Then, I asked myself, "Did I just see someone"?   I was really beginning to feel that something wasn't right. I reached to bang on the door and suddenly he grabbed my hand. My heart was beating so hard. He walked me to the back of the room and said, "Be quiet and just walk!" I thought, "Why me"? He said, "Don't scream!" I looked around. I was only 12 years old and light as a feather, weighing in at approximately 113 pounds. He was very muscular, huge---a senior on the football team, just musty and ugly!

"Please, don't hit me!" is all I could muster up the courage to say. His hands grabbed my neck and he started kissing me. I'd never experienced anything like this before---his mouth tasted so foul. His large hands started rubbing my small chest, and---it felt weird, and I felt funny. He began sucking on my stuff. I was horrified and embarrassed! I wanted to scream, but I froze. There was nothing around to hit him, so I stayed still to avoid additional pain. While still holding on to my neck, he led me on the floor. I was so nervous yet curious, as all of this was so new to me.

All of those girls on the bus were fighting over him because he was sleeping with all of them. Call me naïve, but I had always thought sleeping was just that—lying down in the bed and going to sleep. He then started pulling down my underwear. No boy had ever seen me like this. I hate him! This is private! I started crying. In a barely audible voice, I whimpered, "No." He said, "Shut up!"! I begged with him and said, "Please, no!" He said, "I know that you really want it." His arrogance implied that I had been looking at him with interest, which was not the case at all." He shoved his finger inside of my private spot. I never knew the hole was built like that. He pushed another finger in. It hurt so badly! He positioned his body above mine with his finger still inside. He told me not to scream or that he would hurt me. He took his hand and opened me up down there and then I felt this fat, wet, hard thing, which he pushed into my hole. I had never… He covered my mouth, took his knees, and spread my legs. I couldn't stop crying and tried to push him off of me. But, he was much more muscular and larger than I was. He pinned me to the floor and pushed himself deeper inside of me. The pain was unbearable. I couldn't handle this torture. When he finished, he took off his shirt and cleaned me up down there. Then, he pulled me up to my feet---I hurt so bad fell up against the locker. "If you ever tell on me," he whispered, "I will hurt you and your family." I followed you before and I know where you live," he said. He walked out the locker room as if nothing ever happened. Except that it did.

Since I kept replaying the nightmare over and over again, I started failing in school. So, I was transferred to a middle school. I hated leaving my friends at my current school, and it truly felt like the beginning of the end of my life. You see, at my new school, the kids started jumping me and calling me "white girl," "flat back," and "iron board chest." The kids at my new school looked mutated with their larger-than-life-sized triple DDD- and FFF-sized boobs! They were taller and thicker than I was, too. The good news was that that there were three of us---two Linda's and me. One Lauren was dark-skinned and the other Lauren was light–skinned like me. All three of us had long hair and were very pretty young ladies from good families compared to the other students who loved to abuse us. "Light Lauren" told us that her mom had a mental illness and said that she felt she may develop it when she got older, but we stuck together.

As "The Three Musketeers," we would laugh together, until we got jumped by kids from the middle school. Sometimes, we wondered what would happen if we committed suicide and how those kids would feel then. It was terrible not knowing how many people were going to jump us on a particular day or where they would be hiding to pounce on us. We were nice kids and wanted friends who loved and cared about us like they did with each other. We were about being students and not "street" like them. We didn't smoke and drink like them. We weren't "fast" like them. Our innocence was just taken from us, and not by choice. We couldn't control our fate or circumstances. One Lauren's uncle molested her, I was raped, and the other Lauren knew the same sexual fate as us, but would never say who the family member was---but he or she raped her repeatedly and she was so afraid. She would come to school with bruises and often carry the shame that sexual victims are taught to bear. Why didn't anyone think more of us? Why did "they" feel we should be hurt all the time? One Linda started cutting herself. I begged her to hold on and not give up. I prayed for her, and I begged GOD to keep her safe from hurting herself! The other Lauren began to get depressed. She was spiraling downward. I begged her to hold on. As for myself, I hated myself and everyone else hated me. I could no longer look in the mirror. I was no longer special anymore. HE took "special" from me that day in the locker room and so did that other man who used to follow me every day, begging me to be his girlfriend. I didn't care about myself---not anymore. I sorely needed love and attention, in any way that I could get it. HE told me that HE loved me... HE showed me that HE loved me... and HE gave love to me. I really wanted my mother to tell me that she loved me, but she never did. How could she when *she hated me*? You could see it in her eyes---the resentment and disappointment was so deep! So, I settled for HIS love to feel loved. I was convinced that *HE loved me.*

As I would sleep, I could feel something kick me. I thought I was losing my mind! Again? What the heck?! This went on for some time, and I was clueless. I had no idea what was going on inside of me. Then, one day while watching TV, I saw a lady who was giving birth. "No, this can't be happening to me! Mom would kill me! Should I just kill myself now? What do I do"? I then began to comprehend that a baby was growing inside of me. When the baby would kick, I began to play with it. Are you a girl or a boy? I was so happy now! I finally had someone who I could love and would return that love. I told no one about my pregnancy because I felt it was my responsibility to protect the life inside of me! Then, one day, many months later, Vicky, who I thought was my friend, asked if I was pregnant. I did not respond since she was always so nosy. She pried in everyone's business! Vicky said, "You have to be"! She ran ahead of me, and once again I was jumped by a lot of students. Fighting, I became out of breath protecting myself---the big, black girl, Patches, was wailing all on me, why? I tried to run home and could barely breathe.

I cleaned up my tears and walked home. There she was talking to my mother's husband, the man who hated me. Why was she saying goodbye to him? What did she do? He said, "Your mother is in the house and wants to speak to you." I walked inside of the house and received the beating of my life! I protected my baby, though. My mother said, "You are pregnant and going to get an abortion"! She was also pregnant and said, "You are not going to have your child and I'm not going to take care of two babies." I said, "Put me up for adoption or in foster care. They will help me! But, she said, "No." So, we went to a doctor who confirmed that I was indeed 6-months pregnant. I was so happy because it was too late to do anything---or so I thought. One week later, the counselor asked if I was in agreement with having the procedure or if I wanted to keep my child. I wanted to scream, "Yes, I want to keep my precious blessing!" but had been repeatedly told that I better say "No!" I knew what my consequences would have been, so I said, "Yes, I am in agreement." Otherwise, I would have been homeless.

Later that night, the pain was so intense---I called my mother, and she told me to deal with it. I called the doctor who took his time coming in the room. I never felt pain of that magnitude before. "Push"! "She's finally here," I thought to myself. I did it, and she's alive! She has all of her fingers and toes. My baby is fine. She is not crying like the TV, though. Why? "Let me see her"! I demanded. "No," the doctor team said. After screaming who knows what for how long at them, they wrapped her up and handed her to me. She was so beautiful, dark-brown skin, curly jet-black hair, with all of her fingers and all of her toes. Michelle was so warm. Mommy is here. Wait! Michelle is not moving. Michelle is not kicking. I killed her! I let them kill my daughter! What did I do? I did not defend her. I did not fight for or protect her. I hate myself. Who does this to her child? I hate Vicky! She told on me! GOD, please, just let her breathe. Please!

The doctors sent me home. My mother was pregnant with my sister. I was not pregnant---not anymore. I couldn't take it. They had a lot of people over the house and I was in my room in the bed. I hated myself. I hated that I did not save my child, and I wanted to die. I wanted to be with my daughter. So, I started taking a bottle of pills---1, 2, 3…15, then my aunt came into the room and asked, "What are you doing"? She took the bottle away from me and told my mother what just happened. They all started coming in the room, and pretending that they cared, they told me about their abortion stories. I had just turned 13 years in May, and it was now July 13, 1983. I asked GOD, "Why didn't you just take me"? He answered and said, "Because I LOVE YOU." I cried, felt dirty, used, and lonely. I had just lost me. I had just lost love. I had just killed my baby. And I believed that I was going to hell for murder. That is what the Bible said, "Thou shall not kill." Well---I did it! I had committed a great sin.

One night when my mother was asleep, her husband called me into the kitchen and asked me a series of questions. He asked, "How was it? How was the sex"? He put his hand on my leg and said, "If you ever want to know how to do it right, I will show you." I responded, "I'm telling my mother and I will kill you personally if you ever try to touch me"! Moving forward, I slept with a knife under my pillow, and I left my mother's house when I was 17 years old. I told my mother that he tried to touch me, but she didn't believe me so I just left. She took his word over mine. I knew that if she left me alone around him, he would try to take "it," and I didn't want to go to jail for killing him. I promised myself that the next man who raped me would never breathe again---and I meant it. So, when I moved out, my mother tried to stop me, telling me that I was too young to take care of myself. I told her that she could not protect herself and that I could not stay there and watch her, my younger sister, and my brother be abused anymore. I was so overwhelmed. She made up her mind and chose HIM over ME. She remembered how her father was with her.

I was unable to forgive myself for what I allowed to happen to my daughter---I kept hearing a baby crying and waking up with cold sweats, trembling. I tried to get pregnant again to bring my daughter back but was unable to. I knew that I was punished for life. I moved in with my girlfriend and her mother. I needed air. My baby sister was my daughter in my mind. She looked just like me—exactly like me. I wanted to protect her from everything, just as I should have done for my daughter. I was trying to be balanced. I started working two to three jobs at a time. I finally graduated from high school but was not sleeping because I would still hear my daughter crying for me. Then, I finally found love again---with Duane. We were together for a long time but could not get pregnant. I thought that God was punishing me. His mother told me that he was cheating on me. This was a type of pain---a type of betrayal---that I never wanted to experience. So, I paid him back. Then, I left him!

I started college and was active in the church. I read my Bible and GOD began showing me so many great things! I started singing with a group, and we began doing shows. I managed groups and stayed with my grandmother. While managing a group, one of the limos broke down, so we had to separate. They called me the "little church girl." Everyone was very protective of me and made sure that my safety was a top priority. I went home that night and I was frightened because no one was home. So, I asked one of the members if I could stay with him over at his sister's place so that I would not be in that huge, dark house by myself and he said, "Yes." I was so excited! So we were watching one of the music shows, I was getting sleepy, and started dozing off. I remember him coming back wearing only a condom, and I passed out. I woke up the next morning freaking out and crying. I called him because he had left me at her house. I asked, "Why did you do that to me"? He replied, "Because I wanted it. Besides, I wore a condom so you can't prove anything." What?!?!?

I put my clothes on and ran all the way home. I was so angry and felt so betrayed!

During a practice, one of the men who was very fond of me kept staring at me and asking if something had happened. He wanted to know if anything had happened during the ride home from the show. I was too afraid to tell him and wouldn't answer. He kept asking as if he knew and would go after him or something---I was just too scared. So, I quit as their manager. I just did not have it in me anymore, and I never wanted to put myself in that position ever again.

Eventually, I started taking classes since I felt it was best to further my education. I also wanted a better job. I wanted a better life. I wanted a career. I decided that I never wanted to have children. When I was younger, I wanted to be married at 18 years old. I always wanted to be married, have a white picket fence, have a large family, and live in a large home with me and the love of my life. Sometimes, we as females build castles in our mind and move into them. My castle was knocked down and destroyed! In fact, I met the man who would later be the father to my children in college. I was living with my two roommates who had been friends of mine since we were younger. There he was in my class, with his pearly white teeth and captivating smile. I told my friend to let him know that I was interested. He was very nice looking and dressed extremely well. We all would hang out in the library, sing, and have a great time. We talked on the phone for hours, and I told him about my white picket fence. I wanted to be in a loving relationship—our relationship wasn't about sex. I wanted to love someone and have that person love me. I was now 22 going on 23 years old. I was a Program Coordinator, making big money for my age. I owned my own car and was preparing to start my own business. In the house, we made big money. I also braided hair, typed papers for college students, and tutored individuals. They called me "The Hustler." I did not sell drugs, but I made that money! If I wanted something for myself, I made sure that was able to buy it, and I did. We dated and then agreed we were "an item." We attended church together, read the Bible, talked about our future, and I let him know that if I got pregnant that I would protect my child. If GOD gave me another chance, I would have the baby and raise him or her way better than my mom did with me. I wanted to do better than she did and would ensure that no man would abuse me or my children!

We talked and spent lots of time together! Eventually, we met each other's families. I wanted to ensure this was going to work. He shared his life with me and I shared my life with him. We talked about children and he said he was not sure if he really wanted them because of background. However, if I did get pregnant he assured me that he would love and take care of the child. He seemed genuine. I started feeling weird. So, I made a doctor's appointment to get things checked out. Although I was still having my period, I learned that I was 3 months' pregnant! I had given them the fake name, Sharon, which I thought was sexy. So, when they called my name, I almost missed it! I went to get the results while he was happily reading a magazine. When they told me I was pregnant, my knees started knocking and my heart started protruding through my chest---I was so scared! I couldn't walk over to tell him because my legs had turned into rubber. He was so into the magazine that he couldn't see me gasping for air. Finally, I made it over to him. I smacked the magazine out of his hand and he said, "Why do you look like you've seen a ghost"? I stood there shaking and couldn't speak. He asked again, "Why do you look like you've seen a ghost"? I tried to speak but could only stutter. He said, "Tell me, what's wrong"? I finally managed to say, "I'm pregnant! I can't believe it. How did this happen"? He said, "We're adults—being adults who love each other is how it happened."

I always thought that God was upset with me and that I couldn't have children. So to be pregnant was a great joy---and a huge surprise! Although I was happy and excited, I was so afraid because I never forgot, Michelle Jannai. I never forgot how beautiful she was, I never forgot her fingers, her toes, and her beautiful jet-black, curly hair. So, had God given me the opportunity to really bring another child into this world? I was so happy yet scared at the same time. Every day I wondered, would my child be okay? And as mine grew, I felt the kicks and I knew what it was this time. This time, it wasn't going to be like before when I was younger. I was so happy, every month I grew larger and I was so full of joy. This time, no one could stop or control what God had done! I knew that I was able to finally protect my child. And nobody could stop me in any way, shape, or form. I had all of the control because I was not a little kid---not this time.

I finally realized that GOD was not angry at me and that He loved me. It never felt like it, though, with the nightmares---I remembered everything. But I had another chance, another opportunity to do better than before to protect my baby son or daughter, and to be able to raise him or her. So we had a boy, 8 pounds, 3 ounces. I felt so blessed to have a baby I looked at him, smiled, and told the doctors, "He's going to be six foot four or five." One of the doctor's said,, "You don't know that." I said, "Oh, he's gonna be tall"! And, guess what? Today, he's six feet five inches tall! And almost a year and a half later, GOD blessed me with another son! GOD is so wonderful!

When I was in school working on my master's degree, I learned that I was pregnant with "baby No. 2." While eating with my classmates from NJ at the Clambox, they said, "Little Mama, you got to be pregnant"! I said, "Whatever. I have a baby already." One of my classmates said, "We are over 6 feet tall and 400 lbs. and you are eating more than we are"! You are not even 200 lbs. I thought, "I can't be." I was going back and forth to school and also working for the late Bruce Bolling. So, I bought a pregnancy test. Plus sign. I got dizzy in the ladies room. Are you serious? Soon, I had two children and I was working. I was so happy. But that bubble would soon burst since unbeknownst to me, their father would soon decide that he was going to search for his ex-girlfriend, his first love, because he wanted to see if she still has feelings for him---apparently, he still had feelings for her. I was devastated and crushed. I was 6 months' pregnant with my second child, and he was looking for his high school fetish.

Oh, God, what's going on? Then, I realized that I was going to have to move out and that I was gonna have to live my life. I learned that he was cheating on me with numerous women.

We had an apartment together, and we were supposed to be happy. One day, I went to pick him up from work. One of the women was so excited to see my baby. But I felt uncomfortable, like something wasn't right. I observed his face and his actions, I then learned he was sleeping with her, too. I took my baby and I put my footprints all over her van. I was so hurt. I couldn't understand how someone could have a child with me, say that they love you, and sleep with everyone they come in contact with. I had no choice but to keep my sanity and leave the relationship. Although alone is where I never wanted to be, God blessed me with two children, gave me another chance to have joy. Therefore, I was not going to allow HIM to mess up on that chance for me.

I graduated from college, which was a monumental, joy-filled day. In the same month, I also celebrated my birthday and celebrated Mother's Day as well. I felt like my children graduated with me since they were with me through everything. Their father wasn't there, though. He now lived in Florida and was married to the woman he cheated on me with---and that's okay because I did it, and I did it God's way! Yes, I was supposed to be married, so when he asked me to stay, I said, "No"! I couldn't be stuck with someone cheating on me all the time. It wasn't healthy, and I wanted to live! I left and never looked back!

I then decided to open up my heart to dating again. After my children were older, the father of my children told me that nobody would ever want me because I was big, fat, ugly, and had two kids. He was very mean spirited I later learned that he talked about me very harsh and didn't care what he said to the children. So, that was my other problem and it was really difficult---that he would---in turn---do this to me with children. I realized in relationships, that they weren't turning out as good as I thought they should have. My mom went through her bout of things. And I did not understand why I was going through mine. I thought that I was breaking generational curses, that I was going to be married, and that things were going to be great. However, they weren't after ending the relationship with my children's dad. I dated someone else, and that didn't work out well either---he had women, alcohol, and drama.

I dated someone else and learned that he had someone on the side who he had been involved with from time to time---he, too, had been lying to me.

Then, I was asked for my hand in marriage. I was so happy because I felt the chains were broken, I would have a husband, I would have a full family, and maybe I would have two more children. A young lady introduced me to him who told me that he was really great. We dated and went everywhere together. However, she never told me that he was married. When confronted, he showed me his divorce papers that was filed in the court. Well, he was in the process of divorce. He explained his story, and I gave him a chance to get it straightened out. He hid this for a year. He was so mysterious, yet when you looked in his dark eyes, he portrayed himself as this really nice person, a pastor, who graduated from school and who had all of these wonderful things happening in his life. In fact, he was living his life, he was living his life with another woman and even had her believing she was getting married, too!

I, too, thought I was getting married------tried on different types of wedding dresses, put my lists together, and invited people to the wedding. We spoke to the officiant who was going to marry us, who was a friend of his. I soon realized that things were not lining up and I began to feel like something was off.

I was working with him because he was a General Contracting, I loved to paint, and I loved carpentry work. I was so happy to be able to go into labor in the vineyard with him as we would laugh and joke. But what I didn't know is that he took ME as a joke. He kept saying to me, "You do not know who you are." I didn't know what that meant. He kept letting me know, by saying it repeatedly, "You just don't realize that God made you so special. And it's really sad that you just don't know who you are."

"So," I would ask him, "Who am I?" He responded, "I won't tell you. You have to go to God." And, it made me very sad. I was really nice to him, I was very supportive of him, and I stood by his side. So, one day, I got down on my hands and knees and I really prayed and asked GOD to show me who this man really was. After I got down on my knees, everything was crystal clear! I learned who I was in a relationship with---who the imposter really was. He led me to believe that he was a contractor who had built a huge gym, and someone who had traveled to obtain all of this work. In addition, he convinced me that he was the victim in all of the relationships he had with the women who claimed he had "children" with but he also claimed the other woman's kids so when the onion was unpeeled. He had been married and I helped him to get through the divorce process. So the divorce became final, but she was very upset with me since she wanted to stay in the marriage. In fact, she kept his last name. But as time went on, she accused him of raping her. It's unfortunate because the day that she accused him of raping her, he had picked up his mail earlier and came back to the house and told me they got into an argument because he was finished and left. He said her kids were upset with him but he left and said he would never go back, that he was tired and done.

I knew that he was at the house with me. He stepped out for a little while and he had grabbed some things from the store. I'm not sure if that was the amount of time needed for him to have accomplished the crimes that she accused him of. Who's to say he did them or not? He had an old car that he was driving around and eventually that car disappeared. Eventually, he started driving my truck around telling everybody it belonged to him. Then, I learned that he would stay over at my house during the day, but would stay over at her house at night so that she didn't think it was strange. Soon, he was arrested because he was accused of assaulting his ex-wife and never went to the police station to explain what really happened.

When he arrived, they beat him bad---with a black eye and marks on his chest. The police took the pictures, and when I went to court, I listened to all of the charges they had on him, and I couldn't believe it! My mouth dropped open. Some people had told me that he was great, but this old man said to me, "Do not take no wooden nickels." What did that mean? He said, "You will learn." There were so many things I didn't know. What do you do in this type of situation? I kept praying and ask God to loosen me up from this. I had introduced him to my whole family. My Godmother loved him so much that she begged me to stay with him and even tried to convince me that he was in love with me.

However, I told her as soon as she died that I was leaving him and that he had to go. She couldn't believe it and was devastated. But I didn't care---I wanted out. He was gone all Thanksgiving Day, and I didn't see him until 11:30 pm. He always disappeared at night for certain holidays, and I could never understand why. Then, God began to reveal everything---I learned that he went to jail for 5 years for touching one of his children. He said that it wasn't true. The more I prayed, the more verbally abusive he became. I prayed daily for GOD to remove him from my family and from my life! I didn't want to look at him or for him to come near me or my family! I really couldn't do it anymore. He was just lying about everything, and God was showing me everything. He had to go and when I got on my knees, I said, "Lord, please get me out of this situation." And he told me, "to wait. When I tell you to move, then you follow the directions and instructions." One day, I was in the middle of a project and He said, "Go to the courthouse now and get a restraining order." I stopped what I was doing, drove down to the courthouse, and got the restraining order! I was so happy that they honored it. When I returned home, the police were already at my front door, which was not fully locked. I learned that he ran out the back door, had left the lights on, he left the keys on the bed in the guest room and everything,

I was so happy I called that locksmith. That was the best $600 I had ever spent. After this, I decided to stay single. I was so tired of my heart being broken and hurt, and I have been alone for more than 5 years. I prayed and asked GOD to date again.

I visited a few different states, and during my travels I met this really nice man. Wow! Five years after the imposter drama. I had been by myself getting to know ME, who I am, and the things that I love to do. He really opened up my eyes to a whole new world and a whole new life and helped me to open up my heart again. I spent time with my family, because we needed to heal, together, with doing a lot of prayer, praying, fasting, and I decided to turn my life around. I had already met Samira and everyone in Atlanta, prior to coming to LA. Great people who were all part of the Act Like A Success (ALAS) program. Samira told me about a woman's retreat in Maryland and I informed her that I was interested in attending. Samira sent me the information. I prayed, "Lord, you're gonna have to make a way because I need a change." I had just adopted my new son and my daughter, who are my cousins, as their biological parents were giving me some challenges. I was trying to finish biblical school, dealing with the debris from fallout of the "relationship from the imposter," and of past relationships that failed, thank GOD! And I was praying God, you know, Lord, I tried to do the right things in my life. I just wanted somebody to love me. And, for them to love me, like I do them. And I said I can't put my heart out there anymore. I FELT LIKE I WALKED THROUGH THE FIRE! And I asked GOD to uproot everything that was not like HIM, to cleanse me and wash me and make me as clean as that of freshly fallen snow.

I thank God for healing and experiencing pure joy. I always said when I wrote a book the title would be to "Hold On To Your Dream!? As a child, I always felt unwanted like Cinderella and that I never fit in anywhere. I always desired to be a world-renown inspirational speaker and playwright. I could see it and feel it as a child. I've had several distraction in life but I'm striving toward my dream! I am still her! Words can stump your growth, but you can still go forward! I was told I would never be anything. But GOD said that I am HIS, which makes me special! I want to encourage people to get past the words and live in your purpose. Don't let it take several years to go forward. It was not how Cinderella started. She stayed faithful, she was humble, she believed, and she dreamed. This is like our faith in GOD! Cinderella married the prince and her life changed!! I choose to Hold onto GOD, HE is our Prince of Peace.

Thank you!

Juanita Grant

Fireside Reflections

Keywords and Takeaways:

1. Sexual and physical abuse

2. Losing faith in people

3. Feeling mistreated

4. Despite the several distractions in life still striving toward my dream!

Let's be clear. You must understand that when someone sexually or physically violates you whether it is a peer or adult, it is never okay and it is never your fault. Do not own another person's mess. It may sound easy not to, but subconsciously, many do by way of self-sabotage.

If necessary, seek support through counseling and get the help you need to ensure you have a better chance of having a successful future. Don't stop living! There is plenty of life in you to THRIVE!

Start loving on yourself by creating a self-care routine. Make it all about you. What are some of the things you like to do? Also, don't be afraid to do them alone. *That's actually some of the most relaxing and enjoyable time. Make sure to pencil yourself in DAILY!*

_____

_____

_____

_____

_____

_____

RECIPROCITY ON STAGE

Lisa L. Hartwell, PsyD, RN

"None of us knows beforehand which of our childhood experiences will shape us."

This is the very first sentence that appears in my first published book in 2014, *Bad Apples: How to Feel Good Even When Rotten Things Happen.* After a little over five decades on Mother Earth, I would now add, "None of us knows beforehand which of our *childhood AND adult experiences* will shape us." This is ironic because the whole premise of my book IS about continuing to grow through life experiences with grace (and less anxiety) in a way that is rooted in developmental frameworks as guideposts. I never really knew what congruence meant when I was younger. However, I ALWAYS knew when what I experienced was congruent with who I was as a developing person. This would be a thread that was woven throughout my life right up to my "game-changer" moment of becoming an author and a speaker.

I was "lull'd" in my youth where I was raised in Ashland, Oregon, which is home to the Oregon Shakespearean Festival. My mother introduced us early on to the wonder of theater. Initially, I enjoyed the song, splendor, and ease of the musical and acting, but Shakespeare lured me with his metaphors. At a young age, I saw how written and spoken words can move people. And how powerful teaching with metaphors can be a powerful change agent. To this day, I hold my breath and allow the visions of writers and poets to take me to their banks *"whereon the wild thyme blows."* In the Ashland school district, the study of Shakespeare's works went beyond a cursory reading of Romeo and Juliet's Cliff notes. We were expected to both read and to recite. I played the magic-wielding King Oberon in my elementary school production of "A Midsummer Night's Dream." My long, wavy, dark hair gave me the perfect gender-bending hippie look to be the king of the faeries. King Oberon's magic worked on me just as well as it did on his sleeping wife Titania. I, too, fell in love with what I saw: an ensemble acting together to create fun, laughter, moments of reflection, a story, and engagement with an audience. I found the reciprocity between performers and the audience magical.

And this magic works again and again in my life.

When I decided to put pen to paper and write "Bad Apples," it had already been "written" for years in my head. I've always had an affinity and appreciation for reciprocity in nature, growing up in the Pacific Northwest. There are orchards everywhere! There is an unspoken gratefulness between workers and consumers of the harvested fruit. *Reciprocity in relationship and nature.*

Publishing my book was one of the most challenging and rewarding experiences in my professional development. As it would turn out, it was also a Game Changer for my personal development.

It was late 2013, and I had been getting caught up with some online trainings, including Marketing, Course Creation, and the Ethics of being online as a licensed clinical psychologist. I decided to reach out to a business coach who I had been following and participated in some of his trainings, as I found him easy to follow for my technically challenged brain. Sometimes being a visionary is a deficit when it comes time to know what button to push and when! I decided to book a call with him to see how he could help me create an online course for my current clients and create a marketing strategy to share with potential clients to give them a taste of what it would be like to work with me. During that conversation, he listened and asked lots of questions about what I did and what my ultimate goal was at the time. And then he said it!

"Sounds like you have a book in you wanting to be written." I literally laughed out loud.

You see. I do not consider myself a writer. A dreamer. Yes. Big time! Always have been and always will "have my head in the clouds," as that is where my creation takes place. But this wouldn't be the first time someone has told me this. And every time it happened, I would scoff (under my breath because I'm polite that way), and outwardly I would say *it is not a good time or this seems completely overwhelming and I've never considered myself a "starving artist" either*. I had heard over and over, "Books don't make money and are not a good business model."

I always had people "just show up" throughout my life and tell me, "You need to write." Once, I spent a month in New Zealand in my 20's, having a blast doing hiking tours, kayaking, hostel jumping, and meeting a ton of people. This ambivert (extrovert who loves her introvert quiet time not with people) would always manage to find a quiet, secluded area to write in my journal. I have kept some form of a "diary" or journal since I was young. My mom bought me a "five-year diary" when I was in the fourth grade. The one with four lines per day. And I kept it up! I think about how remarkable that is today!

Looking back at those writings sometimes makes me laugh. And many times makes me cry. Life wasn't always easy and yet there were many, many amazing and joyous times.

On this particular New Zealand trip, I had been walking around one of the many quaint, small towns, grabbed a drink of coffee, and noticed a small walkway between the shops that led to a picnic bench behind all the stores that overlooked the water. And I began to write. I journaled about my experiences, how I felt about those experiences, self-reflection, and…. "Excuse me, may I sit with you?" Oh, for the love of Pete! Really? "Sure, but I'll just be writing." He was an elderly, very polite New Zealander. And yes, my spidey-senses were on alert, traveling in a foreign country as a single woman. My nervous system was calm though. And I've always trusted 'her,' although I have always been one to send out a quick prayer for a protection shield. However, this time was different, as were all the other times this scenario has played out in my life.

"You should keep writing," he said. I looked up and smiled graciously and said, "Oh? I'm not writing, I'm just journaling." He laughed a comforting laugh, not laughing at my need for clarification and most-likely sounding dismissing of his comment. I realized that when he said this next unsolicited opinion, he had been waiting for me to come out of the cloud I was in as I always do when I write. To be honest, his wise timing was spot-on as I had almost forgot he was sitting opposite of me at the bench gazing at the same water.

In the most kind, gentle New Zealand accent, he said, "When you were writing, you were not here. Your mind is somewhere else and it is like you are channeling your thoughts through your pen. And you do not realize you are writing. I just thought I'd share that with you. Have a beautiful day." And he got up and walked back through the walkway between the stores.

What. The. Heck! My head and feet were now firmly planted on the ground, brought back to the current reality in front of me. Now, I've always been a bit on the spiritual side, with a faith firmly rooted since childhood, so I wasn't sure if this was God sending me an angel to coax me along, trying to protect me, or…well, I wasn't sure.

I gathered my things and walked down the walkway that he had just exited to, well, I'm not sure where! My instinct was to thank him for his reflection, but maybe to explore further. But he was nowhere to be found. Since he wasn't walking that fast, I looked inside a few of the shops. But I never saw him again as I walked through the small town. When I shared this experience with a beautiful family I had been staying with later that evening, the "Mum" said, "He was probably a creepy stalker." I've been on the other side of said creepy stalker. This was different. And yet familiar. It happened every single time I went on extended trips during my 20's (my 30's was about getting through graduate school. LOL!). Two months traveling 11 countries in Europe, three months all over Australia and Tasmania, most of the United States, and Japan, it would happen over and over again in one form or another of someone coming up to me (even at airports), and politely try to engage me and leave me with a form of "Well, I'll let you get back to your writing."

But every time I pushed the notion away that I wasn't "writing"---I was journaling. I wasn't writing in a way that someone would get lost in reading anything I wrote the way in which I did in everything I read. I AM one of those readers who reads and gets absorbed into the words that create almost film-like images in my head.

My zest for adventure, while choosing a "stable" income and life, took me to Alaska where I obtained my RN (nursing) degree and license. I worked in trauma, emergency rooms, flight nursing, and obtained my certificate in forensic nursing. I LOVED every part of my nursing career. The science nerd in me feeds and makes my brain thrive. The relationship person in me (relationship with self and other) loved everything about being alongside in the journey of triumphs and agony and death with patients and their loved ones. There is a bit of a sisterhood-brotherhood with nurses. We "get" each other. And we support each other. Because we have triumphed and anguished together. So you can see why it was a BIG decision for me to choose to eventually leave this profession to pursue my doctorate in clinical psychology with a forensic subspecialty. This was related to obtaining my forensic nursing certification, as I thought that was my next step. But what I learned was how another level of multilevel agencies work together to work in the forensic field. I kept having this vision of going above the orchard viewing an entire system working together. Reciprocity again. I knew I did not want to do what I felt was the "mundane" task of processing evidence. Therefore, you could see why I was drawn to forensic psychology, which is the interface of behavior as it relates to the law.

And then my third decade of life, I decided it was time to return to school. I had already been dabbling in other forms of nursing that interested me. I LOVED what I did at the time. I was working as both an emergency room and flight nurse for more than 12 years. That interest took me back to school for a business degree.

But I struggled. A lot. With writing. I vividly remember the first paper I ever received from an instructor. She appeared to be trying to soften the feedback, as my entire paper was marked up in purple pen. Most instructors use red. I guess she didn't want it to look like someone bled all over my paper. I was horrified. Maybe even embarrassed. I certainly felt incongruent. Maybe I shouldn't do this? I had always been mostly an "A" student. She was kind, supportive, and encouraging, so needless to say, I continued to finish, of course finding the financial and international business and business law more to my liking.

And then it happened again. Throughout graduate school, I would labor for hours and days to write papers. Only to have my 50-page research papers marked up (usually in red) with a resultant "B". I excelled at the clinical as you would expect with my nursing and medical background. I remember during one of our first clinical supervision classes the instructor asked what our definition of rapport was and how we do that as a clinician. My mind literally went blank.

I couldn't come up with anything! I think I had embodied "setting up rapport" after 13 years of nursing it had become such an unconscious process. And we all know how hard it is to articulate unconscious processes! I equally struggled how to get my unconscious process from pen to paper.

You see. I am NOT considered a writer. I AM an author. There is a difference. Can I write? Absolutely. Sometimes it flows and sometimes it doesn't. I do not write for a living. I do not particularly find my joy in writing. I find speaking and connecting to others verbally so much more rewarding and effortless, and I find being in-the-moment with the human connection a reciprocal process.

And yet, there I sat on the call, with a potential business coach, which was a stretch for me to think about hiring at the time. But as we talked more, he told me, "Listen to you. If this is what you do with your clients, no wonder they get results. You are so good at talking through it, don't worry about it. I'll teach you the process and how to make it easy for you." Well of course I was good at talking. It's what I do for a living! And I'm Italian so we are ALL good at talking. And I had fine-tuned that skill into teaching and training that felt as comfortable to me as my youth days on stage performing. But what did my speaking skills have to do with writing a book? I was confused.

He then laid it out for me. "This isn't about your book. What is it you REALLY do for your clients and those you want to help?" Well, I said, "I guess it's how to feel good even when rotten things happen and the goal is to keep growing yourself and others along the way." To which he shouted, "Well! There's your title! It's a little long, but we'll work on that!"

"And so HOW do you do that?" And his question sent my mind ablaze! He unlocked that neuron pathway that was now unconsciously established, as I had explained it a thousand times over the last decades of practice. Even as a nurse, I was teaching how to train/retrain patients to better take care of themselves, implement a foreign treatment plan, help them adjust to a new diagnosis, and sometimes transition to death. As a psychologist, that is essentially the ENTIRETY of what I do: teach how to create new neuron pathways to get to a desired feeling state or behavior change.

"So, we are going to schedule times together and I'll ask you questions, we are going to record the whole thing, get it transcribed, edit it a few times, and let's self-publish this first one. Because there will be others." To which you know I laughed out loud. "Then, we will take this book, and it will be your basis for creating programs to offer your clients in new and exciting ways." Spoken like a true business coach! Am I right?

My biggest challenge was that I hated not knowing the steps to take. The technology always eluded me! The disconnect from marketing online was counterintuitive of my need to connect with others. My entire life is based on connection with others, INCLUDING the framework of reciprocity of the orchard metaphor!

But it made sense, and it also fueled something in me, I suppose, I needed all along. I needed a bridge to have someone else believe in me as I transitioned to the other side. After all, that is what all of us therapists, coaches, service providers, and teachers do for a living, right? The difference this time was that it would be yet another financial investment to move me along in my professional path. I had, after all, invested plenty just to arrive at this point as a licensed psychologist.

For my vision to grow and bear 'good apples,' I needed the help and nudging of many people. You see, most people do not just get up one day and decide to write a book. Well, maybe some do. But for me, it was about ONE piece of a much larger vision I had for myself. This exciting and many times unnerving journey needed the skill, dedication, encouragement, blessings, and love of many. And is usual the case when growing, the very thing you need to learn is presented as an opportunity for you to seize, work through, and thrive.

Or not...

There were so many steps during the writing and publishing journey when I asked myself *why are you doing this?* There were SO many times I was "lull'd" into keeping the status quo, which was much more enticing. When I knew it was time for me to expand my reach and to make a difference in lives on a bigger scale. My biggest challenge was discerning the "intellectual inside of me" and putting her for a time on hold so that I might write from the heart. It takes the uncanny ability support and guidance of the chosen audience members eyes (in this case, my business coach) to translate the technical words of a clinician into the relatable words of an author.

The decision was made to go forward!

We got started right away with the process early in 2014. We held weekly meetings on video, with him asking me questions, typing on a mind-map software (another Game Changer by the way!), and me just talking. Somebody was WRITING while I was talking! It was easy. It absolved my fears. The process flowed.

One month later, I made the decision that would lead to my game-changing moment.

I had attended a local workshop in Honolulu, Hawaii, where I live, about the collaboration between all agencies involved in helping victims of crime. The facilitator was an attorney from Washington, DC, who represented a larger agency that was tasked with supporting victims at all levels when a crime has been committed. As part of my profession, I practice as a forensic psychologist, where I am the link for the courts between mental health and the court interface. It is mostly about educating the court about mental health and how this relates to the best recommendations for consumers (victims and perpetrators). During this local workshop, I signed up to be included on their email list as I resonated with their message and vision.

One week later, I received an email to submit a 90-minute workshop proposal for their upcoming conference in September 2014. A national conference? It felt REALLY big for me to decide to submit a proposal. However, THIS was the sort of thing I had just been coached on, and I felt a nudge from my intuition to go for it. Besides, that certainly would provide a deadline for publishing my book if the workshop was going to be about my message! I was also strangely detached from my proposal being chosen. I had done plenty of in-person workshops, but none to that scale. And certainly never at a place where NOBODY knows me! It felt scary and very far-reaching. But, I did it anyway. We shifted the coaching for a couple weeks to finesse the proposal, and it was submitted in February, one month after I had begun the "writing" process for my book.

In March I was chosen! I remember waking up early one morning and checking my email as my husband got ready for work. There it was: "Congratulations! You have been chosen to be a speaker at our 2014 National Center for Victims of Crime Conference." At first, I was dumbfounded. I literally sat there and reread it, thinking I had not read it correctly. I immediately had my husband read the email, and the joy in both of us finally was released! Was this it? Was this REALLY going to happen? All I could think about was, "Oh my, this book HAS to be done AND it really has to be good now!" The conference was in Florida, so being the fun parents that we are, we immediately started planning the "fun" around the conference with a trip to Disneyworld and NASA. We are Disney and rocket nerds in our house.

The first phone call later that morning was of course to my coach. He was ecstatic and also encouraging as would be expected. Immediately, he started to reverse engineer the "publishing" plan. After all, I would need ACTUAL BOOKS if I was going to have a vendor table and sell books at the conference as well as being a speaker!

The next six months consisted of excitement and sheer anxiety. I really had to practice what I preach with, "using anxiety as your ally." There were months of "quiet times" when I didn't hear from my coach or the transcriptionists or the editors. It was nerve-wracking and felt very much out of my control as I waited for step one to be completed before moving on to step two. I kept myself busy with creating the visuals for the book, vendor table tablecloth design, having stress balls made to be given away as swag, booking the trip, and working extra hours to pay for the trip. It all started to feel like we would have better "odds" if we booked a trip to Vegas instead.

Sometimes our lives mirror that which we are trying to teach or do. The process was now beginning to mirror exactly what I had written in "Bad Apples." You see, in nature, especially trees, when "stress" is deliberately place upon an apple tree, as does happens with pruning, as well as rough and windy weather bends and "stresses" the branches. This is IMPERATIVE for growth and thriving. However, when "stress" is placed upon our brain and body system, it was never meant to have this natural "growth system" be used as a way to become stuck to the point we stop growing. It is designed for us to be used to what I refer to as "our ally." Whereas, we can "hold" it and respond differently and know it will pass and is for the sake of our growth. It is always about how it relates to our core. The transformation that happens is much like a thriving orchard. We all have the framework, the tools to ground us and course correct, and the focus are always on a growth mindset.

And yet, then it happened to me. The deadline kept getting closer and closer. I still have the emails and communication from back then. I can read the panic in my writing and remember the sleepless nights of sheer anxiety that this would all turn out to be one big disappointment. Had I invested in something that was going to fall entirely flat on its face? That's not me! I NEVER fall flat on my face. I do not consider anything I have done as a failure. Poor choices maybe? Learning experiences for sure. But I don't fall where I can't get up. Even though there were only two other times in my life I felt like that: in grad school and when we were going through an ectopic pregnancy, failed fertility treatments, followed by failed adoptions. But that is another book for another day! (With a positive ending of a fabulous son who has taught us more as parents than our own lives).

The first week of September was just around the corner. We had everything ready. All arrangements were made. What we did not want to carry in the suitcases, we had shipped directly to the conference hotel.

All except the books!

You've heard the saying I'm sure, "Let Go and Let God." Well, I had nothing else to go on other than the encouragement, mixed with his own fear, of my husband. It's hard to be supportive when you are feeling the same fear. And my anxiety was through the roof, so I'm guessing I wasn't the most pleasant person to be around during that time. I should probably ask him about that one day.

So we took off, hoping and praying the print order books of "Bad Apples: How to Feel Good Even When Rotten Things Happen" would be at our Disney hotel. Yes. You read that right. I was SO worried about not even laying eyes on my book before the conference, we had the boxes shipped to our hotel room.

Florida is a LONG way from Hawaii, and our son was four years old at the time. HE was so excited that he didn't sleep until the LAST two hours of the trip. The sheer exhaustion took away ALL anxiety. Besides, once we were on the plane, there really was nothing else to do but trust the process, which I always have, and this time was no different. All of the emotions of the previous nine months had now turned into fear of disappointment and fear of perception. How would my talk be received? How would my book be received? There were more than 800 people at this national conference, and I knew I had a deep fear of not looking like a fool. All thoughts in my head. I've NEVER been told that. We are so hard on ourselves, aren't we?

The shuttle to the Disney hotel was a long ride with kid and stuff in tow. My husband, even in his tired state, asked the question before me, immediately after giving our check-in name at the hotel. "Do you have a box for Lisa Hartwell?" After handing us our "first time visitor" lapel pins, the receptionist replied, "Well, yes. Actually, it's in your room already." I burst into tears. Right there in front of God, Disney, our son, and everybody waiting to check in! Now, I'm not a crier except behind closed doors during a great movie or with my BFF's. I'm sure they were tears of relief. And exhaustion.

We schlepped all our stuff to the room. And there it was, just like she said. The box sitting on a chair. We opened it, screamed with joy, took pictures with Mickey on the bed, and admired the outcome. The cover, the layout, the words, MY words in actual print! With such relief, we all cleaned up, laid down for a "nap," and woke up four hours later when it was dark. We got up and continued on a relaxing and fun-filled four days with Disney shenanigans, putting aside all the stress and anxiety of the past months, and any fears of the upcoming conference.

After four days, we headed to Miami. We weren't in Kansas anymore Toto! It was a COMPLETELY different vibe than Disney to say the least. Which was a good thing. It helped me refocus, get my head out of the clouds, and prepare for the three-day conference at which I was scheduled to speak on the second day.

It was brilliant. The book was well received. I got VERY good at my 17-second introduction, as there were 50 other vendors there the 800 attendees had to visit! As I started to sell books, my confidence soared. Actually, I would say it returned first, then it soared. The individual conversations were beautiful and intimate and showed me my book needed to be written. My words needed to be put "out there." The stress balls my husband designed and ordered were a big hit as our four-year old son made sure EVERYONE had one! It really takes a village, or in my case, an orchard!

The second day arrived, and I remember waking up early to get ready before the boys were awake. All of the anxiety returned. This was foreign to me as I do not tend to get anxious before speaking. I had to quiet the voices in my head, as there seemed to be a lot riding on my talk. I meditated, prayed, and self-talked my way into believing I was *merely teaching, just as I had done hundreds of times before.*

That was the golden ticket thought reframe. I would just teach! The hubby woke up, wished me good luck, promised to keep our son busy, and reassured me they would be there right after I finished my workshop.

There I stood. I conducted a quick visual scan of the room and quickly counted around 88 people! My heart raced a little, and I just as quickly took a few deep breaths and prayed for grounding and the wisdom and guidance to deliver my message to whomever needed to hear it that day. I looked up and immediately felt peace as I looked around and saw my book on various tables and familiar faces I had spoken to the day prior. I smiled. They smiled back. A calm and familiar stage presence of fun and delivering, washed over me.

It flowed effortlessly. I spoke about how I use the apple as a metaphor to explain how I use developmental growth models for self-examination, sharing Michael Pollen's book, "Botany of Desire." He describes the apple's long journey as a wild and unpalatable fruit in Central Asia to the most common item in every American child's lunchbox. The apple is one of four plants that he discusses that have enticed humans to cultivate them. Evidently, it is a bit of a cult classic for those who are interested in natural resource management!

Our discussions led to the simple fact that the apples we eat derived from an inconsumable wild plant that humans have harnessed and molded to our modern tastes. A large amount of marketing and management went into the apple, for generations as a matter of fact. Over thousands of years, thousands of cultivars have been created for a diversity of purposes. The biodiversity and relationship with humans is what makes apples thrive.

There it was again! Reciprocity.

Talking and relating to all who were in the room, as to the sometimes-challenging professions we all had chosen, was easy. We all "get it." We get how difficult it is to manage stress and anxiety that many times leads to eventual burnout in working with victims and perpetrators. And yet, during my workshop, leading the large group through a guided orchard imagery experiential experience, once in the beginning and again at the end, would prove to be a Game Changer.

It was a moment. It was THE moment.

My orchard metaphor I had used for so many years with clients was finally coming full circle. I wanted to write a book to be used as a guide to help you look deeper into your core so that you can keep growing and thrive no matter what happens to you in life or how you feel about difficult (or joyous!) events in your life. Everyone has some form of stress, anxiety, or relationship problems at some point in their life that may keep them stuck. I realized the development of apple orchards, which was about matching elements together to create the best apple for consumption, was very similar to creating our best-developed selves to create the best life that we can. Both of which are faced with seasons in life, changes in the compounds in the soil (our foundations), and "diseases" that can impact a single tree can wipe out an orchard. I loved the systemic analogy. The systems of human beings are so analogous to the systems of natures.

When I had finished my "performance," the audience clapped in appreciation. I felt the connection as well as relieved as it came down to this moment. And then it happened. I noticed in my peripheral vision, there were half a dozen people lined up on the side. In tears, waiting to talk to me, I walked up to them and the first one couldn't speak. So I hugged her. And she hugged me back. And we just hugged for a few minutes. I suggested she collect herself and come to my vendor table as I would be there the rest of the day and the day after.

And then another audience member. And another.

While this was happening, my husband came up to me and whispered, "I heard in the back of the room you did great!" I had to choke back the tears, as I could see the pride and encouragement in his eyes. As he is quite practical and grounds me, he said, "So, you need to get back to your vendor table now. There are people lined up out there."

And so I headed back to my vendor table. I was always good at holding in my emotions while remaining present. I have spent many years honing this skill. However, all I could think was, "Emotions, don't fail me now!" Over and over again, I listened to more stories of how each person felt during the guided imagery, being in their personal orchard, some not believing who was in their orchard, and others feeling distraught because they couldn't "see" others who they felt should be there. And each one expressing the reminder their clients are individual "trees" within their orchard who are responsible for growing their own orchard. It was a blessing to be able to do this for so many. It was beautiful. It was powerful. It was rewarding.

It Was Game Changing.

I have since gone on to develop self-care resilience and "Using Anxiety as Your Ally" retreats for small groups and coaching programs, all based on the game-changing first book I had ever written. Why do I love what I do? I have learned it's the way I learn about myself through my experiences with others. I do see what I do as a reciprocal relationship with clients. I show up as the most-valued and valuable version of myself, the version of me that really feels like I make a difference. I am doing the thing that is my unique contribution to this world in serving the people who I serve. My clinical practice and all business endeavors are all about serving. I truly believe and embody my own teachings, and this congruency is truly important to me.

In the process of this game-changing life story, I learned I CAN write. I will forever "listen" when strangers randomly show up in my world when my head is in the clouds. My words do have meaning to some, and they are the ones who count.

It was a Game Changer for me to learn that I am in others' orchards, and they are in mine. Together, we take these words and experiences and must grow ourselves for the sake of *self* and *others*.

I learned mostly that reciprocity builds resilience and relationships so that growth continues.

Fireside Reflections

Keywords and Takeaways:

1. None of us knows beforehand which of our *childhood AND adult experiences* will shape us.

2. We take these words and experiences and must grow ourselves for the sake of *self* and *other*

Do you recall any experiences that have shaped you to be the person you are today? How about a discovered gift? What do people tell you that you are good at, yet you either brush it off as not adding up too much or never really thought to see if there was more there to discover?

_____

_____

_____

_____

_____

_____

_____

_____

Our experiences are not to just shape us, but also for us to share ourselves and our qualities with others. Is there anything that you've taken and shared it with the worlds, like become an Author, write a play, start a business. If not, do you desire to do something. What is it?

_____

_____

LEGACY OF LIGHT

LaTonya Knox

[Chorus 1]

This little light of mine, I'm gonna let it shine

This little light of mine, I'm gonna let it shine

This little light of mine, I'm gonna let it shine

Let it shine, Let it shine, Let it shine

[Chorus 2]

Everywhere I go, I'm gonna let it shine

Everywhere I go, I'm gonna let it shine

Everywhere I go, I'm gonna let it shine

Let it shine, Let it shine, Let it shine

--JJ Heller, "Patreon Project"

This is the song that my mom used to sing in the church choir when she was little and even as an adult when I was a child. As a little girl, she belted out this song with the power of an army! She didn't need anyone else to sing the chorus because her voice projected throughout the entire church building like a choir. She also didn't need a microphone because her voice was just that powerful. As I sit here, I can still here her voice singing "This little light of mine." I enjoyed listening to her and was proud to have a mom with such a beautiful voice (granted I wasn't blessed with such exceptional talent, but that's okay). I really never knew how much this song meant to me until now. I never realized that this song described my mom---my mom was singing life into herself (and I really don't think she knew this either). My mom's life reflects precisely what this song says… everywhere she goes, people see her Light, she never hides who she is, and she never dimmed her Light for anyone! This was her song that she sang all the time, with her powerful voice projecting the light of God in the words. Little did she know that these words were giving life to the actual life God would give her later in life, and that light was born May 16, 1981. Please don't misunderstand, my life was and is not a bed of roses. I simply have this tendency to see light in *everything* even in the darkest places. It isn't something that comes easy, you have to desire and want it to the point that you are willing to go get it.

My mom is that woman who everyone wants to get to know. Even in school, my friends and classmates called her mom. I never fully understood why but as I became older I realized that they saw exactly what I saw in her. She possesses a Light that is close to impossible to dim. Even when darkness tried to cover it, she never let her Light dwindle and die. The relationship we have is unlike any other mother-daughter relationship I have ever witnessed. She is my mom. She is my confidant. She is my counselor. She is my first encounter of God. She is the reason why I am the way I am. She is the reason why I love the way I love. She is the reason why I forgive the way I forgive. She is also the reason why I give the way I give. Her unselfishness is unlike no other, as she will give her last to someone in need, she will give the clothing off her back, and she will give the shoes off of her feet. She is that solid foundation of the Word…the Word is LIGHT, the Word is LIFE, and she is that Light (that Word). Even as a bus driver for more than 20 years for children with special needs, she performs her job with the love and patience that most in her shoes could not come close to. She goes to work every day, never complaining---never tired of doing her job. As a matter of fact, I have never heard my mom say she is tired even when she is. I look up to this woman because she is the epitome of a servant. Where did she get that Light, that heart, that loving Spirit? Well, I don't remember my grandmother because she died when I was a toddler…but my grandfather. He was a man who I never saw yelling, he spoke with such a gentle tone that it would soothe your soul. Whenever I would talk to him…Oh man! I can still hear his voice to this very day. He spoke with such love that after one of our conversations, I would feel like the luckiest girl on earth. Even when he was sick, he spoke with joy. I know he possessed that Light as well.

My mom is a woman who God has blessed me with. Even when I did wrong, even when I made mistakes, she always told me how I made her so proud. Even to this day when I tell her my craziest dreams, she says, "Do it, I believe in you." She has never held me back and is also my biggest cheerleader. I could tell her today that I want to be the president of the United States and she would say, *When do we start?* I wouldn't be the woman I am today if it wasn't for her. Her belief in me is what keeps me going and what keeps me fighting. She is my rock and my strength. My mom exemplifies everything that Jesus is---a woman who sacrifices her life, a woman who offers and provides unconditional love, a woman who forgives without holding a grudge, and a woman who believes the best in those around her. No matter the types of mistakes that I made in my life, the wrongs I have done, she has never said to me that she was disappointed in me. She has always said that she was and is proud of me. She never spoke death into me, she always spoke life, and that is why I have the desire to show her that she has every reason to be proud of me. Even when she disciplined me, she did it in a way in which I understood her correction but she never made me feel "less than" for doing wrong. And as I sit here typing this---my story---it makes perfect sense to me why it bothered me so much when I *felt judged* in my relationships about my mistakes. It wasn't because I didn't like hearing the truth about what I did wrong, but my mom never attacked my character or me as person. She helped me *to correct my mistakes*, not *tell me that I am the mistake*. There is a distinct difference, which is what unconditional love looks like---it corrects without judgment, it corrects without hurting, true unconditional agape love *knows the difference* between the behavior and the person. The person is not his or her behavior but what God said he or she is (His Word). And even when I thought my mom was frustrated with me, she would let me know that it is my behavior that needed direction not me. She always let me know that I was perfect just the way I am even when I didn't behave accordingly. That's that God Love!

I have experienced and still experience dark situations in my life, but I have learned to not let them define my life. They are opportunities to trust in God, and moments to let my Light Shine! I wasn't always like this, I was once in the darkness of depression and suicide. When I learned to look at these periods in my life as moments and not as a life sentence, I began to see the Light more and more. Every hurt, every pain, every anger, and every negative emotion I have endured and experienced, I turned it around for the glory of God. Staying stuck in darkness is a choice, and when I learned that I have the power to move, to go forward…I took my power back and said, "No more"! No more will I worry, no more will I stress, and no more will I fill both my heart and my spirit with poison. I must *choose to live* in Light or live in darkness. I must choose to live or die. It is my choice…that's it, it is my choice. No one, not even my enemy, has the power to put me in dark places; I hold the power to be the light! I will be honest, it took a long time for me to embrace this person that I am.

Being a Light in such a dark and cold world is hard because many will not receive someone who sees the beauty in life. Being a Light shows that you are *different* from most, and being different has and always will be frowned on. Being different is looked at in a negative fashion. Being different raises eyebrows. Being someone who loves life and doesn't walk around angry at the world, has many looking at me as *weak. Why is she smiling so much? What does she have to be so happy about? She must have never been through anything in life to be laughing all the time.* **Wrong!** I have been through a great deal in my life, and that's exactly why I laugh, smile, and see the beauty in life. I am still here, still standing, still alive…Why should I be angry when I am no longer where I used to be? It broke me (I hated myself) when I was told that my demeanor, my use of words, my constant smiling and laughing were not deemed "professional" for a businesswoman. I was told that I am "too sweet," that "people would run me over," I spoke "too country," and that "no one would take me seriously." I was told that "no one is that happy all the time." I was told to be like "everybody else" in my profession. And I believed all of that to the point where I was trying to be like those people, dress like those people, act like those people, and behave like those people. But, I wasn't happy at all! I was miserable and became lost and confused. It only caused me to hate myself more than I did before. I confided in a friend, who was also a colleague, and she gave me some great words of encouragement. She said that *who I am is the God in me and to not be ashamed of how He created me.* Even after that I still wasn't sure that people would accept me for me, but when I heard myself say that (whether people would accept me), I realized that I had never accepted myself---and that I had never loved myself. I got lost in the world and forgot the foundation that my mom had created for me. All that I felt were lies from the enemy in using those around me to pull me down because not everyone understood the internal Light that I carry. When people don't understand you, you are viewed as weird and unordinary. But today, I delight in my *weirdness* and my *extraordinariness*! Carrying this Light is a huge responsibility that many are afraid to bear the weight of because it doesn't look like the world, and the world may not accept it. But when you understand how the Light can break bondages, changes lives, heal souls, and set people free, you will no longer worry about the number of people who receive it, *but you will focus on making sure that they receive it*.

Our emotions, our opinions, and our thoughts do not compare with God's Word. Because I feel this is right, because I think this is okay, because in my opinion it should be this way, it does not matter when it does not align with God's Word. The truth is God, God is the truth and some of us cannot handle that because it hurts to see the filth (Isaiah 64:6) in us. But it is necessary for us to see who we truly are in order for us to see that we cannot do it alone. We need a Savior, and there is no exception. We have a choice, and the choice that we make today will affect our tomorrow. All I know is that I am so happy that I chose Him because in that decision I chose Life!! He is life, He is Light, and once you are tired of living in the darkness, you, too, will join me in the Light! God is good. He has pulled me out of places that I would have never thought I would have been. He has been in the fire with me, in the boat during the storm, and each and every time He has saved me---and that I give Him all the Honor and Glory because He loved me even when I didn't love myself. That's how wonderful and awesome God is!

I gave birth to a Light as well, and that Light is my son. There was a period in my life where the light was dimmed; but it never went out. My son is the sweetest, kindest, and most loving boy I have ever known and that is not being biased...well maybe a little (smile). He has a tendency to touch the lives of people who meet him. He brings joy to those people he meets and leaves an everlasting impression on them. When I was pregnant with him, I told God that this baby I was carrying was His and I thanked Him for seeing me worthy of carrying this precious life. I gave my baby to God. I asked God to guide me, to show me how to be the best Mom I could be, and to show me how I could be a positive person in his life. I am by far not a "perfect mom." At times, I have no idea what I am doing or if I am doing it right but my son, no matter what perfection he sees in me. I never knew what love at first sight meant, until I saw my son after I gave birth to him. Now, I wasn't in the best place spiritually or mentally when I was pregnant with my son. I was in a dark place. But because I gave my son to God, the moment I found out I was pregnant, God protected me and my son from the darkness that loomed over me. And I gave birth to a boy who is filled with such joy that sometimes I have to ask myself, *Where in the world did he come from (smiles)*? He is goofy, tells the corniest jokes, and is always trying to make others laugh.

My son's presence is powerful and many cannot handle his Light. He beams with love, he beams with hope, and he beams with Light. He is the epitome of love. He embodies what it means to love others without condition. He sees every person he meets as an opportunity to love on them but his peers are not as receptive to it as adults are, and it hurts him at times. I have to remind him that this world is different, that everyone will not love him, and that it's okay. He is in good company because the world did not love Jesus. And what that means is that Jesus lives in Him and that others may not receive him as he receives them. But I let him know that he should not change his love for others, always protect his Spirit, but should never change because there are people who need his Light in this dark world. It hurts my heart the way others reject him, and it pains me to see him sad. But I tell him that he should be thankful to God for those rejections because God is protecting him from what is trying to destroy him (spiritually and mentally). His heart for others is beyond the comprehension of most people. But then again, people will criticize what they don't understand.

This is a "dog-eat-dog world" in which everyone is out for him or herself and thinking of how to step on each other to get to the next level in life. But all he wants to do is be a fun-loving, playful, and joyful kid. He tries to figure out why people are so mean, why they do what they do, why they hurt each other, and they are so angry. And I tell him because they don't know God. Without a relationship with God, a person cannot know love, peace, or joy. He is always concerned about others well-being, doesn't like to see others being mistreated, and always trying to protect those who cannot protect themselves. He is respectful, always saying *Yes, Ma'am or Sir and No, Ma'am or Sir*, he speaks with such kindness and love in his voice, he asks questions politely, always says *Thank you* for everything, and greets and welcomes everyone with an open heart. No matter where we go, I constantly hear from adults that he is the most respectful and sweetest kid they have ever met. And to be honest with you, as a young black man, this is very important to me and his father. We want to ensure that he is viewed as a respectful young man. God has great plans for him, and I am excited to see God use him in unimaginable ways. My prayer is for him to always remain the positive young man he is today to carry the Light inside of him so that the world can see there is hope and love. I pray that he carries this Light unto his children and shows them that it's okay to be different, to love different, to see life in ways others cannot, and that it's okay to be that which God has called you to be.

My son is a direct reflection of me and, at times, a greater version of me. It's amazing how God uses our children to teach us. And God said to me, *"You are, your son is a reflection of you, but you have let the world tell you to be someone you are not."* That was the knock over the head that I needed to WAKE UP! I made the decision to be the *goofy me* (I make others laugh), the *too sweet me* (someone needs to know that they are loved), the *speak too country me* (southern hospitality), the *happy me* (why not?), the *joyful me* (people need to know there is joy even in the storm), and the *imperfect me* (I am clumsy, I make mistakes, but they *do NOT* define me)...and if anyone has any problem with her, they can politely leave from her presence. And what is so funny is that those very same people who criticized me now love those things about me (that's God at work). I wake up each morning and tell my fear that I will walk in my shoes (not anyone else's stilettos, flats, or boots) without apologies. I have a purpose, and I cannot walk in it worrying about the opinions of others...what they think of me is none of my business, but what I think of myself is, and I love every part of me. My son was that reminder that loving him was loving me.

See…many families speak of their generational curses (diabetes, high blood pressure, etc.) and generational blessings such as money and businesses. But what my family has is Light---that is our generational legacy, it is the foundation of the life we live, our purpose. Life will hit you, life will not be fair, life will distract you, life will give you pain, life will throw everything at you…but that's it. You have life, a life of abundance, and if you purposely learn to look at your life as light, you will live life as a light. Remember this journey we are on is not about us, but about what we can do to be that light, hope, and love for others. Everything storm, every mountain, every valley…it is a setup for your faith and for your strength to shine. That little light of yours, let it shine!!

When you have been in darkness for so long, you have to decide what you are going to do. Are you going to remain in darkness and let it take over you OR are you going to stand up and move into the light? Darkness is the absence of light. What is it like in darkness? It looks endless, it looks as though there is no way out. Have you ever noticed that if you turn all of the lights off in your house at night and walk down the hall that it seems like you are walking forever, but as soon as you switch the light on, you see that the bedroom or bathroom door is closer than you thought? That is what it's like to be in spiritual darkness. It seems unending, you are thinking that you have a long way to go when in reality it's right there. *You just have to reach for it!*

The Word of God is Light, and it reveals the truest intent of the heart. You can't run from God's Word, meaning you can't run from the Light (the truth). Light always overpowers darkness! (For the Word of God is alive and active. Sharper than any double-edged sword, it penetrates even to dividing soul and spirit, joints and marrow; it judges the thoughts and attitudes of the heart. - Hebrews 4:12) To truly see the Light, you have to be ready to embrace the truth. You may not like---no scratch that---you won't like hearing the truth, but you need it to set yourself free from bondage.

I have various journals of thoughts, dreams, and prayers, and here is an entry I wrote last year:

July 25, 2018

Today, I was reflecting on this storm I have been going through the past few months and you know what reality hit me square in the face? These storms keep coming so that my faith will build. Each storm that has come into my life I have to ask myself the question, *What have I learned from it*? This past storm I have endured has brought to my attention that of how I have allowed people to determine my worth, to define who I am. I gave my God-gifted power to others and allowed what they say to me to destroy my God-worth...I cannot focus on my self-worth because that changes like the weather, but when I allow myself to know my God-worth---THAT IS POWERFUL!! My God-worth is in the Word and it never changes. Y'all I have been such a big ole' mess and didn't realize it! I have allowed past mistakes, past words, *past, past, past* define me. And in doing that I allow myself to throw this pity freaking party, wallowing in my self-pity, forgetting that every moment I sulked, every moment I am swam in my tears, I wasted time being the Light for those who need me. I know this was all a distraction from the enemy that I fell for once again. Delaying the vision God has given me to live in His purpose. But it's not the time to beat myself up for it---I just need to wake up and move forward. One thing I am learning is that it is okay to fall as long as you get back up...some get up quicker than others, and it's okay! This is not a race, as each of us have our own path to walk. Woe is me doesn't live here anymore...but I know that another storm will come. I cannot have a testimony without a test. I allowed the enemy to use my former mental illness against me, my former past as a weapon to pull me into his foolery. What I have learned is that when you take ownership of your mistakes, ownership of your past, ownership of your flaws and imperfections---YOU TAKE

POWER BACK. The enemy no longer can throw it back into your face because you have taken ownership of it---you now have the power. We have to stop giving the enemy the power that God has given to us. The enemy, in truth, has zero power...the power he receives is what we freely give him. Yes, he comes to steal, kill, and destroy but it is by the power we give him that he is able to do this...not of his own. God stripped the enemy of all power and authority, and we received that through Jesus Christ. Playing victim comes from us believing that we have no power or authority over the enemy's tactics and tricks."

Why did I share this journal entry with you? Because this was a part of my process in walking in my Light. I had to look at myself and see where I allowed the negativity and toxicity to enter into my spirit.

Your purpose is found in that Light, and it is time to step into the light, to step into your greatness, and to step into your power. The Light is where your blessings flow, and where joy, peace, and comfort are found. *Be intentional, be purposeful.* It will not happen by chance but you have to WANT it just as much as God wants it for you and your family. Do you already have that Light? You do but just as the Holy Spirit is already in us, we have to open the door to receive it...the same applies to the light. You have it to open it up. Think of it as a present you were given; you have it wrapped in pretty paper with a beautiful big bow...inside of that box is exactly what you asked for, but until you open it (that is the work) it will always been hidden and absent from your presence, and it will remain in the dark. You have the gift of Light. You have the power to walk in your gift but you have to unwrap that gift and open it up. Without darkness, there would be no light. When God created the heavens and the earth, it was pure darkness until He spoke light. When you begin to change your mind set by renewing your thoughts, you begin to see a light of hope. You are not your situation, you are not your past...you are victorious. Speak life, speak light into you. Your faith has to be greater than your fear, not faith in yourself but faith in God---your creator. As I mentioned earlier, people criticize what they don't understand. So, be prepared to experience negativity. But it's not because of you, it's because of them. What others can't comprehend, they will judge and try to explain with their limited understanding and knowledge why you are not responding and behaving in a way they think is 'normal.' But you cannot allow their lack of understanding deter you from walking in YOUR Light.

Darkness cannot drive out darkness…only light can. When you understand that the trials, storms, and mountains in your life were not put in front of you to drive you into a permanent dark place but to guide you through the dark tunnel into a light, you will fully comprehend that you are right now is not your destiny (it has already been written in God's Word)---it is only a current situation. What you see today is not your tomorrow.

I think it's crazy that we are so comfortable with being in darkness, that we're so comfortable being negative, and that we actually do fear the Light because it reveals the truth within us. Let's think about this: most wrongdoings are done in the dark and at night because the "Light" shows everything! It shows who we truly are, what we truly think, and what we truly feel not only about ourselves but about others around us.

When you finally decide to take that step into the Light, that is when you are ready to embrace your imperfections, your shortcomings, and your weaknesses, you are ready to love every single thing about yourself, including the rights and the wrongs, you are ready to look yourself in the face and say *Hey, you! I love every single inch and bit of you without apologies Without Regrets*.

Personally, I have been called a pushover and labeled as weak because I am a person who smiles and laughs a lot because I LOVE LIFE! But, if that's one of the downfalls of being a person who walks in the Light, then so be it. But, I am far from naive about what's going on in the world, and I have never been through anything that I am ignorant about either. The truth is that I've been through so much in my life that I got to the point that I'm tired of walking angry, mad, sad, and depressed. After a while, it gets tiresome and is exhausting. Who wants to live life like that? Come on! What is the point of living like that---in that state of mind? For self-pity. What does self- pity do for you? I tell you what it did for me, absolutely nothing. All it did was keep me in the prison I built for myself. Self-pity blinds you of what God already ordained for you. It keeps you hidden. You see, the blessings of God are hidden in His Word. But then again, it's not really hidden because His Word is so accessible to us that in reality it's not a secret. We hide ourselves from what He has for us because we are walking in shame and guilt and we are just a ball of emotions keeping us from what already belongs to us. *We* are blocking ourselves from the Light.

You see, what many people don't understand about me is that I smile because I cried. I laugh because I've been hurt. I find joy because I lived in sorrow. I am at peace because I played in noise. I dance because I fell a lot. I rejoice because I've been delivered. I sing because I couldn't talk. You see, what I want you to understand is that on the side of all that you are going through---on the other side of the storms, on the other side of the mountain, on the other side--- there is joy, peace, love, happiness, healing, and restoration. What you need is on the other side of whatever you are going through--- but you have to get through it to get to it. You see, this Light that I walk in is not an easy walk. Even though many think it is because in their mind they are saying *Well, she's just walking around laughing and smiling because it's easier to do that than it is to deal with life.* Walking with a smile and with a positive attitude is not easy when you are going through a storm. But I know that I am not alone in the storm. I know who is holding my hand through the storm. I know who is walking in front of me through this storm. I know that as the winds blow the rainforest down, I know that I am covered and protected, and that this storm will not harm me in any way. That is why I can walk with a smile. That is why I can walk and speak with confidence. Because I no longer am confident in me, but confident in my Creator---I have confidence in my Father, knowing that He has me in His hands. His love runs so deep for me that I have nothing to worry about even when there is something to worry about!

I cannot say that I've been delivered. I cannot say that I'm a woman of God and yet I am a walking with a dark cloud over my head, upset at the world. I cannot. I am a Light for others to use. With everything that I've been through, all of the hurt, the pain, the sadness, and the anger, all of that is for God's glory. That's what I use it for. I am no longer in this season of negativity. I am in a season of Light, and when you are ready to walk in your purpose and in the greatness that is within you, that's when you are ready to be a Light for others out here who need exactly what you have. I cannot allow the judgment and the criticism from others to keep me off of my mission, purpose, and path in my journey. The longer I stay in the darkness, the longer that I complain about my life and what I've been through, the longer I hold onto my mistakes, the longer I hold those responsible for my struggles and my pain, the longer I do all those things is the longer that I keep myself from the promises of God. And when you begin to see this, that's when you begin to tell yourself *I am not a victim of my circumstance, I am victorious, I am more than an overcomer, I have the power to get out of the pit.*

This Little Light of Mine, I'm gonna let it shine. Admittedly, these are simple words, yet they deliver a powerful message. Each one of us has a special Light inside of us, and that light is yearning to be released because it wants to be seen. This Light has to be seen. This light must be seen. Remember before God created the heavens and the Earth it was dark, complete darkness. Until He spoke it and said *Let there be light.* Stop dimming that light for others. Shine bright, let them see that there is hope, even when they can't see their light is their Hope.

Begin to break the generational curses in your family and start creating generational blessings not of money, not a material things, but spiritually because those will live on until eternity. Let's stop speaking what is wrong with it and start speaking what is right in it.

Leave a legacy of Light for your family! Don't wait until tomorrow. Start today because today is a new day. It is another day of God's grace, His Mercy, and His everlasting love. No more taking ownership over those things that God never meant for us, instead take the power and authority back that was given to us more than 2,000 years ago as if they are because my love they are. We all know that we reap what we sow... Are you sowing light or are you sowing darkness? Look at every area in your life and ask yourself what you are planting into the lives of others around you. Love is a light force that projects the Spirit of God. Live in His Word and drown in His presence. Walking in Light is walking in hope, walking in hope is walking in faith, and walking in faith is believing and trusting in what God has spoken to you through His Word. Walking in Light is walking in love, a selfless love that does not revolve around you, but revolves around God. Loving God first and loving others is the foundation of living a life of Light. This world is full of hopelessness. Why not be that Light for someone else? If you say you are a Christian, then the proof is not in the Scriptures you have memorized or how well you are able to avoid situations, but in your testimony. The proof is in your faith in God, how you took your hands off the steering wheel and allowed God to direct your paths. You cannot be a Light in this world if you have never experienced any darkness. You cannot say God is good if you never experienced the bad. You cannot say you have faith if your faith has never been tested. You cannot come out as gold if you have never been in the fire.

What is so beautiful about the relationship I have with my mom is that we play off of each other's strengths; we know when the other needs the other. It is a bond that is more than physical you know by the blood it is a spiritual bond. We know when the other is hurting without even saying one word. We protect each other. My mom has never made me feel that I was obligated to love her because she's my mother. She always made me feel that I was and am still a blessing to her. She always made me feel special without putting me on a pedestal for me to think highly of myself always ensured that I kept myself humble. Pride is something she never displayed even when people complimented. She's always kept herself as a humble servant to others. And I know that's where I get my serving ways from. I LOVE to serve. I don't and never have viewed serving as being beneath someone because my mom was an example of someone who humbly served. I always tell people that my mom was that first example of "juice." When people wonder why I am the way that I am, I always say *because of her, my first relationship of knowing who Jesus is was through my mom*. My mom not only served the church, but showed her Light when she slept outside the church or through her jobs with people who she didn't even know.

To this day I am always amazed at how strangers just walk up to her and tell her that they just see something so beautiful within her. It still amazes me how people are just attracted to her. No matter where we go, my mom ministers to people. She's not a pastor, she's not a bench, and no she's not a prophet---no, she's none of these things, but she is a woman after God's heart and is constantly blessing people. Everything she does is from a selfless heart and is never about her. She sees a need and wants to fulfill that need. When family and friends are going through anything, who do they call? My mom. When they are looking for advice to help them solve a particular problem, they know that my mom gives it with love and no judgment or criticism, just love. No offense is taken by what she says because the words that she uses do not tear the person down. She doesn't make a person feel stupid or belittled for their mistakes because the one thing that she's shown me is that when someone is going through something, they already feel beaten down, so why are we going to beat them down even more? We are all going to make mistakes, and we all are going to do wrong, and all of our actions will not always be pleasing to God. But it doesn't stop you from being loved by Tyga and so that is my mom. My mom can be upset with you because she still is human. So, yes, she will be upset for a minute but then All Is Forgiven and she moves on. She doesn't hold grudges. She doesn't beat people in the head about what they've done to her. She loves unconditionally. The kids who my mom 20 + years ago, and who are now adults, all remember the one time she said they having her in their lives made an incredible difference. It touches my heart to know that's the impact my mom had on people. The one thing I know for sure is that my mom is leaving a Legacy of Light when she leaves this Earth, and my goal, mission, and purpose is seeing that light passed on to my children so that they, too, will leave that Legacy of a Light on this Earth.

Wow, it just hit me just now but whenever I pray over my daughter the one thing I do say and speak into her is that she is the Light of this world. This is because that's what I want her to be, and that's why I know she will be. She has her own testimony to tell when she is older and ready to share.

Legacy of Light---Who would have thought that God would choose my family, who is neither rich, famous, and not what the world would see as extraordinary (three generations and counting) to be what the world needs! So, now it's up to me to bring this Light out for others to see and to impact the nations. Because *This little light of mine oh, I'm gonna let it shine and Everywhere I go, I'm gonna let it shine.* When you put God first in your life, Blessings pour all around you...I can testify to that! Thank you, Father, for all you have done and will continue to do for me! Thank you, Father for your Love, Grace, Mercy, Redemption, and Salvation! I will continue to let my Light shine so the world can see that Jesus lives in ME!

Repeat after me: *God has blessed me beyond measure...He has given me a life that I don't deserve but because His love for me is Great, He continues to lead me, guide me, and make every crooked path straight. With every breath I take I praise Him for He is worthy. He is my Counselor, my Comforter, my Shelter, my Rock, my Fortress...He protects me from my enemies and keeps me safe. He is my Light in darkness. He is my Father, and I boast in Him only because without Him I could not be the person He has called me to be. I can do all things through Christ who strengthens me! I am more than a conqueror, I am the child of the MOST HIGH. I am a joint heir with Christ. I am not my situation but I am who God says I am.*

I am VICTORIOUS!

Fireside Reflections

Keywords and Takeaways:

1. This little light of mine, I'm gonna let it shine

2. Legacy of Light

The takeaway here is that it is okay to let your light shine. Your light is your gift and anyone who takes issue with that... that is their business and not yours. LaTonya's Mom always showed her love and encouraged her to be true to herself, and as we discussed learned behavior earlier in Cyndilu's chapter, this is also an example of that. Not all learned behavior is negative.

Because of the legacy LaTonya's mom has instilled in her, she was able to do the same for her son. Do you have any great qualities that were passed down in your family? If so, what are they? If not, why not start today? What would you like them to be and why?

_____

_____

_____

_____

_____

_____

_____

_____

GAME–CHANGING REFLECTIONS

Melanie Pieters

As far back as I can remember, I've had to deal with a lot of traumatic events in my life. My earliest recollection is of my dad. He left us on a misty, early morning, in the South Dade area of Miami, Florida. I don't know how old I was, but I was extremely young. We ended up moving from South Dade to where they called it down South and currently what is now referred to as the historical area of Overtown, in Miami. I distinctly remember my mom being with this man, and that he was very abusive. He used to hit her. So, when she would leave and go to work, that's when the physical abuse would start with me. He was extremely mean. He also sexually abused me when I was around the age of 3, 4, or 5. I'm not quite sure, but I was very young. I don't know how long the abuse went on, but as long as he lived there, with us, it would happen. So, those are some of my earliest memories, which are pretty shocking for a child to begin her life with. Just growing up in that environment was very rough. There were lots of shootings, drugs, and gambling. The rich history of Overtown includes being the home to many movie stars and famous people, including mostly African American actors and singers and those who were in the entertainment business. However, it also had a dark side to it.

Although my childhood was rough, somehow, I survived. I had three brothers, and I was the oldest. So, of course I was their caretaker. Anything they needed, I took care of for them. I basically raised them; I fed them, I clothed them, I dressed them, and I got them ready for school. I was their mom as a child. So if they got into a fight, I would come to see who started the fight, and I was the one to finish the fight for them. So, at a very early age, I was always taking care of them as well as cleaning the house and all of the other chores that a mom would normally do. As a little girl, I did play, but I didn't have a "normal" childhood because I already had the responsibilities of an adult in raising my brothers. So, I snatched a little piece of childhood here and there to try my best just being a child. In the meantime, I was doing my best to survive in that area. I knew that I didn't want to get caught up in the traps of the men. Lots of older men were always after the younger girls back then.

I was also really into athletics. Having been blessed with four brothers, I played a lot of sports, and I truly believe that was one of the mechanisms that I used to protect myself. I didn't know this back then, but I know it now. As long as I dressed up and looked like a dude, like a boy, the older men wouldn't want to be with me. I didn't look like the other little girls, you know. So, I did all the things that the guys did. I shot pool, threw dice, played poker, all of the card games---I did a little bit of everything! I even climbed up the mango trees and on the tops of the cars and played football---I really did almost all of the athletic things that guys did. I was naturally athletic and even lifted weights as a young girl. I really loved sports and love to play them in school. I remember, though, not ever really having the full support of my mom. Even when I was in elementary school, and would win a ton of awards and honored with certificates, she rarely showed up to the event. I guess it was because she worked. However, it can be devastating when children don't have anybody to support them in their accomplishments. I remember one typical morning. On our way to school, someone had gotten shot in the head, and we saw their brains splattered all over the sidewalk. That was just a typical day, seeing the brains on the sidewalk as you walk to school. There was always something traumatic and violent happening in our neighborhood. We would hear people in the hallway at night and in the alleyway, we called it the alleyway back then, in the back of the building getting beat up. You could hear all kinds of violence. We stayed on the second floor at one point, then moved to the first floor, then moved again to the second floor on the other side of the building. We lived in building 268 on 11th Street. Everything transpired in that back alleyway. The buildings were really close, with one in back of the other or adjacent to the next to the side of the other. Where we lived was like a mini-New York. No one ever slept and bustling activity continued, whether it was day or night. I remember at one point there were these two guys who tried to kidnap me, and take me through a window because back then, the windows were long, rectangular type of window panes and, you could literally lift the slots that they were in. So, I think my mom must have heard something, and she came in during the attempted kidnaping because they literally had me halfway out of the window! That's kind of weird thinking about that. She squashed their attempt, and to this day, I don't think she knew who they were. But, she was a single mom, so they probably had been watching her comings and goings for a while.

Anyway, there's been a force that has been protecting me for a very long time, all of my life. And even though all of those things happened, there's something that has just always been trying literally to take me out. From there, I went to Douglas Elementary School. I remember my principal, Mr. Oliver, as well as my favorite teachers, Ms. Crawford and Ms. Brown. I was a high achiever in school and as stated previously, always won awards and got good grades. A's and B's or just straight A's. I also remember that I started having seizures at a young age, so I used to pass out a lot, and they were something that I just had to learn how to deal with. I'd be standing up waiting for the bell to ring or outside waiting on the bus to leave for school. The next thing I know, I'm on the ground and passed out. After elementary school, I ended up going to junior high school, which was another transition, not only because it signaled that I was getting older and moving toward high school, but because we had to move from a black neighborhood to an all Hispanic neighborhood now. That was a cultural shock. The school was located quite a distance from where we stayed, which I suppose was their form of busing, I guess. But, I was still pretty much in love with school. So, right after that, we moved. Well, let me back up. As I said previously, I grew up and by the fourth, fifth, and sixth grades, my mom's boyfriend had moved out. I later discovered that he was my dad's best friend and that she also had a baby by this guy. This meant that I now had a younger brother from the same guy who was molesting me. So, now I'm in middle school and using all of my survival techniques to make it in a pretty crazy environment. I remember that I used to get on the bus, I think it was 35 cents to ride the bus at the time, and one day the bus driver said, "You know, young man, you owe me some more money." I just looked at him. That kind of hit me hard because I wasn't a little boy! I was a little girl who had trained herself to be a male because that was my protection from being violated and from all of the men who always went after the young girls. I did this as a repellant, to push them away, so they wouldn't want me, I figured if I looked like a dude, they wouldn't harass or desire me as much. The façade pretty much worked because I ended up becoming a little hustler. I liked hanging out with a lot of the drug boys, the pimps, the players, and the hustlers. I ran their errands and made money---that was just my survival mode. And because I was pretty athletic, I ran everywhere that I went---Anything I had to do, I just ran! I would run from point A to point B to point C to point D. Even when I used to have to go to the corner store and buy my mom's cigarettes, I'd run to the store and run back. I remember distinctly one time when she sent me to the store. These two guys walked into the store and robbed it. Since I was there during the robbery, I couldn't leave until they finished. So, again, the hand of God, saved me because anything could have happened to me that day. When I think about things now, how I continued to be protected, I remember all of these traumatic events. I remember when we were young, and I was small. As stated previously, my three brothers and I used to want to go and visit my dad, who would never come to see us. So, we would have to go to him. My mama would never take us. So, she would put us on the Greyhound, and we would ride all the way down south from the city of Miami to the southern part, which is like the country part of Miami down towards homestead area.

You could just imagine, elementary school kids going to see their dad all by themselves!

Yet, here I was watching over my brothers again, as we set out to find our daddy. This happened several times. I remember when we went to see my dad and my mom used a neighbor's phone to make the call. The man raped her. But, I remember being made to feel like it was my fault, and that I was the cause of her assault since she wouldn't have gone to his house to make the call for us to ensure we got to our destination. I carried that around with me for a very long time. Eventually, I remember wanting to become a cop so that I could work with rape victims.

I also remember wanting to go to the Air Force to become a military police officer. I had my little life mapped out! I was going to have my kids and stay in the Air Force for 20 years, then retire. But, things didn't happen that way. My life took a lot of dramatic turns, which I'll visit as move on with the story. So, I remember moving around a little bit in junior high, and that one time Muhammad Ali visited our school to film his movie. "The Greatest Boxer of all Time" needed some extras in his movie. And, although it ended up on the cutting room floor, *I was in the Muhammad Ali movie!* I was one of the people who was chosen to be in the movie and that was a big deal for me because Muhammad Ali was one of my heroes. I literally taught myself how to fight, and I was a good fighter by the way, watching Muhammad Ali box in the ring. He was one of my "superheroes" at the time, and I'll never forget that moment. It was the absolute biggest thing for me to be selected to appear in that movie.

But there was still a lot of bad stuff that happened like clockwork. Every other night, or at least once or twice a week, the Swat Team would put the whole building on lockdown because they were looking for the drug dealers who lived in the building. They'd flash their big, bright lights into everybody's apartments and would go through and ransack certain apartments. The Swat Team would jump out of at big, black truck, and people would be laying on the ground, handcuffed behind their back. Oh, God, it was always something dealing with crime, something with drugs, sex, and violence. Someone was always getting shot, and I always saw somebody getting beat up in the alley. So, you survived or you didn't survive. You know, kill or be killed! That's the type of environment it was. You always had to be four or five steps ahead.

We didn't really go to church a lot. The few times that we did go, mom would send us to church, but she wouldn't go with us. And it was soooo boring and there was zero excitement! So, I would end up leaving and walk to the drugstore across the street to buy some candy. To this day, I do not like a boring church! The preacher had a monotone voice that would literally put you to sleep, which I hope I'm not doing to you right now! I think the church was Presbyterian, but to be honest, I really don't know. What I do remember is that it was boring. So, from there, we eventually ended up moving away from Overtown to a community by the name of Brownsville.

At an early age, I felt that my mom always had an issue toward me. She would just get angry with me for no reason, curse me out, and call me all kinds of names. It seemed like I would make her so angry and disgusted for no good reason. Then, she would make me go stay with other people. Certain women just took to me and they became like a mom when she didn't want to be a mom to me. I would go stay with them for a few days until she wasn't mad with me anymore. I'm being honest with you because I was a child, and there is really nothing that bad that a little girl can do to you to make you resentful and angry, especially when I wasn't running around, I wasn't being grown, and I wasn't being "promiscuous . I always appeared to be a problem for my mom. She would get very angry sometimes and didn't want me around. Those are my earliest recollections of my relationship with her. I need to say though, that living in that building, whether it was good or bad, it felt like a never-ending, *bad* rolling movie!

My mom started dating different men. It seemed like whenever I looked up, a new one was around. But, there was one who always had his eyes on me, but he never got the opportunity to do anything. Plus, I couldn't stand him. He disgusted me. She also always had some type of drinking going on. I was like Cinderella, always cleaning up after everybody. I was the little maid, the little cook, and the cleanup girl. So, they'd have all of these parties, and I would be the one dumping the ashtrays and throwing the Budweiser and Miller beer bottles away. Because of all of my mom's boyfriends being around all the time, I always had to be on guard, for myself and for my body. Only one of my mom's "boyfriends" ever tried to molest me, but he didn't succeed. For some reason my mom used to tell people that she was my aunt or my sister. She did not want people to notice that I was her daughter. So, I watched her pretend to be my sister or my aunt in front of other people. I had no other choice but to play along, which was very awkward, very uncomfortable for me. That never really settled with me in the right way because how can you pretend you're an aunt or a sister instead of the mom that you supposed to be? So, she would just tell people, "I'm your aunt or I'm telling your mom on you." Please don't tell them I'm your Mama. That was very upsetting for me. Frequently, I just went along with it because that's what she asked me to do, but I didn't like it AND I didn't agree with it. I had to deal with a lot of women in the building who didn't like her because of their boyfriends or husbands who liked or wanted to be with her. My experiences growing up with women were a challenge. On one hand, she denied me a mother. But on the other hand, here it is. I would literally hear women talking about her in a bad way but she was still my mom. That was very conflicting for me and also quite embarrassing to have other women talking about her. Frequently, they'd be talking about her with me, her child, standing right there. It was like they didn't care or they wanted me to hear those nasty words. Sometimes I think they just couldn't help themselves. But if truth be told, what was I going to do? What was I going to say? *Don't be talking about my mama, grown, angry, aggressive women because somebody is talking to your boyfriend or to your husband,* you know?

I remember my mom allowing her youngest brothers to come stay with us because they didn't have anywhere else to stay. Again, one of her youngest brothers began to violate me, sexually. So, I was violated by quite a few people that she placed me with, and I couldn't get away from that person because it would happen when I was asleep. When you're a child and being molested, what do you do? You freeze. When you wake up to somebody, you know, violating you in that way. Sometime the year before, I confronted an uncle during Thanksgiving. God kept telling me to confront him. When you have been violated, it puts you in a state of fear and you avoid confronting the person who has hurt you at all costs. You feel like you can't move sometimes or you can't talk. It took many, many years to build up the strength and the courage to confront this individual. I said to him, "I know what you did to me." And of course he tried to deny it. I tried to tell them what he had done to me, and he was in shock. So, how can you deny it, but you're in shock? Right there, he told on himself. I continued and said, "You know you're a child molester. You're going to be judged and punished for what you've done to me. You've never even said that you were sorry for what you did because you're trying to deny it now!" He replied, "No, that didn't happen. I didn't do that." I replied, "Yes, you did," and I told him that I did not like him as a person.

I really did not want to see him at any more of the family functions. Period. I told him I did not want him coming around because he made me feel extremely uncomfortable. I didn't even like seeing him around the other children, the female children especially. With people who violate children, I've learned that if they are never confronted or if they're never caught or if they're never any consequences to what they do, they just continue with the same pattern. They just keep going and going and always find a way to find another victim to abuse and to violate. For many years, I had to deal with physical and sexual abuse from different men who visited or stayed in our home or that my mom dated or were related to me. The first incident, which I previously described, was with my mom's boyfriend, who is my youngest brother's father. He was very physically abusive. He would fight and beat her and then molest me when she would go to work. Here it is again, I was being molested by her brother, who was my uncle.

So, you know, it was just a lot to deal with. On top of it, I was not having the nicest experience with my mother. Through the years, even during elementary school, she would get angry and start cussing me out, calling me the "B" word, whore, "MF," just cussing me out. You know, and I was just a straight A student, and I was always trying to please her, but nothing was never good enough for her. So, growing up in that type of environment, was like survival of the fittest. I always had to survive and stay a few steps ahead of danger, or what I considered danger.

I did little things like I said, to make money because hey, what else is there to do and in that type of environment. Was I playing with baby dolls? Not really. I wasn't doing things that little girls do. Back in the day, it was a given for you would take care of your little brothers and sisters. Today, this generation of kids don't think that's a part of their responsibility. It probably isn't, but that was the thing to do way back then! You were just expected to take care of your younger siblings.

When I was in the eighth grade, we moved from Overtown to a place called Brown subs in Miami or Brownsville, as they liked to call it, on 50th Street and 22nd Avenue. One of my aunts, my mom's sister, had a stroke and ended up staying with us. I remember I was forced to take care of her, so, there were days that I was made to stay home from school to take care of her. I hated that because I really loved school, and this did not make me very happy. So here I am as a child, taking care of a 50-something-year-old woman, who was a paraplegic now because the stroke was so severe. I had to give her a bath, feed her, and lift her up, all of these things that one does to take care of a sick person. I learned how to take care of sick people, which came natural to me. That's also one of the things that made me want to become a nurse. I distinctly remember every time that I want to be a nurse that she would say, "What you want to do that for?" But, I had also told her that I wanted to be a model. You guessed it! She would ask, "Why would do you want to be a model?" So, *anything that I ever wanted to be* in life and achieve was always met with zero support, immediately shot down, and always discouraged. *I was never encouraged.* I never heard *Go for it!* Never, none of that! It was more like *Go sit down over there on your own. You'll need to do that. That isn't for you.* I wanted to be a nurse, I wanted to be a model, and I wanted to be a cop. All of these things are naturally inside of me, but they were never cultivated. They were never encouraged. They were never watered. Water was poured on them to drown and kill the dream that was inside of me. To be honest, I believe that if I would have been encouraged, I would have accomplished two out of the three, if not all three of those accomplishments. I even became a candy striper at Miami Jackson Hospital, learning how to fold hospital corners on beds, because I really want to be a nurse. Of course, those things didn't happen because life began to take another turn, and it wasn't for the best to me.

I was still having seizures, so I was still passing out, still rolling up in my head, swallowing my tongue, and all of those kinds of things falling out. Waking up, my face would be scraped or something got broken because when you pass out, there's not really anything to grab on to and you're going to hit the ground HARD with this type of deep convulsion. I used to be so embarrassed after every seizure. But. I was never was taken to the hospital because of my serious condition and I don't remember going to the doctor for any type of treatment.

I recently discovered, however, that I have a new health challenge, and I asked my mom why didn't you ever tell me. I also asked if she ever knew that I had this issue? And she responded, "Yeah, I knew." When I looked at her like, *why didn't you ever tell me?* She never gave me an answer. So, I doubt if I went to the hospital to identify what the problem was or if I was taken to the doctor to receive any type of seizure medication. At this point, I was 13 or 14 years old, and things were difficult to say the least! Living with her and taking care of my aunt, it was just miserable for a 13- or 14-year-old girl. I always felt like I didn't have a life, and that I had been living someone else's life---I literally felt that my life had been taken away. Here I am taking care of a stroke victim, and dealing with my mom's drinking and violent behavior toward me when she would drink. All of her anger would spew out at me. She would always refer to me as a slut or whore, when she would allow the alcohol to express her true emotions and thoughts about me.

One day, I ended up going to the park because they use to have these jams where they would play music. I ended up meeting my first husband at the time. We weren't married; however, but we were being sly and dating when we weren't supposed to be. My mom didn't like him because she was prejudice. He was of Puerto Rican descent and part black. She was just very prejudice. She hated him, and she still hates him to this day. Other than him dating her daughter, just didn't like him, period. In his mind, he thought he was rescuing me from a bad situation because he saw what I dealt with and knew what I was going through, living and being with her. I always felt like her personal maid and even at times her own house slave. (Always cooking, cleaning, and taking care of everybody and everything in the house, while at the same time being cussed out at the drop of a hat.)

So, with this in his mind, he felt as though he was rescuing me. I became pregnant at a very young age, and I believe I either told her or that somehow she found out. She made me have an abortion. I truly didn't want to go through with it. She forced me to do it. She was very angry about me being pregnant at such a young age. I really couldn't comprehend how my mom, the woman who gave me life, could be upset about me being pregnant at an early age. But, I was aware of all of the people who sexually violated me and her being content with that and not accepting responsibility for my past due to her inability or to protect me from my violators. The physical aspect of the abortion was difficult to process, but the emotional trauma felt like someone cut my heart deep and left it to bleed out. After the abortion, she wanted me to stop seeing him. I wouldn't, and I couldn't! So due to my choices, which didn't align with what she wanted me to do, she threw me out again!

I ended up having to stay with a guy and I was barely in high school. I thought I was in love, but I didn't know any better. I didn't have anything or anyone else to hold on to that could provide me with the proper guidance on what authentic love is. The one thing I always realized about being a young girl is that she should never feel unloved in a world that already doesn't love her. She becomes vulnerable to anything and anybody. At a young age, I never felt loved. I never received love. I was never told I LOVE *YOU.* I never was told *YOU'RE DOING A GOOD JOB.* I was never given any type of acknowledgment for my achievements in school or in sports.

I just think it's important for a child to receive validation, but most importantly genuine love from his or her parents. This is a vital component. If they do not, then it leaves wide gaps and voids, which allow anything or anyone to come along and fill those gaps and voids for them. If filled by the wrong people, they can take advantage. Honestly, I believe that's what happened with me. My mom never provided me with validation and love. She never provided me with the proper nourishment to my heart, soul, and mind, as a young girl.

This is why it is important to seek help when there are underlying problems in our lives, because what we do not deal with, will eventually deal with us. The even more unfortunate part of that is it can affect generations.

That is why I feel so blessed today, to be able to work as a family and parent specialist with young children and their parents, coaching them along the way, showing them how to build healthy, positive relationships.

Fireside Reflections

Keywords and Takeaways:

The great takeaway here is to be mindful and vigilant when it comes to the care and well-being of children, because children learn from their parents first and are much like sponges, meaning that they absorb those things that they are exposed to. Luckily in Melanie's case, she was able to take her pain and turn it around for the good of other children and parents although she was not taught those skills and qualities in her own home. BIG Kudos to you Melanie!

Let's do a self-reflection. What are some of the ways that you can improve your

communication and presence in the lives of your children?

_____

_____

_____

_____

_____

_____

_____

_____

_____

_____

_____

_____

_____

_____

_____

PICK ME UP AND PLACE ME SOFTLY

Princess Mapp

At 5 years old, you usually have no idea your future will require endurance to finish the race. You can barely get through the meter run around the track, let alone beat your cousins in a race from the broken wood brown fence you just got a splinter from in your thumb, after proving you were faster and stronger. In reality, you just tried to fit in. You had to because every other year, not really knowing when that year would start, you would be shuffled back onto a plane with a stewardess smiling in your face, making sure you received extra bags of peanuts, as you flew over the bluest waters only to land in paradise again. You just had to keep reminding the boys that you were better. Or were you? Paradise was where you realized you were just a fragile, lost, and confused girl looking for happiness in between the tears.

Before I landed, I squeezed my hands tight and folded them into a prayer position, closing my eyes tighter only to wish and hope that

God heard me better since I was in the blue sky, thinking that I was closer to Him. I said, *"Please pick me up and place me softly."* When my eyes opened, the big, white-looking Chester cat flight attendant was in my space smiling. "Are you ready little Princess?" Grabbing my bags I hurried off to be greeted by my grandmother. Barely 4'11, she may have had a diminutive stature, but she was strong as an ox though too. I remember seeing her grab one of her husbands by the neck and pick him up off the ground. Of course, she had a lot of anger inside of her when she did that, so maybe that is why she was so strong then. I realize her strength turned to putty through the years because the things that were totally wrong to do, she allowed him to do. Oh him...I've got to tell you about him! But, first, let me rewind this memory bank and take you to the mainland.

To California, Northern California in a city called Oakland. Home of the crack heads, hustlers, pimps, and prostitutes. Oh! And let's not forget to mention Huey P. Newton of the famous Black Panthers! Well, that is where I am originally from Oakland, California. Back then were the days of innocence, fun, and living fancy free. We would play till the street lights came on. I remember my brothers and I had this mountain we would walk up to and slide down---that dry, brown grass. Each of us had a cardboard box. We called it Speedy Joe Mountain. There was no telling what would happen at the end. Some of us hit trees or cars or slipped off the cardboard. Man, we had a blast! We would go between different aunt's houses, my grandma's, and ours to visit. Playing football, tag, and hide and go seek was our thing! I was officially a tomboy! I loved it! In the 80s, those days were the best days of my life---for a minute. Then, one day, things became gloomy when my grandma met this guy 10 years younger than she was---grandma was always was into those military men. She lived in a city near Oakland called Bayfarm Island, and worked on the military bases as a civilian. It was cool and didn't bother me at all. That was the big people's world, and we were the little people. We knew how to stay in our place. Well, at least I tried until things shifted for me with no warning.

One time when I was about 5 years old, my whole world of being a kid was snatched right from under me. Now, keep in mind by this time I kind of had what I describe as a rough life. I had a sister who was murdered at 9 years old. And my parents, they lived in the Indy Five Hundred lane of life. My dad was a known pimp and my mother, as she would say, was a "high-class call girl." They both came from the East coast and story would have it that they met in the Bay Area. My mother was the prettiest of them all! Long, silky black hair, little waist, and a big booty. My dad was a fox! He was so incredibly handsome and also a ladies man. I only heard the rumors of my grandma not caring much for either one of them. My mother ran away at a young age from Philly and never looked back. I was actually conceived the year before my sister's murder and, to top it off, my mother's tubes were actually tied. So, yep, I am first, a miracle. Then, I realized maybe I was here for a reason. But that was not until I became an adult and reflected on everything.

So, let's fast forward and understand why I whispered and prayed before I got off that plane---again in paradise to a living hell on earth. No fairy tales at all. Sometimes I am so baffled why I have the name Princess and not the lifestyle. Back in 1975 on BayFarm Island, I knew I wasn't a real Princess. As a matter of fact, my grandmother's boyfriend wanted me to think I was a woman at 5 years old. My grandmother had to run to the store and asked this man who she barely knew as far as I was concerned, to watch me. But wait, I was about 5 years old and wasn't supposed to know. Wasn't my grandmother supposed to have the common sense to not leave her grandbaby with a stranger? Who does that? Unless maybe the grandchild was prey? Well at 5 years old, I had no clue, but that day, that gloomy day that the sun shined through the window and as he sat on the couch. That day, that afternoon, he called me over as he kept peeping through the curtains and window to see if my grandmother would pull up. As I thought about it later, I understood it all. But that day, that day I had no clue. As a child you are told to listen to you elders and to all adults. Do what they say. My grandmother apparently felt okay leaving me at the age of 5 with this man so I felt okay, too, until he called me over to the couch. As I approached, I could see that his private part was sticking straight up out of his dingy blue shorts and he was rubbing it. He told me to sit on the couch and he grabbed my hand and showed me what he wanted me to do. As his hands wrapped around mine, his hips moved up and down. I didn't know what to do! All the while, I was also feeling like this was bad and that I am going to get in trouble. What is happening? I held my head down and can remember like it was yesterday---his leg. He had a white, rubbery looking leg. It was burnt with hole imprints resembling an iron on it. After sitting there doing that horrible thing, which seemed like forever, it wasn't long before he told me, "Go into the bathroom and don't say anything!"

I ran to the bathroom. From that day, I was a walking zombie trying to understand what happened and scared to tell. I remember vaguely my grandma coming in with bags and hearing the sound of keys and laughter. She was playful and happy, and that man got off that couch and acted like nothing just happened. I peeked through a dark bathroom door scared to come out. As I reflect, I wish I could hug me and tell me that it is okay to tell. That secret stayed inside of me years after off and on as I flew back and forth to paradise and crack nation. My grandmother ended up marrying that creep and things just got a little worse. But my prayer never changed…*Please God pick me up and place me softly…*

Now that you have an idea what my life was like at the age of 5, let me bring you up to speed. Yes, the day I witnessed my grandma pick that man up was him. The inappropriate pervert was at it again. Screaming from the bathroom my aunt yelled, "Get out! Mom he's at it again!" as she took a shower. My grandmother rushed upstairs and wrapped her hands around this man's neck and slammed him into the wall. She said, "I told you to stop that shit"! Dropping him like a sack of potatoes, he hunched over and just shook it off. What kind of monster was this guy? Although the years became insufferable with so many indecent acts toward me, what was even more horrific in my eyes was the fact that it was finally confirmed my grandmother knew this man was a real monster, and that hurt the most.

The lady who had cared for me because I was so much younger, my grandmother, was deceiving me and everyone else. She gave me security and what I thought was a safe place till now. When I think about the aunt who tried to address some issues, who took her daughter out after doing indecent things to my aunt, her mom. Yes, trying to kiss your mommy in the mouth with your tongue was every red flag that something just wasn't right. As an adult, I still did not understand this power he had over me or why I felt the need to respect them and visit. Walking into that house every time made me cringe. I was just as guilty since I acted like I didn't see the porn magazines the kids' little feet ran across that laid spread open on the floor near the computer in my grandma's room. How about when my young cousin, who was 4 years old, would run to every male who entered the home goggling naked. Was I the only one who thought this was wrong? I boiled with silence and still could not muster up any boldness to confront this demon. Strangely enough I was an adult. No one was putting their hands over my mouth. No one was telling me to be quiet and to act like nothing happened. For whatever reason, I was paralyzed only in my mouth, and the silence was better---as if the sickness would go away.

Yes, I can recall several of the indecent things I would have to go through with regularity. I did wonder what was going on in this house with these children. On one occasion when I visited, it was like I was reliving the nightmare because of how similar the home was shaped. The kitchen wrapped around to the living room, then into the family room, like one big circle. I remember I used to play so much. I liked to scare everyone and make them laugh. I was a prankster.

Well, this one time I think I was borderline trying to be funny but serious at the same time, and got caught in a web of confusion and terror all at once. This one time, I was home alone with my grandma's husband and he was watching this channel. This was back in the day when Robosize was on, an exercise show where the women looked very sexy. Well, I called myself being funny and turned the channel. I told him that I was going to tell my grandmother what he was watching. I can't recall how old I was, maybe in the 10th grade at this time. So, I walked across the room to turn the channel, he told me to stop, and kept turning it back. He told me if I didn't stop that he would get me. I was pushing the envelope yet again, and being funny one more time, when he jumped up and started to chase me. Running faster and faster in circles you can only imagine my adrenaline because I really didn't know what would happen. I ran and started to scream. While I was running, he told me he would put a sock in my mouth if I didn't shut up. When he caught me, he threw me on the floor and sat on my arms and was on my stomach. I started to cry and pleaded for him to get up. I yelled at him, "Please stop it"! He immediately pulled a ball of folded socks out of the back of his shorts and shoved it hard into my mouth hard and sat there. He was a Caucasian man and had started to turn pink. He said, "I told you I would catch you." I was squirming like never before. He looked down at me and, yes, it was as if he was trying to decide what to do. He has caught his prey finally and now, should he do it now…violate me? I was a kid, crying and trying to figure out what he was going to do. Helpless, with tears rolling down my face, and screaming at the top of my lungs, with this human muzzle from this sick man wanting to hurt me. This must have been a moment that God looked down over him and made him get off of me. I ran as fast as I could and pushed every piece of furniture against the door crying, scared, as well as helpless. Yes, that day God remembered my little prayer and not only picked me up and placed me softly, but He pushed that creep off of me!

So, you can only imagine my thoughts, as I stood in my grandmother's house and watched my younger cousins playing and laughing and running around while my grandmother fixed him another Bloody Mary before taking a big gulp herself and serving him. Her security blanket. That is the only conclusion I came to as to why you would allow this mother f'er to harm me and your daughters. By this time I had no clue what was really going on but my own suspicion.

You can really imagine how I had my own hang ups with man problems and trust issues. Fortunately, my boyfriend from high school became my saving grace in the midst of all that BS. Of course, he wanted to kill him, but we had a plan to get away. After all of the indecent ways he would walk around the house, with his private hanging out, to come behind me and grab a glass above me or play with himself in the corner as my grandmother drifted off to sleep, while I sat there watching TV until I found the nerve to get out of the damn room. I was even hospitalized for undiagnosed belly aches and pains, but ultimately, I believe it was the stress and the silence that almost killed me.

At the end of my junior year, I finally begged my mother to come to Hawaii and help me finish school. My grandmother and her pedophile husband were moving to Paris and tried to convince me that they wanted to adopt me and take me there. I was so relieved when my mother showed up and decided to stay. It was a new beginning for her, too. We really hadn't had a normal relationship up to this point. I knew she wanted a new life and was trying to reinvent herself, so the idea was perfect. In addition, although I never spoke of the things that happened, there's that mother's instinct that simply can't be denied. When I later told her what happened, she explained to me that she had her pistol that she carried from Oakland, California on a plane, contemplating murder. Now, my mom was pretty gangster and probably would have if she knew the truth.

Living all those years as if nothing happened followed me as an adult and my fabulous, well let's say *less life*. I couldn't keep up with all the times God really did pick me up and place me softly. However, we can revisit the nightmare of that unforgettable tale later. I think it is important to fast forward and try to understand why I made the choices that I did with men and how I could never fully be free of the God-awful debris of memories from my past. I searched most of my life looking for love in all the wrong places. But, I did marry my first love. We had a son together who was my heart and kept me on my knees in prayer as pieces of my heart chipped away from his decisions and his growing pains.

The oddest thing occurred several years later when my oldest son was about 12 years old. He was visiting my aunt who lived near my grandmother. He had about 4 young cousins who were his age, and the one who I would see run around the house and act promiscuous was among them. So, as he was visiting they ended up talking about one of the kid's teachers who was kicked out of school because of some "pornographic things" and violation of girls. This prompted the conversation from my son, who had no idea that I was victimized as a child. He was quite the protector and when they started to talk about everything he said, "Yeah, like Bob." You see all of them saw the nasty magazines by the computer but never knew there were darker secrets until this day. When my son asked, "He doesn't touch you does he?" One of my cousins screamed at the top of her lungs and ran down the stairs crying. My son said, "Call my aunt now." They all cried and said, "No." But this was the day the truth came out, and the lies could no longer be sweep under the rug.

Yes, you guessed it. My grandmother was still in denial. As all the facts surfaced, it was as if God heard my silent cries and prayers. I was asked to present what happened to me on the stand over 20 years ago. Although I was too afraid to tell the truth, through the years I was relieved to know that it would be my testimony that hammered the nail into his coffin. *He was sentenced to life in prison.* My grandmother suffered in silence. Now, an alcoholic finding out the truth would have set her free and God would have supplied her needs, not her perverted husband. God rest her soul for she is gone now. But she taught me and my mother to love…albeit a strange love. I think that love is what had me choose love over and over in dysfunctional situations. I was either cheated on, lied to, the other woman, or beat up verbally, mentally, and physically throughout my desires to have a family. *The brokenness became my normal.*

I had longed for a normal life…The white picket fence, the husband, the kids, the big house, and the car were on my young adult bucket list. If I ended up pregnant, then we were having a shotgun wedding. We can talk about that four kids later. Now listen, I planned to be with my first husband forever. That was the way it was supposed to be. You don't get married to get divorced. That was not the plan. Surely, I never thought I would be in an adulterous relationship for more than 10 years of my life. And, these were just the first two men who I thought would be in my life forever. By the time I was in my mid-20s, the world was my oyster and I had just landed smack dab in the middle of Hollywood. Fine as ever, I was chasing "the dream" with one kid in hand and beating down Hollywood Blvd. to just get discovered and make it.

At the turn of the century, I ran away from Oakland when crack was just hitting the streets. I had no clue what crack was until my auntie kept peeking out of the window asking if I *saw the fire* as she would sit on my lap in a huge room, which had more than enough space for both of us and 10 other folk if need be. I had just arrived from Hawaii and was as green as green could get. I spoke "proper English," and as others would say, I sounded "like a white girl." I knew that I wanted a life, that I wanted it all now, and that I was going to figure out how to get there. A house, a car, money, and a man were all in my success chart, but as reality would have it, I didn't know a thing. So, the big, bad wolf easily could smell me from a mile away. That was when I met my mentor, who was 10 years older, although I was still married to my high school sweetheart, who had also become a real challenge. He was tempted by the fast money that crack bought into our lives. He chose to sell dope rather than keep his good job at UPS because selling crack on the weekends got him a better return. I tried so desperately to stay the girlfriend-turned-wife with our new baby boy and to keep the relationship like it was---a high school dream. But the responsibilities pulled us in opposite directions. As he was coming home in the morning from selling dope all night, I was preparing for work to sell HMO policies to families. I wasn't sure if we grew apart, or if the guy who worked with me put a spell on me, because not too long afterward I divorced the love of my life and became someone else's mistress.

Two decades later, with three kids by three different men, my walls had caved in. I was losing my car dealership and wondering how to catch my third husband cheating on me with the flower designer and Spanish-speaking assistant, who I had hired. My choice for love was horrible. But I think I was just got caught up in the idea of love. I was always chasing a perfect love story in the hopes I would be the star of the show. After my third child was born, the girl I always wanted, I decided to risk it all and move back to the Bay area into my girlfriend's house, which I was going to flip. It was huge. It sat on a golf course just on the outskirts of Sacramento. I thought I was dreaming! I was anxious to make the big flip so that I could make a ton of money and get back to the life I once knew before the kids. But you know what I have found out? Sometimes you may want what God feels you aren't yet ready for. In this case, I found out pretty fast that my life was not ready for an upgrade.

Well, as time and destiny would have it, I ended up falling face first into a pile of crap. My girlfriend's house started to foreclose. Here I was giving up everything and only had the clothes on my back. I thought *Wow! What have I done?* I was homeless with two babies now. I high-tailed it back to Los Angeles and couldn't believe myself. I couldn't believe my choices, my decisions, or my actions. What was I going to do? This is what rang in my head night and day. I bargained with a few friends and was literally homeless.

All a girl wanted was love. I wanted to love and to be loved. I wanted the American pie. I wanted success on my level. I wanted to be "Ghetto Fabulous!" You are talking about a lady who had a dealership, owned income property that was a duplex, purchased cars from various auctions to flip and make a dollar out of 15 cents. A lady who drove a Mercedes Benz, BMW, Corvette, Porsche, and Range Rover on various occasions because I lived that life that many will never see. I, Princess, had nothing. I had no place to go and actually had to squat in a house that an ex-co-worker lived in and offered me as a place to stay. Did I appreciate it when I had it all? Maybe not! Would I change a thing? More than likely not. In spite of it all, the perseverance gave me the character to endure what others may not be able to. Facing homelessness was the Game Changer. I had come so far in life to just end up with nothing. But sometimes God will silence everything around you to get your full attention. Well, He definitely had mine!

Just think about it. I had to move back to the unknown and hope to have a place to rest my heavy heart and weary head. There was no way I could face many people or even look at my own kids in the eyes with mommy's decisions. I know it was like yesterday. As a matter of fact, I started writing in my journal then.

Let's turn the page and take a look back to see if God still was in the business to pick me up and place me softly.

Wednesday, August 22, 2007, 1:20 am

Man, man, man you would think u person becomes tired of chasing her tail. Well that's a dog Right? Looking in this smoky, smeared mirror one could only guess who sat and looked in it before. I have been to hell and back within the last 45 days. But that's nothing new; you can pretty much smell the stench of the smoke in my clothes after my emerging from the pit time and time again. I get to the top and a crawfish crab grabs my leg and tries to take me out. The sad thing is that this time I may have been the crab who pinched me. Now, I'm laying across a king-sized bed that is draped in two sheets, one belonging to my good friend, and by now I guess it's okay to call her my big sister, Cheryl, Cheryl Rich. Cheryl is almost a replica of my mom. Strange thing is that they walked in similar shoes, and I guess that's why I ran from her in the beginning only to come back when I felt like calling 911. The other flower-printed sheet belongs to my new roomy, Sean. Sean was my ex-partner at my previous job. He was actually someone who I went off on during the height of my climbing success in the mortgage world. This, of course, came after he worked for me at my auto dealership, which folded months before. That's another chapter we'll get to later. I can clearly see me throwing my hands up and waving them up and down since I was so adamant about the fact that there was no way he would be getting a percentage of my commission because we weren't partners anymore. As a matter of fact in the real world I insisted he wasn't pimping me. He politely apologized and bowed down, backing up discretely. Now keep in mind I had five deals on the table, and he had maybe one if that. Wow! Who would have ever figured that the tables would and could turn? So much has me huffing and puffing! God apparently had another plan. Mind you, I had just had a baby 3 months prior and was single, no baby daddy, well let me give him his respect, no father of my child, around. Sean, of course, had his eyes on me. He was a good guy, but not the one for me.

How did I get here? Here in this green bedroom with all of my bags, garbage bags at that, gathered around the room, with clothes in one corner and papers, over stuffed in a couple of boxes, in the other.

Hanging from the once well taken care of curtain rods were light-blue curtains, which were so thin and dingy I have to figure out which corner to stand in so that no one can see me outside when I change. To top it off, God knows I don't want to know what thing was killed by what appeared

to be a whole can of raid with about four huge stain-dripped spots on this money green wall. No, it really isn't money green, I was trying to sike myself out, and it is throw-up green. I don't know what's worse, the filthy carpet that has mildew stains crawling up the walls or the broken knobs on the doors that I have to touch, hoping to avoid getting a splinter in my finger. Oh my goodness, am I complaining? Shoot it looks like it! God, forgive me! I am oh-so appreciative, but come on. I must keep it real.

By now I am fighting every day with this pride thing, and all that rings in my spirit is that God loves a humble person. I love God so much that I quickly silence the complaining and reflect on his goodness in my life and take a deep breath and remember the test is for the testimony. I keep pushing to the fact that there is a soul attached to this mind-boggling journey.

Oh, someone will see that the good Lord has seen me through and realize in the sometimes God awful journey he will see you through to the end and ultimately you rise to a place that usually ends up better than before. All things work together for the good of the Lord who are called according to His purpose. So, despite the facts, I must press through it to get to it. Besides, I am at that crossroad where time is running out, my baby just started to crawl, but there's no way I'm letting her touch this floor. I wonder if there is a stage where she can just walk and skip the crawling part.

Oops, am I complaining? Let me quit while I'm ahead. I can't complain. I'm half a second from being in the cold. When I say cold, I mean cold like homeless. Shoot, looking around all this mess, I see why it's all worth it. In the mess, I must remember I'm blessed. My two precious angels, Little Princess and my Prince, give me every reason to appreciate every step of this journey. I pray these days will be faint to them, leaving no traces of goop in their mind. By now I'm tough as nails but this last episode took the cake, ice cream, and everything else. I didn't even want to write this story because I figured hey when I get settled I'll do what I am called to do and I'll get to it but man I'm in living color and the story only thickens as I go, so what did Cheryl say? Write, right now, write!

Have you ever been in this position? Well, man if I had, I would know what to do right. I need a manual that could tell me what to do if your best friend was really your enemy? Or better yet, Stop Being Your Own Enemy and Become Your Best Critic for Dummies. The best thing is that God protects his children at all times and does make a way of escape. I just escaped from the land of milk and honey, and there was major wickedness. Well, at least I thought it was the land of milk and honey, as it was camouflaged. Lesson number 700,056,000 and still counting.

Always, and I mean always, have several plans in place when dealing with individuals who offer everything to you on a silver platter. If it looks and sounds too good to be true---it usually is.

Sunday, August 26, 2007 1:50 am

Today, my dear friends, I walked around the African Market Place with my little sugar baby Princess in the stroller and a cute basket draped in checker-red cloth, selling cakes, Lemon Jell-O, Chocolate, Sock It to Me, and Sour Cream. Why? Well, honey if you don't remember the devastation that occurred, then I can't say. Wait a minute, I may not have told you.

Man, I really hate airing out my dirty draws, but I'll say it again. It was only my testimony.

Anyway, I think I made a good $175.00 today on the fluke. Raising this money for Cheryl and Leila's non-profit is a great idea. At least I get a kick back. Oh, the heck with it! I'm flipping cakes to survive, and Cheryl is letting me keep the profit. I got a little break, as Josh went over to his dad's house for the weekend. Therefore, I was able to hit the cement a little harder. Not as hard as my 17-year-old Ikaika, who is also known as Young Boss, constantly clowning me and saying that I don't have it anymore. Well, I think if you try pushing out three babies, by three different baby daddies, you did it because you lack self-confidence and want nothing more than to be loved. I think Eddie Murphy said it better as Buck Wheat on Saturday Night Live, "Knucking Por Nub in All Da Rong Pwaces." Why? Why? Why? Do I ask about this love thing? It has engulfed my whole being through the years. It isn't like I felt I wasn't loved as a child but not like a mommy's love or a daddy's girl love. It was a strange love, kind of cold.

You see, growing up I was always on the go, on the move, from house to house, and from relative to relative.

After my sister was murdered, it was as if the intentions of my family were to protect me. Unfortunately, the ones who were supposed to protect me were actually the predators waiting to hurt me. You see I don't remember much, and I never saw any baby pictures of me. So, being a child is a very vague memory. I do remember some things, things like when my grandmother's boyfriend at the time called me over to the couch. As he sat on the couch, he had his pants down and his penis was erected. He grabbed my hand, placed it on his penis, and began to rub it up and down, telling me to do this. It was very weird and strange, something inside of me just didn't feel right. I think I was around 3 or 4 years old. The memory is so vivid because I remember his leg looking like rubber with holes in it. You see he had a burnt leg, and it was gross. He constantly looked out the window to watch for my grandmother. As soon as she approached, he told me to go in the bathroom and don't say anything. Man you talk about a little girl who was frightened and scared as I remember peeking through the bathroom door, and as I stood in the dark hiding as if I did something wrong. That day was the beginning of me knowing better than ever that I didn't want them to adopt me, and I was never going to accept my grandmother's husband as my grandfather. He was younger than my mother, who was the oldest, alive, and not crazy, as they always tried to convince me of---that ill-conceived boldface lie. Not to mention I would never be convinced it was better to find a white man to marry than one my own race. Stay away from black men is what seemed to be my grandmothers' direction of choice although all seven of her daughters were from black men, if I'm correct it was around 4or 5 different ones. Well I'm not going to complain I'm going to share truth that might set someone free.

If you are a grandmother reading this or even a mother and you may be in a situation of the sort, let me be the first to tell you it hurts that baby granddaughter or grandson to know you know the truth and you won't stand up for that baby, that innocent child shouldn't be given to the wolves for a sense of your own selfish gratitude and security. Understand that you cannot entertain the devils playground and mix your seed to justify your own selfish actions. If you think not, think again because God will not allow that sort of sickness to go on. For one what you do in the dark comes to light, and his word says suffer not the little children. To allow their innocence to be ripped from them is a horrible shame that you will and must repent from. For your sake be silenced no more, the truth will set you free and know that God is Jehovah Jireh your provider not man. Your help will change destiny and break that generational curse that has been swept under the rug.

I'm going to sleep. It is now 2:42 am, and I've got to go to church in the morning.

That was my reality for a few months. It didn't last long and it was in these God-awful moments I slowly had to see my self-worth through it all. I had to realize my life was not over and I had a lot going on that needed to come to the surface again. We sometimes go through the fire to be shaped and refined. My mother, God rest her soul, Jeanne Maria would say pressure made the diamond. I have survived it all. I made every conscious decision because of my experiences in life to say, "You know what? I will serve the Lord." Making a commitment to love and lean on the Lord was my Game-Changing moment through all of the bad times. He never left me like His word says. He was always there…it was me trying to figure a few things out. Do not run from Him in dark times, I run to Him. Why? Because He will be your Game-Changing Moment. He needs you to get in the earth… I see the great you coming forth just like myself. And even when I didn't even have a clue…He always picked me up and placed me softly.

Fireside Reflections

Keywords and Takeaways:

1. Looking for love in all the wrong places

2. Come so far in life to just end up with nothing

3. Sometimes God will silence everything around you to get your full attention

Princess nearly experienced it all, which ultimately shaped her life's decisions with looking for love in all of the wrong places and obtaining what she felt was the good life, to later learn was a temporary moment before it was all snatched away.

What I know for sure is that when life feels like a rug that has been snatched up from underneath our feet, like Princess mentioned either God wants our attention, and hc wants our attention to be focused on him

Can you recall a moment when you felt life was snatched from you? What did you do ? What did you discover in the process?

_____

_____

_____

_____

_____

_____

_____

_____

_____

_____

RISING BROKEN

Kori Jay

Today, if you meet me, you meet a woman who is full of peace and joy, self-love, and strong confidence. I am courageous, and I have my smile. I have my voice back, I sing again, and I allow creativity to flow through me daily. I am driven and determined to be happy, and open to receiving all that the universe has to offer me in this life. But that is not who I always was. The story you are going to read paints a picture of a much different woman because during the time I was living this story, I was unrecognizable to the woman I am now.

I have gone through many nights of tears, prayer, faith, and consistent affirmation of self to get to this place of peace that cannot be shaken. Getting to this place of not only self-love, but also self-respect, was a long, dark process, and it all started with a relationship that I was in for 6 years with a man who was very troubled, abusive, and extremely Narcissistic. Now of course when I met him I had a pretty high level of self-confidence, but nowhere near what you see today.

When I met him, I was extremely independent and self-reliant, and in him I thought I had met my perfect match. I call him *The Charmed One* because he knew how to knock my socks off in ways I had never experienced before. He was attentive and caring, you know, everything a person could want in a partner, or so it seemed.

He appeared to be the perfect gentleman, and over time I grew to love him deeply. As you read this story, you will come to understand why my opening statement is so important, how that came to be, you'll learn who I was before, and how I rediscovered ME.

The Charmed One

Seven years ago, I met him, The Charmed One. The one who could burn a hole in my soul just by looking at me. He had me and he had me good, but not at first. When we met I was not all that intrigued by him, however, over time he grew on me. Initially, we didn't speak everyday so I didn't really pay him any mind. But then, one day everything changed. We were having a funny conversation via email and we exchanged numbers or the first time—the rest was history. We spoke every day for a few times a day, and he became my best friend. Initially, we were inseparable, and we did just about everything together when I was home (I travel for a living). And when I went off to work, he appeared to be so into me that I thought that I had found the ONE.

I believed that we were going to be together forever over time, as most of us do when you feel that you've found real love. I call him The Charmed One because he was good at telling me what he assumed I wanted to hear to get the desired results he had in mind. Now, of course I did not know that then, and I believed everything he said to me. Not because I'm gullible but because at the time I had no reason to second guess his words. I trusted The Charmed One completely to say the least. He told me he was a Doctor of Neurology, he had a house on seven acres of land that HE owned, he was well traveled, his family was well to do, and he was very well spoken and highly educated (that meant nothing to me at all). In hearing all of this, you're thinking just like I did. What isn't there to love about all of that? He was the perfect gentlemen it seemed as I stated earlier. Opening doors for me, pulling out my chairs, the works! He did all of the things that make a woman feel special and loved. Then one day something changed. The Charmed One was into anything freaky so he invited me to go to Key West, Florida, our first year together to experience fantasy fest. I had never been and it seemed interesting, so I agreed to go.

I believe that we all have a little freak in us and that it just takes the right person to bring it out. He promised to pay my ticket and cover all expenses; however, I paid my own way. He didn't know that at first because I wanted to see if he was actually going to keep his word. What I received instead was an apology as to why he was not able to cover anything that he had promised. *He had to pay his parents' mortgage that month* he said. What woman in her right mind is going to argue with anything like that? It was then that I let him know that I had already paid for my flight.

Little did I know Mr. Charming had a totally different agenda. Another woman showed up in Miami as just a friend who needed to stay with us because her friends cancelled, leaving her stuck. Well honey, before the weekend was over the entire situation blew up in his face! As it turned out, she flew down to Miami thinking the same thing I did because he lied to us both. He had told her the same lame story about me that I heard about her. I asked her one question during a ladies break in the bathroom, "HOW LONG HAVE YOU TWO KNOWN EACH OTHER?" and the weekend went downhill from there. Later that night, she confronted him about me, and instead of being honest he evaded the entire question all together by blowing up and getting loud with her, which is what most toxic people do.

He kicked her out of the hotel with nowhere to go and proceeded to confess that he paid her way, apologizing to me and asking me not to leave him. He promised to never do that again and begged my forgiveness—and unfortunately, I did forgive him. I know some of you reading this now are screaming on the inside about how you would have responded. Please, don't judge me. I loved him, and I did *what I thought* was the right thing as his woman to make him happy. I believed that he was genuine and sincere. He was crying a little bit, so you know of course it was easy to believe him. This trip should have been the end of anything between us. I mean he humiliated me after all. But I chose to give him another shot to do right by me, at least so I thought. For the next year and a half we were inseparable when I was home from work. We spent day in and day out together like most couples do when you enjoy being with the person you are in a relationship with.

Everything between us appeared to be real, and I was a loyal woman to him for that reason as most of us are when we love someone. That moment in Miami I chose to stay with him, knowing what he was a little capable of when challenged by the truth, and I chose to overlook that to stay with him. I should have left his ass high and dry right there to sort out his own mess because what follows is a lot of ugliness in between fake beautiful moments.

He continued to charm and gain his way deep into my heart, my son's heart, and of course into my bed. He had us right in the palm of his hands where he wanted us, charmed and under his spell. I won't lie, I was stuck on the sex at first. I had been single for two years prior to meeting him, and that was by choice. I hadn't even been touched by a man in two years sexually, so he knew he had hit the jackpot with me.

I was such an easy target being, vulnerable to the right man, saying the rights things, and certainly doing the right things to make me stick around. I wasn't in love right away, and truth be told, I wasn't all that attracted to him when we finally met in person. But we had become amazing friends so I stuck around. I had become pregnant in this early part of our relationship, and with me being a single mom already, I didn't want to deal with another child all by myself. So unfortunately, I chose to terminate the pregnancy. He was all for it, and this is when the subtle verbal abuse started in 2013. He began to call me a breeder of children and tell me that all I was good for was giving birth and that having my children were my biggest accomplishments. Of course I would get in my feelings about it, however, I didn't consider it abuse at the time because I already was insecure about the fact that I had three children and they all had different fathers. I mean, people close to me would make me feel bad about it sometimes, so it was easy for me to look at it not as abuse but as a known fact. During this charming stage, which with the Narcissistic person or the Narcissistic Sociopath, they call this stage love bombing. They pile on the love and compliments for a while and when the subtle hits come, you really think nothing of it.

He began to take all of the things that he knew were my insecurities or a sore point with me and use them subtly to control me; control the way that I thought about myself, my life as it was, and all of the things that my life was not. He would share a little narcissistic joke here or there at first, then it became a regular thing later on in the relationship. You see, there are different phases to narcissism. When the narcissist is in a relationship, love bombing is just something they do to keep reeling you back in and keeping you in a vicious cycle of control and abuse.

I am sharing this experience with all of you because like me I am sure there is someone going through this but had no idea it was Narcissistic Abuse. It took about 4 years to really comprehend what was going on. He would go from loving me to hating me all in a split second if I didn't do something he wanted me to do and the exact way he wanted it done. Narcissistic abuse if the worst form of abuse there is because it not only breaks you down emotionally, but mentally you are so exhausted you don't even want to get out of bed and most people who actually survive it are never the same.

This kind of abuse will have you so broken that you want to die. You literally want to disappear off the face of the earth and never exist again just to never have to deal with this type of person ever again in life. Some feel the only escape from their Narcissist is death, *and they egg you on*. They encourage you to kill yourself or they threaten to kill you themselves just to get away with the lies and all of the deceit that they dish out daily. Again, they are charming individuals, so they know just what to say to keep you staying around even though you already know you need to get out.

Love Bombing

As mentioned previously, Love Bombing is the first phase of Narcissistic Abuse, and it is the worst phase for you but the best phase for them because that is when they snag their victim. They play their best mind games and I mean they are so clever with it and so good at pretending to care about you, when really they have an ulterior motive and that is to get whatever they can out of you, to drain you of every ounce of goodness in you. During this phase of my relationship with DOCTOR WHO (he lied about being a doctor), he made sure to be generous, super kind, and extremely complimentary, making me feel like the most beautiful woman in the world.

The Narcissist will only focus on their goal at hand, whatever that may be, and most times it is totally self-serving. The male Narcissist is obsessed with sex most of the time, which ultimately leads to multiple sex partners with men and/or women partners. Male Narcissists are uber concerned with having a beautiful woman on his arms to validate him as a man among his peers. They feed off of the accolades of others. The reason that LOVE BOMBING is the worst phase of the relationship for the victim is because they truly do NOT mean one word of what they are saying to you during this time. They are incapable of loving anything or anyone, including themselves. They have no connection to emotion at all, but they do connect with completing their task, with winning. It is all a game to them.

Now, as their victim you are clueless that they are completely leading you on, which is why when the real them surfaces it take you by total surprise, leaving you in utter shock. Narcissists are the type of people who are demanding and want you to give up everything just so you can become their nothing. They really want to become the center of your world, your everything, isolating you from all that you know to be real, just so you can live in the bubble of false reality they have created for themselves. They make sure you are totally reliant on them.

It starts off with the small things such as doing all of the things they now know no one has ever done for you in a relationship. Then it moves to doing the things that your family and close friends may have left you hanging on throughout your life. They want you to worship them and give them everything, including your mind, body, soul, and spirit just so they can suck the life out of you and move on to the next victim. They know that if they pick up the slack of others, you will be endearing to them and that is when they know they can get whatever they want out of you.

I came from a broken home, had daddy and mommy issues, been married and divorced by the time I was 22 years old, and that man was abusive. So, DOCTOR WHO comes along telling me everything I want to hear and gets me to open up and let my guard down telling him my heart, my hurts and disappointments, everything. Later on, those things became his tools to control me. Narcissists also use this phase of the relationship or the entire relationship, depending on their victim, to absolutely boost their ego. The men love to have beautiful women on their arm, and the women love to have new shiny trinkets they can show off to the world.

He won me over real good by making me believe that he was in my corner and the only support that I had and needed. I never told him no, and I always gave him whatever he asked for until one day he showed me a picture of another woman and asked what I thought of her. I didn't think she was as pretty as he did and he started to change toward me for a second. Made a joke about her being lighter than me and that ultimately made her more beautiful than me.

That moment was the beginning of the end of the Love Bombing stage. It was as if I was not allowed to actually think for myself because God forbid I had a thought or opinion of my own! It was a verbal take down by him with saying the most hurtful things he could think of saying to me. Then, he would turn around and say how much he loved me and that he didn't mean it. He had a bad day and he didn't mean to take it out on me and would go right back to Love Bombing me. He normally would take me on a nice date or surprise me with a gift, something that I needed for the house or something.

With Narcissists, their spending on you depends on your outward accomplishments. If you had a high-profile career, then they will go all out for you with expensive gifts. But if you didn't have a college degree, most times your gifts will be what they think your own money can afford to buy. I don't have my Bachelor's degree yet, and I noticed after some years passed that his gifts were normally always from the Goodwill or from his closet of things he had never used. Don't get me wrong, I love shopping at the Goodwill, especially on delivery days; however, I just noticed that to him I wasn't worth MORE than the Goodwill. I recall when he had given me a Coach bag for our first Valentine's Day together. It was a used Diaper bag and the only way I knew that was because there were stale Cheetos at the bottom of the bag.

I am not complaining. I am just explaining how the Narcissist views their victims. I was grateful for the gift and was happy he thought of me in that way because we all know that Coach is not cheap. I never let him know that I knew it was used. About a year later we were heading to the gym (he was stuck on being fit although he used the gym to snag more victims), and I didn't have a proper gym bag. I used the diaper bag because it was big enough to serve the purpose of a gym bag. He proceeded to say that I needed to get a real gym bag so that I don't ruin that "LV" because he remembered how much he paid for it. I looked at the bag, and then I looked at him and I asked him to repeat himself. And he did.

I said, "Well, I guess you're in luck, because the bag you bought me is Coach." Now, what did I go and say that for? Correcting a Narcissists is the worst thing anyone can do because they always have to be right. It was that moment that I knew he was more than likely cheating on me and that he valued this other woman way more than me since she was worth a new "LV" bag and all that I got was the used diaper bag with stale Cheetos at the bottom.

I didn't ask him if he was cheating. However, in that moment he had just told on himself, realized I knew it, and that the Love Bombing stage was now temporarily over. I say temporarily because Narcissists go through each phase of relationship, torment, and abuse several times before they discard you permanently. The Narcissist is also calculated and predictable once you catch on to their patterns, and DOCTOR WHO stayed at least 6 steps ahead of me.

He knew what to say to get the desired responses out of me and it would always work like he planned. It took me a total of 4 out of the 5.5 years we were together to figure out what was happening and how I needed to deal with it. It is not easy to tell what is happening. All you know is that one day your mate is sweet and kind and then all of a sudden they are straight from hell, and the nightmare begins. For a short time that is, but long enough to create permanent damage to your mind. When I say nightmare, I really mean a real live nightmare. They are one way in front of people and an entirely different person behind closed doors.

Most Narcissists live a fake life. They create this false image of themselves that they want others to believe or they keep in their minds an image of a life they once lived but no longer exists. For me, I had no idea that people actually live this way. It was an utter shock to my life as I knew it because this was the kind of stuff that you saw on TV only, not in real life. The rug was absolutely pulled out from under my feet when I found out the very harsh truth about DOCTOR WHO.

Narcissists have three stages they go through in a relationship, and all of them with the intent to conquer and eventually destroy their targeted victim. The IDEALIZE stage, LOVE BOMBING, which is what I have mentioned in this chapter. The other stages are important but this beginning stage is the most crucial. DOCTOR WHO set the stage with this phase. He knew he had me within the first year right where he needed me to be to go in for the kill. He treated me according to the value he thought I had for his supply. Meaning whatever he could get out of me for his own personal gain. I started a business for him during this phase of the relationship, so I was of high value to him, I was high on demand because I made him money. He had use for me until he found someone else to duplicate what I created for him, ultimately making him a lot more money, plus she gave him a son and a daughter who he denies having. See, some Narcissists are pathological liars and cheaters, but I will address that in the next chapter.

I said it right, he cheated and had babies with this woman, with whom he ultimately took my business and put into her hands. But this was during the next phase of the relationship, the DEVALUE stage.

I Thought You Loved Me

For three years I was absolutely in the dark about what was really going on. I'd love for that to have been the truth but it isn't. My intuition and my dreams were kicking in so strong to make me aware something wasn't right, but I just could not put my finger on what it was. I would bring up my suspicions and of course that made me the "Jealous One" or I was told I was "Crazy" for even bringing that to him. How dare I ask if he was cheating because he has drastically changed toward me right? God forbid! He went from hot to cold, and cold to hot often during this stage on purpose to throw me off and bring confusion. I started questioning myself during this stage because he made me feel that anything I felt and thought about in life was just Dumb and Stupid.

He would make me feel as if I was just an *uneducated, black nigga bitch, who was only good at giving birth and breeding the next generation*. That is just one example of the verbal abuse I endured from DOCTOR WHO. He would make comments, such as, "I have never met anyone as uneducated as you," I mean all of my exes at least had one Master's degree or a PhD." He would say that they were *more his equal*.

Of course, the insecurities began to get deeper and deeper. He was cheating and that is why he had to begin to devalue me in his own mind. He needed to feel justified in some way that he was doing the right thing and I was not good for him. He even went as far with his close friends to tell them that I had three children all by different men and that gave them a very distorted view of me. In 6 years, I never met any of them. Well, he never met anyone in my family either but a cousin of mine.

During the Devalue stage, he made sure to destroy any ounce of confidence I had within myself. That is what they do. DOCTOR WHO took any and everything that I was passionate about and made me feel like I was nothing for loving those things. He knew that I loved to sing and perform on stage. He would say, "Wow, not only are you an uneducated nigga bitch but you also follow what other niggas do, take the easy way out of life. You're too stupid to finish school, so you thought you'd go sing somewhere. Typical nigga. I need a real woman who will be equal to me."

So, what do I do? *Work hard to be his equal. Work hard to prove MY worthiness to him.* I had to work harder than the rest of his women because I had the least number of accomplishments in his eyes. The more women he cheated with, the more he devalued me. Most of us abuse victims are completely unaware this stage has even begun. All we know is that something is drastically different. The person who was once warm, loving, and inviting, is now cold, heartless, and downright evil. DOCTOR WHO went through great lengths to destroy me.

During this stage, I lost everything not once but twice. Now, I will tell you why things went downhill and why I call him DOCTOR WHO. He told me when we first met that he was a neurologist who worked for the Atlanta VA Hospital. He would travel telling me he had job interviews or medical conferences out of town. I believed him for years, I mean, what woman is going to question a man who says he is at work or has to travel for work? I sure wasn't and I didn't until one day everything began to change. I began to feel inside that something wasn't right and that he was indeed cheating and lying to me, but I just didn't have clarity.

I began to ask God to show me what was going on and to reveal the truth to me. I don't know why I did that because for the next year and a half God wouldn't stop letting me in on what he was doing. Some of you may not believe in such a thing but I am an empath and a psychic medium, so there are things that I see that not many people can. Many people do not realize that sexual energy is very strong. He was one of those people.

He would come to my house during the week after he had supposedly gotten off work and as soon as he would kiss me, I would back up and ask if he was okay. More than likely it was late at this time so my son would be asleep already. The first thing I would do is go for sex, if he had just had sex with someone, he would give me the excuse that he was tired from a long day at work; however, if he hadn't, he was certainly all over me.

DOCTOR WHO would even use studying or his boards as a way to go cheat and spend time with one of his many women he was cheating on me with. The first time I realized he was really lying to me was one day he said he had to fly to New York for a job interview. I believed him so I asked no questions. He turned his phone off as if he was on a flight but forgot to stay off of social media. He had posted something and forgot to turn his location off. *He was still in Atlanta.*

I called him when I realized this and proceeded to ask how his interview was going.

He didn't answer the question yet proceeded to say he was in a rush and had to leave. Then, I received a message from one of his Frat brothers who said, "I just spoke to DOCTOR WHO." And whatever else he said after that was a complete blur. All I thought was this SOB had time for his bro but didn't have time for me. What I found out was he had one of his women fly in to see him. That was just one of many times. He would fly out to other cities and meet up with other women during this devaluing stage, making them believe either I knew about them or that he was completely single.

I recall one particular night, after I had lost my house to foreclosure, I was drained and he didn't help, kicking me while I was down. But, on this night I felt like something just wasn't right. I had moved into an apartment and he was in such a rush to leave when in my opinion he could have been a bit more consoling than he was. To explain, he had also become so abusive physically during this stage that I couldn't always go to work. He was also abusive to my son, and if I defended him neither one of us were leaving the house for a few days. So, there went my income needing to take leave from work, or winding up on workers comp because I got injured on the job and being just plain old exhausted. Workers comp was not enough, and DOCTOR WHO decided I wasn't worth helping financially because he had it, right? He was a NEUROLOGIST after all, right? Then, why would a real man who is a DOCTOR sit back and watch his woman lose everything?

Back to that night, so something didn't feel right in my gut, but my intuition was kicking in. I slept on it and prayed about it, asking God once again to let me see the truth. The next day I found my old phone that I had when DOCTOR WHO and I first met. I looked through all of our text messages and for a second began to feel a bit nostalgic, wondering why things had changed so much. Then I came across this picture that he sent me from what he said was his office. I am looking and my mouth fell open because as I looked at the picture, mind you we had been together 4 plus years at this point, the conversation was about how the phone sex we had was amazing while he was at work IN HIS OFFICE. Files on the desk, lab coat on, and penis out for me to see.

The kicker was his powder-blue walls. In the text, I had mentioned the blue walls and that it was nice of the hospital to allow him to paint his walls such a pretty blue. He replied that his assistant, who was an older woman, had painted it for him with her husband one day. They wanted to do something nice for him because he was such a great guy. Now, don't judge me for having phone sex during office hours! At the time, my office was at home so I did whatever I wanted during my lunch.

Well, looking back at the picture the blue walls were in his bedroom at home, not his office at all. I never said a word to him but I certainly began to really question who he was and what he did for a living. He was good about saying he was at the office from a certain time to a certain time, he was writing orders for patients and dropping them to the nurses' station He would even go as far to say he was doing rounds late at the hospital and staying late to do lecture.

Now, I am absolutely confused and very afraid that the man that I had been with and loved and tolerated for all of these years was living a fake life and I was caught in the middle. When I say he was good, he was good at covering up his lies, and fake life. Meanwhile, I find out during this time he had two more children while he was with me. Oh, he was really good ya'll. He stayed 10 steps ahead, so his lies were very calculated and precise.

The devaluing of me got worse as I started probing a bit. He would call me saying he was back in his office after morning rounds and I would ask him how they went. *Were your rounds all you needed them to be?* Then, he would start speaking in an extremely soft-spoken voice, and I would ask, "Honey, are you okay? Why did you just start whispering?" He would tell me that his office door was open and he didn't want the nurses to hear his conversation. *I thought the nurses station was own that hall*? That is what he said. Of course, then it was *you're too uneducated to ask as many questions as you're asking!* He didn't have to answer to me, and if I knew what was good for me, I'd be quiet. Well, now knowing he was sitting at the office across from his bed in his bedroom that he had when he was a child, I was even more intrigued about who the hell I was with. By this time, we were 4.5 years in and nothing was adding up anymore.

He stopped wanting to spend time with me, always saying he had to work on the weekends to be a team player and even on my birthdays leaving me to spend most of the day alone. He would stop by my house and wash the dirty towels and rags one of his women had used to wash with. As an empath, one who feels and absorbs all energy, I felt it all. I would smell alcohol on his breath after coming from so-called work and doing rounds at the hospital. One night, again I woke up out of my sleep feeling like something wasn't right. With all of these signs popping up, why the hell did I stay? That is true, however, by this time I had already been emotionally and physically abused by him and I was pretty depressed. If I was unworthy for a man, who apparently lived a lie every day. Then, I felt no one would really genuinely love me.

The next day he told me that he was going to be working late to fill in for one the rotation doctors that night and he had to do lecture at 9:30 pm. I didn't have a car at the time, so my ass hopped in an Uber to his house because I just knew he was lying. His house sat far on the property behind an iron gate. I found my way inside of the property. I remember asking God to allow his car to be gone and not in the drive way because if he was home that night, everything as I knew it was gonna get much worse. But sure enough he was home. Car right there in the driveway. Lights on in the house. I could even see him from the kitchen window.

My heart sank, and I took my walk of shame back to the Uber and cried. Then, he called me and asked where was I, and if I was okay.

I brushed it off and pretended to be okay. I wanted to slice his tires, key his car, knock on the door, and just let him see me walk away, but because he was abusive, and I knew he had guns, I left. That moment was the beginning of the worst times between he and I and also the worst time emotionally for me.

I had to confirm that he wasn't who he told me he was. So the next day I told him that I had sent an edible arrangement to his office and asked whether he had received it. When I tell you he ghosted me for about 4 hours, I knew I was about to get it and bad. He didn't come by this night, he just went into the final phase of relationship for the Narcissist, which is the discard stage. Oh, he was ready to get rid of me, but first he had to let me know what he really thought of me.

He knew in that moment that I knew and he was determined to destroy me before I could destroy him with the truth. I even called the hospital he claimed to work at and asked if it was okay to send Dr. WHO flowers. Now, the kicker is there was a doctor who worked there with his last name but *she* was a woman. I called and had gotten this sweet older African American lady and she could hear in my voice something was not right. She asked me if I was okay, and before I could say no she said, "You know what baby? I'm going to help you find what you need. How can I help you?" I gave her his name and she proceeded to look in their data base.

"Oh, no," she says, "There is no one who works here with his title or his first name." He didn't exist in their system as a doctor, but a surgical tech in Tampa, Florida, 6 years prior to me meeting him. They had no clue otherwise who he was. He would tell me he was on the research team at Emory Hospital. Well, I called them, too, and they had never heard of DOCTOR WHO. None of their research staff had ever heard of him, ever. Did I say they didn't know who he was? Let the discarding begin.

I Don't Need You

I created a huge problem for him because as long as he could use the "being the team player card" and the "late nights at the hospital card," he was good with me, but the minute I found out the truth, he would treat me like I was shit at the bottom of his shoe and he was out to take my ass down. In the Discard stage, the Narcissist has to defame your name and annihilate your character, making YOU out to be crazy, a psycho bitch, and mentally unstable.

They hone in on all of your insecurities so that you can argue with them. They start a big fight right before they fulfill their plans with another person so they can feel justified in their lies. DOCTOR WHO didn't even have a license to practice medicine in the state of Georgia. So this whole time he was lying to me about everything, and I mean everything, from where he worked and what his career was, to lying about having children, and his parents didn't know about any of them.

The abuse got worse emotionally and mentally so much so that I actually wanted to commit suicide. I wanted to disappear off the face of the earth and never return. I started feeling like I was just no good as he said I was, and that my boys would be better off without me. I felt like if this man can make me feel this about myself and he was the one living a lie every day, maybe I should kill myself.

I may not have had the perfect life, and yes I lost a lot while I was with him, but I lived in my truth. The reality of my truth had been so distorted by his verbal abuse I couldn't even see the good in that. I felt so broken and so betrayed. It really took me months before I even felt like a human being worth loving again.

He began to really do some harm to the business I had built for him. He took the blue print and started it with his kid's mother. They would host events around fraternity and sorority events, ultimately making way more money, and he used my name to do it. He used my networks, via email and social media, and the website that had been created for the business.

His abuse got so bad that he beat me down real bad one night and broke my nose and damn near broke my jaw all because he was afraid I was going to ruin his image to another woman he had been cheating on me with. Really, I was the other woman, and this other woman who started off as the other woman was now his everything while he was discarding me into nothing. When I realized what was going on, I silently started taking control back of my life and picking myself up from out of the ashes, which he thought was my life. I began to put my broken pieces back together.

He was even bringing other women around his parents and going out with them on double dates, as if he and I were already broken up. After he had broken my nose, I ended it, and then I took him back because he made me feel like he needed me and was never going to put his hands on me again. They all say that and hardly ever really mean it. I used that time to really learn the way he thought, his patterns, his movements, and when he would make his change from nice guy to Satan.

He had already began to smear my name with his family, making them think I was falsely accusing him of having kids, and making me appear to be the one causing all of the trouble in the relationship. No, I didn't press charges on him for beating me down the night he broke my nose, but to this day I wish I had. He began to tell me that he didn't need me, but would still want to come around, and after a while I got tired of hearing that, so I started reversing it. He would say it to me and I would turn around and say, "Well, I don't need you either."

I really started standing up for myself and not backing down. He would go as far as to pretend he would be talking to another woman but he was taking to his father just to get me in my feelings. Sometimes he would really be talking to his kid's mother right in front of me, smirking as if he had gotten away with it. I guess in many ways he did. He got away with all of it, and here I was starting over yet again.

If he even fixed his lips to speak crazy to me, I started really standing up for myself. He did not like that. With a Narcissist, they hate to be caught. The worst thing to them is to be found out, and with him and I, he had nowhere to hide.

Rising Broken

I call this section Rising Broken because I finally made the choice to pick up all of my pieces and put my life back together, while still broken. I can't say put it back in order because I had no longer known what order was, at least normal order, because of the fake life that I lived right along with him. Nothing was real, and I was on a mission to connect with everything that was real and tangible to me.

The first thing I did to take my power back was shut down the business he was doing with her because they stole it from me. More important, I took a hot bath, grabbed a glass of red wine, lit a few candles, turned my music on, and I cried for about an hour. I cried not really because I was hurt anymore by him, I was. However, I cried because in that moment I had decided to finally put myself first.

I knew what I had to do to heal and be whole again. I started being busy. I sent my son to live with other family members for one year prior to DOCTOR WHO breaking my nose so he was not around for all of this. I was on a mission for my boys and myself to live and to live happy.

My youngest had seen his mommy unhappy for way too long. While he was away, I got busy working a lot and was determined to get my life back. I worked a lot of OT on the job, I was flying about 130 hours per month, which only gave me maybe 8 days at home per month. So, there was no time to really spend with DOCTOR WHO. I would see him at this time maybe one weekend a month, and I was home for two full days out of the month.

My baths when I got home would be everything to me. I would rush home just to have that quiet time alone. He tried to turn up the heat when he realized that I interfered with him making money with this other woman, but I did not budge. I stood my ground. He would argue with me and make threats if I didn't comply, and my attitude became, "Oh well, you do what you gotta do, and I will do what I gotta do!"

I started saving each and every message he sent me in case I needed them for future reference. During this time, I became the most important person in my life. I put myself even before my kids. How could I be the mom they needed in such an unhealthy state? I couldn't be any good for anyone, not even me. I started really enjoying waking up without the burden of having to be on eggshells because I didn't know if I was going to get the nice him or if Satan was going to rear his ugly face that day.

It was nice doing what I wanted to without being judged for it. It was nice to not have to hear about how everyone else was a loser and a buster or fat with a belly. Mind you, he was a bit juicy himself, but yet he worked out every day or every other day. Of course, he did. He only lost weight when he met someone new. That is how I could tell, that and the countless infections I would get from him using no condoms while sleeping with other women.

While rising broken, I had to rediscover me. I had to reintroduce myself to me all over again. Many nights of throwing things and self-blame, and the tears were endless, but perseverance was a must. He saw my descent, and I was determined to let him watch me rise from the ashes of what he thought was my life. I was determined to rise from the brokenness because I knew I was better than that. I was beautifully and wonderfully made, I just had to see it for myself.

I now see that I had to go through all of that just to become the woman who I was always meant to be: a woman of courage, strength, a woman of great faith. A woman of talent and many gifts. A woman who was meant to touch many lives around the world. A mother who can love fearlessly. A mother who can give to her children a new way of loving themselves, a mother who builds up her children and who doesn't break them down. A friend who many can count on, a counselor who can be trusted, a voice for those who cannot speak even from the grave. A free woman who can teach other people how to live free also, and one day, a wife to the man that God sends, and I will be marrow to his bones and he will breathe life into my lungs.

This experience birthed a woman who now understands what it means to have peace that surpasses all understanding, I have taken back my power. I have been given my life back. Leaving wasn't easy, but living made it worth it. He tried to take my life many nights but the one thing he couldn't do was take my will to survive.

There are three major ways you know that you're dating a **Narcissist.** The first is that the person is both self-functioning and interpersonal functioning. This means that they gain their self-worth from others. The Narcissist is all about public image, and everything they do will be done with grandiosity and attention-seeking behaviors. Narcissists have low levels of empathy and they do not consider the effects that their behaviors have on others. In addition, their relationships are shallow and are a means to an end, and that end is satisfaction of self-esteem. The second is that the narcissist will insist that he or she is the best at everything they do, exhibiting grandiosity, giving the appearance of the thought they are better than others, and acting condescending toward others almost regularly, including you. Narcissists are extremely self-centered. They talk about themselves more than anything. If your mate never lets you get a word in edgewise during a conversation, or they high-jack your conversation with a story about him/herself, you may be dating a narcissist.

Third, gas lighting. This is when the Narcissist makes someone distrust his or her own view of reality through mental and emotional manipulation. They do this because they need to feel *smarter* than you. If you express a thought or an opinion, please beware because the Narcissist will do everything in his or her power to get you to change your mind to think like them.

Dear reader, I hope this story has been a Light for you on your own path of discovery, healing and living your best life, and being the person you were created to be. Find the courage to be you, to stand up for yourself, and take your power back from anyone who has taken it. You deserve to have ALL of the things that are promised to you from before the day you were born, but to get it, you gotta get up. Let them watch you rise! You do not stand alone, because I stand with you.

Fireside Reflections

1. I was unrecognizable to the woman I am now.

2. I really started standing up for myself and not backing down

This is the voice of a woman who was hidden in deceit for so long to the point of losing her own identity. It took coming from an abusive relationship and seeking understand by educating herself to know what it was that she was a living part of. It took Keren to stand up for herself to live the freedom and experience the joy that she does today.

If you or someone you know, recognizes any of the signs of narcissistic abuse, please seek support. You deserve it.

Not sure, but know that something doesn't feel quite right? Start to jot those things down and make a note of what is happening. Also confide in someone you trust to share these details with as well in the event that they may need to give some back story about your relationship.

Notes:_____

_____

_____

_____

_____

_____

_____

_____

_____

_____

_____

REFLECTIONS FROM
SAMIRA JONES

These Authors have opened up their lives, not just for themselves, but also for you, the reader who is no different than they are. The purpose here was to share a message. That is what our goal is as this book continues to be read, to share a message that someone can use to either shift their perspective or support their circumstance.

Although the stories ranged in differences, they each were also unique in terms of what there was to embrace on the receiving end. Some may have made you sad, or angry, while others may have made you smile.

In any case, these were real people, with real Game Changer Life experiences who had a story and was brave enough to share that story. As humans we connect through story every day. So always remember that there is someone who can benefit from your story as well.

I want to thank each Author who contributed to this piece of work. I do understand that not every story was an easy story to share. However, I do hope and pray that doing so supports you in your journey and healing.

Til Volume II

Be Blessed,

Samira Jones

RESOURCES

Rape Abuse Incest National Network

RAINN (Rape, Abuse & Incest National Network) is the nation's largest anti-sexual violence organization. RAINN created and operates the National Sexual Assault Hotline 800.656.HOPE,

online.rainn.org & **rainn.org/es** in partnership with more than 1,000 local sexual assault service providers across the country.

Visit, https://www.rainn.org/ for more information and resources.

State Laws on Reporting and Responding to Child Abuse and Neglect

The following Child Welfare Information Gateway products and other resources offer information about State laws related to reporting and responding to child abuse and neglect.

https://www.childwelfare.gov/topics/systemwide/laws-policies/can/reporting/

Mandatory Reporting Laws: Child Abuse and Neglect.

Incidences of child abuse and neglect have a profound effect on the lives of many children across the United States. Therefore, all states have set in place variations of mandatory reporting laws in order to decrease and prevent these incidents from occurring. These laws help ensure that cases of child abuse are reported to the proper authorities.

Mandatory reporting laws differ for each state when it comes to child abuse – which includes physical abuse, sexual abuse, and emotional abuse.

https://criminal.findlaw.com/criminal-charges/mandatory-reporting-laws-child-abuse-and-neglect.html

The Domestic Violence Hotline

Operating around the clock, seven days a week, confidential and free of cost, the National Domestic Violence Hotline provides lifesaving tools and immediate support to enable victims to find safety and live lives free of abuse. Callers to The Hotline at 1-800-799-SAFE (7233) can expect highly trained, experienced advocates to offer compass-ionate support, crisis intervention information, educational services and referral services in more than 200 languages. Visitors to this site can find information about domestic violence, online instruct-ional materials, safety planning, local resources and ways to support the organization.

https://www.thehotline.org/